American Food
by the Decades

American Food
by the Decades

Sherri Liberman, Editor

GREENWOOD

AN IMPRINT OF ABC-CLIO, LLC
Santa Barbara, California • Denver, Colorado • Oxford, England

M

The publisher has done its best to make sure the instructions and/or recipes in this book are correct. However, users should apply judgment and experience when preparing recipes, especially parents and teachers working with young people. The publisher accepts no responsibility for the outcome of any recipe included in this volume.

Library of Congress Cataloging-in-Publication Data

American food by the decades / Sherri Liberman, editor.
   p. cm.
   Includes bibliographical references and index.
   ISBN 978–0–313–37698–6 (hard copy : acid-free paper) — ISBN 978–0–313–37699–3 (ebook)
1. Food—United States—History—20th century. 2. Cooking, American—History—20th century. 3. Food habits—United States—History—20th century. 4. Food industry and trade—United States—History—20th century. 5. United States—Social life and customs—20th century. 6. United States—Economic conditions—20th century. I. Liberman, Sherri.
TX360.U6A755   2011
641.5973—dc22   2011009483

ISBN: 978–0–313–37698–6
EISBN: 978–0–313–37699–3

15 14 13 12 11   1 2 3 4 5

This book is also available on the World Wide Web as an eBook.
Visit www.abc-clio.com for details.

Greenwood
An Imprint of ABC-CLIO, LLC

ABC-CLIO, LLC
130 Cremona Drive, P.O. Box 1911
Santa Barbara, California 93116-1911

This book is printed on acid-free paper ∞

Manufactured in the United States of America

Contents

Preface

Tracing the arc of American food trends from the early twentieth century to the dawn of the millennium, this book will follow as a decade-by-decade analysis of American food tastes and innovations. What we consume says volumes about who we are as a people and as a nation. This reference book, organized in a decade-by-decade format, will examine the impact of commercial, ethnic, and cultural forces on the American diet. A narrative will begin each chapter describing the overall historical and social factors contributing to dietary choices, followed by an alphabetical arrangement of entries. A list of books, journal articles, and websites at the end of each chapter will provide an opportunity for deeper exploration of the topics covered. The scope of the text will touch upon brand histories, agriculture, government intervention, historical inevitabilities, and social movements contributing to the American diet and dining habits. The book also includes information on innovations that took place in the kitchen, particularly appliances and technology that affected food preparation and choices. The rise of celebrity chefs, influential American food writers and editors, and TV personalities in the food world are also given priority.

Acknowledgments

This book would not exist without my having met Vince Burns at the ALA Conference in Anaheim, CA, in June 2008. Many thanks to editors David Paige and George Butler for ushering this work through to fruition. I want to express my gratitude to Rosen Publishing for publishing my first forays into nonfiction. Research institutions and resources that were invaluable were the Conrad Hilton Library at the Culinary Institute of America, NYU Fales Library Food and Cookery Collection, and The General Research Collection of New York Public Library's Stephen A. Schwartzman Building. Experts Lynn Olver of the Food Timeline, *Oxford Encyclopedia of American Food and Drink* editor Barry Popik, and menu collector Harley Spiller (one among many hats) were key inspirations and mentors in this process. I could never have kept up the momentum to research and write this book without the love and support of Rebecca Anguin-Cohen, Ginny Chu, Sharon Festinger, Lauren Fortuna and Robert Arrighi, Jonathon Gordon, Derek King, Hank and Loretta Liberman, Anjanette Morton, Jennifer Steffey and Chris Gallagher, Shana Tribiano, Kaman Tse, and last but not least, contributors Margaret Haerens, Hilary Schenker, Margaret Siggillino, and Judy Yablonski, without whom this book may have not been written.

Introduction

The American diet of the twentieth century evolved from a table with red meat at center stage to a mélange of new cultural tastes brought by waves of immigration, advances in nutrition, improved methods of food storage, and a focus on health. Vegetables and condiments played second fiddle, as meat, potatoes, cake, and pie were dietary staples, regardless of the region within the nation. During the first two decades of the twentieth century, plump figures were considered fashionable and a sign of good health. Eventually, improved food production methods and refrigeration resulted in higher-quality foods. Railways that fanned out and connected the major cities provided easier access to a wider variety of foodstuffs. Commercially manufactured and packaged foods began to appear under the brand names Heinz, Nabisco, and Campbell's, all to become household names.

Employment of women outside the home and the nature of meals and mealtimes were also among the significant factors in the changing American diet over the course of the twentieth century. At the turn of the century, working women were generally employed as maids, textile workers, typists, or telephone switchboard operators. Most were expected to marry and be homemakers. Technological advances and the women's liberation movement changed all that. By 1982, more than half of all females were employed outside the home. Tasks in the home were eventually more commonly shared among partners. Frozen foods became a permanent feature of home life in the 1950s, as were microwave ovens in the 1980s. By the latter part of the century, families on the go subsisted on a diet of take-out food. Take-out could be fast food, French, Italian, and, more recently, Thai or Indian.

The modern fast-food world took root post–World War I, first with BBQ chains in Texas featuring "carhop" service. The first White Castle opened in 1921 in Wichita, Kansas, featuring an ultra-clean setup near trolley stands to feed workers. They could buy burgers by the bag for a nickel apiece. By the 1930s, drive-ins serviced by uniformed waitresses appeared. Among the pioneers was McDonald's of California. Counter service was added to McDonald's post–World War II, with an all-male staff. Ray Croc bought the McDonald's business in 1954 and franchised the chain with the famous golden arches. He banned jukeboxes, telephones, and vending machines to discourage teens from hanging out. Most fast-food places did not open until lunchtime, but McDonald's saw that the market for breakfast food was wide open and marketed Herb Peterson's Egg McMuffin in 1972. Other chains copied the idea, and sales of fast food grew to $102 billion in 1998.

Federally designated food standards were a benchmark of improvement in the American diet during the twentieth century. Upton Sinclair's serialized novel *The Jungle* deplored the unsafe practices of the meat-packing industry, which brought about the Meat Inspection Act of 1906. The health food movement was born in the early decades of the century as well, stressing smaller meal size. Food faddists such as Dr. Horace Fletcher pitched a "mastication diet," which espoused the value of chewing food thoroughly. Dr. John Harvey Kellogg strictly prescribed patients at his Michigan sanitarium a low-protein, high-fiber diet, rich in a variety of nuts and vegetable products. The slender Gibson Girl aesthetic soon replaced the robust feminine physique. Wilbur O. Atwater discovered the caloric equivalency of proteins, fats, and carbohydrates and researched the composition of foods for the USDA in the early 1900s. Home economics classes were introduced into public schools. The government began to worry about the diets of the working class and tried to convince laborers to eat more beans, legumes, and cheaper cuts of meat, which were just as full of protein. This push was met with resentment from the working class and was seen as an effort to keep the prime cuts of meat for the elite. Another unfortunate misuse of the push for nutritional health occurred when it was used as ammunition against the influx of ethnic foods to decry immigration. Pastrami, borscht, pierogi, and other salty, meat-based ethnic foods were targeted as unhealthy, for the wrong reasons.

Vitamin deficiencies were discovered to be the cause of bodily harm and disease. In 1913, Elmer McCollum and Marguerite Davis found a fat-soluble nutrient called vitamin A that could cure rickets. In 1916, it was proven that a deficiency in vitamin B1 was the cause of beriberi. These scientific discoveries led to a vitamin craze, with people thinking that taking vitamins could do anything from improving their sexual health to preventing the common cold. Products such as Ovaltine and Kellogg's cereals boasted their high vitamin content in order to increase sales. Cod liver oil, milk, and yeast were touted for their health benefits. Despite the new obsession with vitamins and health, candy and novelty sweets flourished during the first two decades of the century—soda pop, ice cream, and candy bars had an insatiable audience.

In addition to the onslaught of advice from nutritionists, the onset of World War I forced Americans to reduce their food intake. A massive health survey undertaken during wartime introduced immigrants and regional soldiers to simpler, more nutritious meals, and vice versa—spaghetti and meatballs became more popular as Italy was a U.S. ally during World War I. There was a struggle between integrating foreign foods into the American diet and, conversely, the Americanization of foreign diets. Eventually, German meats such as bratwurst evolved into hot dogs, and Chinese American and Italian American foods became more mainstream in the American diet. But the drive to influence immigrants to eat more Americanized foods was compounded by the restrictions set by the Immigration Act of 1924. Assimilation, including diet, was encouraged by public school home economics regimes. During the 1920s and 1930s, the concept of an "American" meal became more standardized.

Food conglomerates expanded; the giants of industry were General Foods, Standard Foods, General Mills, and Sunkist. By the 1920s, food manufacturers were the largest manufacturing industry in the nation and had higher earnings than the iron, steel, auto, and textile industries. Women's magazines flourished in the 1920s, and advertisements strongly influenced family shopping. By the 1930s, things had gone too far when a Betty Crocker ad defending white bread as health food led nutritionists to critique the industry. Medical faculty from Yale University claimed that the food industry had derailed its integrity by making false health claims about certain foodstuffs. In their campaigns, advertisers never mentioned negative consequences of consuming processed foods.

The cost of food dropped in the 1920s. Americans ate more in 1928 than they did in 1914, particularly more refined sugar. Orange juice was now available year round. Refrigerators were more commonplace in the home. Convenience was the name of the game. Packaged foods and popular brands such as Wonder Bread, Wheaties, and Velveeta debuted. The focus of breakfast moved from meat and bread to citrus fruit and dry cereal with milk or eggs with toast. A typical lunch comprised a light sandwich, soup, or a salad. Dinner did not change much from the standard roast or broiled meat, with potato, vegetable, and dessert, but portions became smaller. Special dinners included shrimp cocktail, vegetable soup, Yorkshire pudding, roasted potatoes, stuffed tomatoes, with a dessert of peaches. Casseroles, shepherd's pie, Jell-O salads, mayonnaise, and canned soup were commonly part of a hearty American middle-class meal. Frozen foods were a fashionable choice, popularized by the BirdsEye brand during the 1920s. But not everyone enjoyed these culinary innovations. The Southern and Appalachian diets still comprised salted pork, cornmeal, and molasses. These regions had access to fruits and vegetables during spring and summer but had sparse access to flour and fat in wintertime.

Prohibition, which lasted from 1920 to 1933, had a strong impact on both drinking and dining out habits. Soft drinks became more popular and were needed as a draw for hotels and restaurants that would soon see their doors shuttered due to shrinking customer numbers. Speakeasies flourished nevertheless, illegally serving alcohol often coupled with entertainment. The Great Depression was at its worst during 1934, when one-quarter to one-third of American workers were unemployed. The middle class, however, was not as severely affected and actually benefitted from the lowered cost of food. The Art Deco aesthetic of the 1930s heavily influenced kitchen design, for those who could afford to take advantage of it, during the Great Depression. Stainless steel and chrome appliances were the style, culminating in the 1939 World's Fair, featuring the best of technological innovation of that decade. Franklin D. Roosevelt's New Deal instituted federal social programs to help the nation out of the crippling effects of the Great Depression. In this vein, a federally funded school lunch program, created especially to provide milk to inner-city children, was instituted in Chicago in 1940.

By the 1940s, Americans were eating more dried and canned food, despite improved refrigeration methods, and consuming almost as much canned as fresh produce. With America's entry into World War II came a nationwide food-rationing program. Americans were shocked. How could there be rations after the farm surpluses of the 1930s? One reason was the panic of sugar buying that ensued after the bombing of Pearl Harbor in December 1941. The Office of Price Administration mandated ration books to American families in May 1942, including coffee, sugar, meats, fats, butter, and oil. Americans were encouraged to grow their own vegetables, and victory gardens were successfully cultivated. By 1943, 40 percent of all vegetables were home grown. The production necessary to fuel the war machine of World War II brought almost full employment. Southerners fled to the north in search of defense work, a better life, and better food. Since most American males were enlisted in the army, the army diet helped improve their overall health.

Americans saw great prosperity in the years following the end of World War II. Veterans could receive a higher education through the GI Bill, resulting in higher incomes. They bought homes at a lower federal mortgage rate, married, and produced the Baby Boomer generation. Ads on TV and in magazines portrayed the image of the happy homemaker, with lots of kitchen and home conveniences. This was a myth however, as 50 percent of women returned to work in the 1950s. Frozen food became indispensable because of working families. Clarke Swanson's TV dinners provided a quick and easily heated meat, starch, and veggie meal. The demand for processed food resulted in the creation of more than 400 synthetic chemical additives during the 1950s. Breeding chickens were exposed to extra vitamins, antibiotics, and growth hormones, which made the birds appear plumper. In packaging, they were separated into thighs, wings, and so on, which were much easier to prepare than whole, feathered chickens. Accordingly, the price per pound of chicken increased.

American pastimes of the 1950s, such as BBQ and grilling, are still popular today. The flight from cities to suburbia provided the backyard and social space for this trend to flourish. Convenience foods such as orange juice from concentrate, Lipton's Onion Soup Mix, Cheez Whiz, and Eggo Frozen Waffles are just a few of the popular packaged items that emerged from the 1950s. Television advertising strongly influenced American dietary consumer choices, as families gathered around the tube to watch the *Ed Sullivan Show* and *I Love Lucy.* TV cooking shows also had a stronghold on the American homemaker psyche, demonstrating exotic techniques and daring women to try more complicated dishes. Women's magazines and newspapers were also populated with recipes and ads that enticed women to try both unfamiliar packaged goods and gourmet meals.

The detrimental health effects of processed foods eventually took a toll that required government intervention. In 1958, the Delaney Amendment was passed, restricting the use of food additives and banning any substance that could be shown to cause cancer in animals. Rachel Carson's *Silent Spring* debuted in 1962. Her claims that DDT destroyed bird populations had huge implications for agribusiness. The effect of cholesterol on cardiovascular health was documented in medical journals. Land-grant colleges were charged with showing farmers how to produce leaner animals. Again the pop culture female image changed from the curvaceous Jayne Mansfield and Marilyn Monroe to the slender Audrey Hepburn.

By the 1960s, the nuclear family had replaced the extended family as the typical American living unit. The decade began as a stable and prosperous era, which was rocked by massive societal changes. The space race, the Cold War, the roots of feminism, the civil rights movement, and a growing sense of environmental responsibility all influenced the American diet.

Freeze-dried foods such as those the astronauts took on their space missions could now be found on supermarket shelves. Peg Bracken's *I Hate to Cook Book* of 1960 dared to suggest that all homemakers were not necessarily willing to spend hours in a kitchen and was filled with recipes that used ready-made ingredients and could be prepared quickly. The health food movement grew in tandem with the antiestablishment trends of 1960s youth. Organic produce, raw milk products, brown rice, and homemade bread were traded for bleached white flour, processed cheese, and canned vegetables. African Americans began to get in touch with their southern cooking roots in the late 1960s. Afros were in. Southern dishes such as black-eyed peas, BBQ ribs, corn bread, and collard greens were now served up in soul food restaurants.

The politically tumultuous 1970s shook America's apple-pie image throughout the world. The Vietnam War and Watergate undermined people's faith in the U.S. government. The energy crisis resulted in fuel shortages and long gas lines at the pump. World hunger became a prominent political issue, and food stamp and free school lunch programs resulted. The "Me" decade was awash in contradictions. While agribusiness and fast food expanded, vegetarianism and organic farming moved beyond the scope of hippie communes into the mainstream. Gourmet cookery still stood staunchly behind Julia Child, who had by now become legend and was broadcast on color TV. Hidden Valley Ranch Dressing, Hamburger Helper, and Cocoa Pebbles were created; rich, saucy foods were highly coveted. However, throughout the 1970s, the number of low-salt and lite versions of popular packaged goods grew as well.

The United States emerged from the recession of the 1970s to a period of strong economic growth and prosperity during the 1980s. A new breed of workers, called Yuppies, or young urban professionals, set the benchmark for success. Lee Bailey penned cookbooks full of gourmet multicourse meals, suitable for large-scale entertaining. People ate out more at restaurants. It was the era of the celebrity chef, with Wolfgang Puck at the head of the pack. Americans demanded higher-quality alcohol, and California wines were now competing with French wines in terms of quality. Health food was still a strong subset of the American diet, though obesity steadily grew throughout the 1980s, most alarmingly in children and adolescents. As more "latchkey" kids came home to an empty house with both parents working, decadent chocolate desserts, Ben & Jerry's ice cream, fast food, and snack chips were easily available substitutes to the family meal.

As middle-class families gained more buying power in the 1990s, meal standards were raised. Home cooking became more popular, with gourmet grocers more commonly opening. While nostalgia for brands such as Kraft Macaroni & Cheese revitalized sales, there were more and healthier choices for frozen and packaged foods. Consumers also demanded to know where their food came from. Biotech giants such as Monsanto introduced GM, or genetically modified foods, to the public in the early 1990s. A force against GM foods grew as consumers saw the potential environmental and health risks of consuming bioengineered products. The Organic Food Production Act was instituted under the Farm Bill of 1990, which outlined the standards for handling and production of organically grown produce. Groups such as PETA brought the humane treatment of animals into public awareness, with more individuals choosing a vegan lifestyle, free of all animal by-products in their diet.

Both food professionals and consumers became more interested in food science during the 1990s, and the debut of the Food Network in 1993 revitalized the nation's interest in cooking from both low-brow and gourmet perspectives. Emeril Lagasse, Bobby Flay, Mario Batali, and Alton Brown became household names. *Gourmet* and *Bon Appetit* saw an increase in subscriptions.

What does the future hold for the diet of Americans? The nation's populace is now wealthier, older, more educated, and more ethnically diverse than a century before, and food choices will reflect those changes. Demographic and income projections from the Economic Research Service of the USDA in 2002 predicted per capita increases in consumption of fruits and vegetables through 2020. An ethnically diverse and relatively well-off society will demand a variety of food choices offered in both supermarkets and restaurants. Items such as tofu-grade soybeans and vine-ripened tomatoes will be the expectation, not the exception, resulting in a consumer-driven agricultural sector. And the shift in racial and ethnic composition of the United States will have a direct impact on consumer choices, notably, an increase in the variety of fruits, seeds, eggs, poultry, and fish and a move away from red meat and potatoes. What a difference a century makes.

I

1900s

Sherri Liberman

The dawn of the twentieth century brought with it a revolution in the way Americans lived, worked, traveled, and dined. The rapid rise of industrialization, the urbanization and growth of American cities, and new waves of immigration increased not only ethnic diversity but dietary variety as well. The culmination of westward expansion in the nineteenth century, coupled with the creation of a nationwide railroad network, allowed for faster transport of agricultural and manufactured foodstuffs. And the introduction of the Model T Ford in 1908 made the automobile the ultimate symbol of American independence, spawning the rise of the drive-to and drive-through fast-food establishments.

The shift of women's employment roles from the hearth to the workplace instigated a new era of convenience foods, for the busy housewife had fewer hours a day to prepare nutritious meals for the whole family. Food culture in the United States was also influenced by the new way laborers were eating, seeking out venues to eat and socialize with other workers, on the way to and from the home. Thus a new market developed for the food and restaurant industry, requiring others to prepare and serve meals. A canyon-like gap existed in the way the lower, middle, and upper classes dined at the turn of the century. The expansion of a lower middle class, made of office and shop workers, created a need for venues that were neither brash saloons nor high-end classy restaurants. Thus, urban diners, casual restaurants, and lunch counters sprouted along streetcar routes, which became the model for future roadside fast-food dining.

Nearly one million new people per year were entering the United States in the 1900s. It was the height of mass migration, with immigration streaming in primarily from eastern and southern Europe and from China. Famine, crop failure, and poverty were major motivators in the mass European exodus. And with these newest Americans came a mélange of culinary styles, traditions, and beliefs. Whole grain breads such as rye and pumpernickel, smoked fish and meats, and pickled vegetables were radical departures from the American palate at the time, which favored bleached white breads and the simplicity of boiled meats and potatoes. Italian immigration mainstreamed the acceptance of vegetables, pasta, pizza, olive oil, ice cream, espresso, and wine in the American diet. Before the early twentieth century, nutritional researchers preached that fruits and vegetables had little to no nutritional value because of their high water content, but Italian culinary tradition did not bend to these false assumptions. Russians and eastern Europeans from Poland, Hungary, and Romania introduced New York to pastrami, corned beef, and the bubbly delights of seltzer water. German delicatessens offered up prepared salads, jelly donuts, and smoked sausages, which later inspired the great American hot dog. In 1905, Frank Buckhurst began supplying deli meats and provisions to New York delicatessens, which later became the Boar's Head brand of meats. German delicatessens often sported a wild boar in the window of their establishments to symbolize abundance and prosperity. German delicatessens were later replaced in many cities by Jewish delis, which served only kosher meats or dairy products. The knish, dill pickles, chopped liver, gefilte fish, and lox added another dimension to the culinary landscape of urban America. Meanwhile, in the South, Galatoire's Restaurant opened in 1905 in New Orleans, ushering a now century-old tradition in French Creole cookery.

The influence and interchange of culture went both ways, and many immigrants found themselves willingly, or unwillingly, adopting the eating habits of Americans. A greater variety of meats was available in the United States than in Europe, and a startling array of sweets. Coffee and bread replaced soup as the breakfast of choice for many eastern Europeans, the easy availability of coffee being a new luxury as well. But despite the availability of an increased array of canned goods, many immigrant women continued to can and preserve their own vegetables and wouldn't be caught dead putting store-brought bread on the table. The concept of table etiquette also varied widely. Boston society women founded the Louisa May Alcott Club for young immigrant girls in order to school them in the norms of American housekeeping and manners.

Business models in the food industry began to morph during the age of monopoly. The formation of food processing giants such as Domino Sugar symbolized the new food oligarchy and wielded the influence of industry over consumer choices. Domino mounted a media campaign to convince the public of the possibly unsanitary nature of eating unrefined brown sugar in favor of white, refined sugar. By using photos of unattractive but ultimately harmless microbes, Domino was able to manipulate the public into believing that eating brown sugar could be dangerous to one's health. An obsession with health in general was trumped up by brands such as Kellogg's through promotion of its Corn Flakes and Postum's Grape Nuts cereals. Kellogg's Corn Flakes carried with it the weight of being a product of the famous Kellogg brothers of the Battle Creek Sanitarium, a Seventh Day Adventist health facility in Michigan. Charles W. Post, once a patient himself at the sanitarium, invented and promoted Grape Nuts cereal, even going so far as moving to Battle Creek, Michigan, in order to gain credibility as a health force to be reckoned with.

In addition to a newfangled focus on dietary health, the arena of cooking science expanded as well at the turn of the twentieth century. Fannie Farmer, author of the *Boston Cooking School Cookbook*, opened her own school of cooking in 1902. Known as the "mother of level measurements," Farmer stressed precise and standardized measurements in all her recipes. Until that time, recipes would often use vague descriptions such as "a piece of butter the size of an egg" or "a teacup of milk." She articulated the chemical processes that would occur during cooking in her explications. A passionate proponent of proper nutrition for the sick, she felt that the appearance, presentation, and taste of food were as important for the infirm as they were for the healthy.

Food safety was a major and legitimate concern during the early 1900s. Food, milk, and water contamination caused a host of foodborne illnesses, including typhoid fever, tuberculosis, and botulism. Upton Sinclair's *The Jungle*, published in 1906, exposed the unsanitary and dangerous practices of a Chicago meat-packing facility, leading to the passage of the Meat Inspection Act. Public awareness of the problem had been piqued, and in 1906, the first Pure Food and Drug Act was passed. Methods to contain illness such as hand washing, improved sanitation, refrigeration, and pasteurization were promoted. As a result, the incidence of typhoid fever decreased from 100 cases per 100,000 in 1900 to approximately 34 per 100,000 in 1920, before the proliferation of vaccines and antibiotics. And in 1908, the city of Chicago passed the first compulsory milk pasteurization law.

During this time, diet fads emerged, most notably the dubious claims of Horace Fletcher. His mantra was the low-protein diet, reduced food intake, and thorough mastication, or chewing, as a path to good health. "Fletcherization" entailed chewing each piece of food until it was devoid of taste, at least 100 times, and keeping liquids in the mouth for up to 30 seconds. To his credit, Fletcher used his vast personal wealth to fund scientific research to test his nutritional theories. Fletcher, along with John Harvey Kellogg, eschewed the concept of eating for pleasure in favor of a rigorous, disciplined approach to diet. This severity in diet stood in stark contrast to the messy, boisterous, social way that many of America's newest arrivals ate.

American produce became more varied as a result of expanded rail routes, refrigerated railcars, and scientific research and development. Agricultural scientists developed the strain of lettuce known as *iceberg* in 1902, which was to become the quintessential salad lettuce, in vogue for much of the twentieth century. Before then, lettuce was considered a delicacy, consumed primarily by the upper classes, due to its lack of hardiness during transport. But the sturdy crisphead iceberg lettuce rivaled cabbage in its firmness. Food critic James Beard commented, "Many people damn it, but it adds good flavor and a wonderfully crisp texture to a salad."

At the other end of the spectrum was the explosion of candy and snack food that went along with increased time for leisure activities. The 1904 St. Louis World's Fair introduced a novelty-hungry public to some of the key staples of American food culture. Peanut butter, ice cream cones, lemonade, iced tea, and hamburgers with buns were all hot sellers during the centennial celebration of the Lewis and Clark voyage. The Fair featured more than 125 concessionaires and five restaurants seating more than 2,000 people. The Fair also promoted foods from around the world and exemplified the cultural melting pot that was being stirred up all over the United States. Chilies and tamales were featured at the Streets of Mexico exhibit, tea was poured into delicate cups at Fair Japan, and savory stew was served up at the Darkest Africa village. Although curiosity about other world cultures was a positive attribute of the exhibition, the portrayal of African and Native American "savages" was far from culturally sensitive by today's standards. Wholesomeness and healthfulness of food consumption was a major theme for many of the exhibitors, such as Quaker Oats, whose claim was that eating their cereal led to good health, urging the public to eat less meat and more oats. Despite this new obsession with health food, the turn of the century saw the burgeoning explosion in canned and packaged goods. Canned soups, instant cereals, and

Diners enjoy an open-air luncheon at the Temple Inn during the 1904 World's Fair in St. Louis. (Library of Congress)

packaged desserts all became commonplace during the first decade of the century.

Packaging and advertising also became tantamount to creating consumer allure, and product image was now as important as the quality and performance of the goods themselves. The Heinz brand capitalized on a niche of products traditionally produced at home before the twentieth century, such as pickles and other condiments. Heinz was the first company to erect an electric sign in New York City, a six-story pickle, ringing in the era of large-scale advertising. Heinz also pioneered the concept of vertical integration, controlling all aspects of production from seed to shelf. Henry Heinz engineered his own strain of cucumber seeds for his pickles, contracted farmers to grow them, delivered the seeds to farmers in freighters and tankers owned by Heinz, and then packaged and preserved the pickles in bottles, also made by Heinz.

Health foods, novelty foods, ethnic foods, and corporate branding were the culinary key notes of the 1900s. These threads evolved and grew more elaborate as the century progressed.

Entries

Animal Crackers

Sweetened biscuits in the shape of animal forms began appearing in the United States around the late 1880s. Originally imported from England, a menagerie of critters were soon sold in local U.S. bakeries and were touted in 1876 as Zoologicals at the Centennial Exposition in Philadelphia. Demand for animal biscuits apparently grew after P.T. Barnum's circus visited England in 1889, and capitalizing on the popularity of both the circus and the cookie, food companies in the United States such as Hetfield & Ducker of Brooklyn and Vanderveer & Holmes Biscuit Company began the mass production of the cracker under the name Animals. These firms later became the New York Biscuit Company, and Animals helped them prosper. P.T. Barnum apparently never saw a cent from the mass marketing of his circus-inspired cookies. The National Biscuit Company, a.k.a. Nabisco, became the manufacturer and distributor of Barnum's Animals in 1902, later Barnum's Animal Crackers in 1948. These crackers had a distinctive zoo and performance animal bent. As eye-catching packaging began to blossom in the early twentieth century, executives at Nabisco knew that Barnum's Animals had to set themselves apart. Previously, cookies had mainly been distributed in tins called cracker barrels. The iconic red circus wagon with the string on top was unveiled just in time for Christmas of 1902, so that the cookie box could be hung as a Christmas ornament. Sold for 5 cents a pop, the bright red and green circus wagon sporting exotic caged animals was eye-catching and a huge hit. Over the past century, 54 different animal species have paced around the cage of the circus box, from tigers, giraffes, and zebras, to the most recent addition, the koala bear, chosen by a 48 percent consumer voter margin in 2002 over competitors such as the penguin, which was the runner up, as well as the walrus and cobra. Animal Crackers evoke a sweet nostalgia in American pop culture, being the name of the eponymous 1930 Marx brothers film—and and the subject of Shirley Temple's 1935 tune "Animal Crackers in My Soup." Nabisco currently produces 7 million Animal Crackers a day.

Automats

The opening in Philadelphia of the first Horn & Hardart automat in 1902 signified a sea change in American dining out. Just steps from Independence Hall, the first Horn & Hardart automat represented a harkening of a new era, the edible version of the assembly line. The Manhattan chain opened in 1912. Blending the concepts of vending machine and cafeteria and ultimately predicting the fast-food chain, automats were sleek, chrome-plated temples of modernism. The chain was originally founded by Joseph Horn and Frank Hardart, who modeled the self-service eatery after an automat based in Germany. Customers would exchange three nickels with women called "nickel throwers" for coins to be inserted into a slot. With a twist of a porcelain-centered chrome knob, one could access a fully prepared hot snack, meal, or drink caged behind a glass hatch. Typical food served at automats included sandwiches, macaroni and cheese, and coffee dispensed from an Art Deco–style urn. Food was served on dishes, with metal utensils like in a restaurant, but without a waiter in sight, and no tip necessary. Kitchen staff hid behind the wall of glass-encased food, ready to refill containers the moment their contents were emptied. The vast, cavernous automats flourished in northern industrial

Diners enjoy an "automatic" meal at the Horn & Hardart Baking Company automat in Philadelphia, Pennsylvania, in the early 1900s. Diners select the food they want by inserting coins into vending machine–style kiosks. (Horn & Hardart Baking Company)

cities where there was a large lunchtime base from both blue- and white-collar working communities. Seeing food behind shiny glass doors projected a sanitary image in an age of many health and food scares. The Horn & Hardart slogan "Less work for Mother" embodied the ideal of fast food. Socially, the automat was a meeting place for all classes; both the unemployed and the lawyer could sit side by side at the same table. At their height of popularity, Horn & Hardart automats served 800,000 people in one day, making it the world's largest restaurant chain. By 1979, only two remained, the rest converted to Burger King chains. The last Horn & Hardart automat shuttered its doors in 1991, ending a symbol of a bygone era.

Banana Splits

A chasm still exists between the two men who claim to be the inventor of the over-the-top sundae known as the banana split. Variations abound on this a-peeling dessert treat, but at its core, the banana split entails a scoop each of vanilla, chocolate, and strawberry ice creams, framed by a single vertically sliced banana, ultimately bejeweled with chopped nuts, syrup, maraschino cherries, and whipped cream. The earliest story posits that 23-year-old Latrobe, PA, drugstore soda-slinger and budding pharmacist David Evan Strickler invented the dessert in 1904 at the Tassel Pharmacy. Strickler enjoyed experimenting with different concoctions, particularly the exotic banana, which was still fairly new to U.S. audiences at the turn of the century. The banana split sundae, costing twice as much as other iced desserts at 10 cents a pop, appealed to the youthful student clientele of nearby St. Vincent's College. Strickler reportedly ordered long boat-shaped glass-blown bowls to accommodate his tasty new invention, though none of these bowls have remained in existence. In the winter of 1907, unaware of Strickler's innovation, Wilmington, OH, restaurateur Ernest Hazard encouraged his employees to invent a new dessert treat, giving them carte blanche to use all the ingredients available in the kitchen. Hazard was looking for a new dessert to capture the hearts and stomachs of his primarily college-aged clientele from local Wilmington College. The winning combination was a treat based on a split banana, accompanied by a variety of ice cream flavors and toppings. The winner of this contest? Ernest Hazard! Unfortunately, the Hazard theory has been debunked by printed evidence, which indicates that when the National Association of Retail Druggists met in Boston in 1905, the industry newspaper *The Soda Fountain* had already published a reference to a "banana split." Regardless, Wilmington, OH, holds steadfast to the claim that their city is the true spiritual home of the banana split, as Wilmington has long been the host of the annual banana split festival. This yearly summer bacchanal includes a make-your-own banana split booth, celebrity impersonators, a bull lassoing competition, and of course, a banana split eating contest. More than 2,000 banana splits are typically sold during the festival. In 2004, the National Ice Cream Retailers Association certified Latrobe, PA, as the birthplace of the banana split. No matter what town is legitimately the home of banana splits, one fact remains indisputable—their delicious appeal survives to this day.

Classic Banana Split

1 Banana—peeled and split lengthwise
1 Scoop each of chocolate, vanilla, and strawberry ice cream
Chocolate syrup
Strawberry sauce
Pineapple topping

Crushed nuts
Whipped cream
Maraschino cherries

Place banana halves in a long dish, with scoops of ice cream in between or on top of the banana halves. Drizzle chocolate syrup on top of the chocolate ice cream, strawberry sauce on the strawberry ice cream, and pineapple topping on the vanilla ice cream. Sprinkle crushed nuts on top; embellish with whipped cream and maraschino cherries.

Canned Tuna

Tuna fish first came into the limelight as a popular canned item after playing second fiddle to the more desirable tinned sardine for many years. Tuna, a member of the *Strombidae* family that also includes mackerel and bonito, was originally considered a nuisance fish whose catch distracted from commercial fishermen's more profitable enterprise, the sardine. But as the story goes, according to the National Fisheries Institute, the waters of San Pedro Bay did not yield enough sardines to meet the canning quota of 1903, so Southern Californian canner Alfred P. Halfhill was forced to find a way to fill the empty tins. Halfhill experimented with albacore tuna and discovered that it "turned white and tasted delicious when steam cooked." He took a chance and stuffed his remaining sardine tins with albacore instead. He sold 700 cases the first year, and by the outbreak of

World War I, production was up to 400,000 cases annually. In 1914, Frank Van Camp and his son bought the California Tuna Canning Company, later to become the famous Chicken of the Sea brand in 1952. World War I was a boon for the canned tuna industry, as the protein-rich, portable product became a staple of American soldiers overseas in Europe. The demand grew, and commercial fishermen began to expand their territory from Southern California northward and westward. By 1917, Van Camp began canning yellowfin tuna. Meanwhile, in Oregon, the Columbia River Packers Association (CRPA), primarily involved in salmon canning, finally jumped into the canned tuna waters around 1932, once albacore was discovered in abundance off the coast of Oregon. By 1938, the CRPA was canning as much tuna as it did salmon and adopted the BumbleBee seafoods label. Recent evidence revealing the presence of elevated mercury levels in canned tuna, especially in yellowfin tuna, caused the U.S. FDA to issue guidelines advising reduced intake of tuna consumption for pregnant women, nursing mothers, and children. The skipjack and eastern little tuna are currently recommended as lower-mercury alternatives to the yellowfin, rife with heavy metal.

Club Sandwich

Gentlemen's clubs were popular establishments and social pastimes for the centuries' wealthy, professional classes of the late nineteenth and early twentieth centuries. Originally the provenance of the English upper class, gentlemen's clubs spread to many of the English-speaking nations, including the United States. Whiling away the afternoon hours discussing politics, sport, and travel was a typical feature of clubhouse culture. What better accompaniment to feed the upper crust while playing parlor games and gambling than a tasty sandwich? A trail of crumbs leads to the Saratoga Clubhouse in Saratoga Springs, NY, as the birthplace that popularized the club sandwich in 1894 (coincidentally, the Saratoga Club is also the home of the potato chip, invented in 1853 by George Crum). There are as many versions of the club sandwich story as there are possible layers of toast in said sandwich. Marion H. Neil posits in her 1916 book *Salads, Sandwiches, and Chafing Dish Recipes* that the club sandwich emerged out of a combination of hunger and necessity. Club sandwich lore has it that a man stumbled into the pantry of his estate late at night, after the family and servants had retired. He pilfered through the pantry offerings: toast, butter, mayonnaise, bacon, cold chicken, and a slice of tomato were what he could conjure up. Layering the ingredients between two levels of toast, he created the club

The Saratoga Clubhouse at the race track in Saratoga Springs, New York, is the alleged birthplace of the club sandwich. (Library of Congress)

sandwich. The inventor of the sandwich belonged to the Saratoga Clubhouse, and after telling his mates of the snack, they began requesting it at the club, thus anointing it the club or clubhouse sandwich. Variants on the sandwich can include having from one to five layers of toast and using turkey instead of chicken. The first appearance of a recipe for the club sandwich was in the *Good Housekeeping Everyday Cook Book* by Isabel Gordon Curtis in 1903, and four major restaurants at the 1904 St. Louis World's Fair featured the sandwich on their menus. James Beard, the renowned American food writer, says of it: "It is one of the greatest sandwiches of all time and has swept its way around the world after an American beginning."

Corn Flakes

Brothers Will Keith and Dr. John Harvey Kellogg are credited with the innovation that produced the natural, crunchy breakfast cereal we know and love as Corn Flakes. Their story, however, is not quite as wholesome. Dr. John Harvey Kellogg became chief physician and medical director of the Battle Creek (MI) Sanitarium in 1866. His leadership advocated a healthy dietary regimen that eliminated meat, alcohol, tobacco, and caffeine from patients' diets while promoting the consumption of whole grains, nuts, fruits, and legumes. His other beliefs and practices were a bit more eccentric, such as requiring daily yogurt enemas for patients, and a fixation on the use of food to control patients' sexual urges. Will Keith was the business manager and jack-of-all-trades around the "San" and assisted brother J. H. with his nutritional experiments in the name of wellness. One of their goals was to create a digestible substitute for bread. Will accidently left a pot of boiled wheat soaking overnight, but not letting a useful thing go to waste, Kellogg forced the boiled grain through a machine with rollers. The product that emerged was a flattened, thin flake. Baking the flakes turned them crisp, and thus the first incarnation of a Kellogg's flaked cereal was created. It was served to sanitarium patients with positive feedback. In 1902, the Kelloggs used corn to produce a malt-flavored flake, which they thought would improve the taste, but it wasn't until four years later that the public outside the San walls got its first spoonful of Kellogg's Toasted Corn Flakes. Will Keith started the Battle Creek Toasted Corn Flake Company and in 1906 parted ways with his brother, who did not believe there was a market for breakfast cereals. Starting with just 44 employees, Kellogg's today boasts 32,000 employees in more than 19 countries.

Cotton Candy

Candy floss, which is also known as fairy floss, refers to the air-spun cloud of sugar known as cotton candy. Cotton candy, a carnival favorite, was revolutionized by mechanization in the United States by William Morrison and John C. Warton of Tennessee, who introduced the sticky fluff during the St. Louis World's Fair of 1904. It sold for a whopping 25 cents a bag, half the cost of admission to the fair. However, spun sugar has a lengthy history. The confectionary process was invented in Italy during the fourteenth century by first melting sugar in a pan, then using a fork to make strings over an upside-down bowl. The sugar was then allowed to dry, producing strands of a willowy, sweet dessert. In 1897, Morrison and Warton created an electric machine that would melt sugar with flavoring and dye, which was then pushed through a screen by centrifugal force to create the strands of sugar, the "cotton" of the candy. These strands were twirled around a paper cone and served up ready to eat. They received a patent for the machine in 1899. Morrison and Warton sold 68,655 boxes at the World's Fair, where it was touted as "candy floss" or "spun sugar." But there was competition lurking in the wings. Thomas

Patton invented his own cotton candy maker, a contraption that used caramelized sugar that formed threads—through a fork! A rotating gas-fired plate spun the threads into the requisite cone. Patton sold his airy confection at the Ringling Brothers Circus, and it quickly became a favorite among circus-going children. It was not until 1920 that the name "cotton candy" became a recognizable entity. In 1949, Gold Medal products premiered their cotton-candy making machine with a spring base, which operated with more reliability than previous models. Cotton candy remained a circus and carnival favorite until the 1970s, when automation allowed cotton candy production and packaging to become more streamlined. It was then also sold in stores and shopping malls. However, its popularity as a carnival, circus, and amusement park delight persists a century later.

Hershey's Chocolate Bars

Milton Hershey began his long, sweet, illustrious career in confections as a teenager, apprenticing in a candy store in Lancaster, PA. After studying the craft of caramel making in Denver, CO, Milton Hershey returned to Lancaster in 1883 to become a caramel purveyor. Enamored with the German chocolate-making machines he saw at the 1893 World's Columbian Exposition (Chicago World's Fair), Hershey bought some of these machines for his Lancaster plant and began using chocolate as a sweet coating for the caramels. Hershey also produced breakfast cocoa and baking chocolate during this time. Pleased with the results of his chocolate experiments, Hershey sold off the Lancaster Caramel Co. in 1900 for $1 million in order to concentrate solely on the chocolate end of his business. Hershey began producing milk chocolate in the form of bars and wafers at a lower cost per unit through mass production. Hershey made milk chocolate, formerly a high-end item only available through Swiss chocolatiers, an affordable luxury in America for all. As the demand for milk chocolate grew, Hershey saw a need to expand his chocolate production facilities. He constructed what was to become the largest chocolate factory in the world on a stretch of farmland near the place of his birth in Derry Township, PA. Hershey's Chocolate Company was a utopia of sorts. Dairy farms abounded in Derry Township, perfect for providing the milk for milk chocolate, while the hard-working people of Central Pennsylvania supplied the labor. Being close to the port cities of Philadelphia and New York allowed for easy access to sugar and cocoa shipments. In 1907, Hershey's Kisses debuted, rumored to have gotten their name from the sound the chocolate made while being deposited during the manufacturing process. These bite-sized treats were first individually hand wrapped in silver foil. In 1924, the Kiss became machine wrapped and donned its paper plume. Milton Hershey' made a sweet contribution to society not only in the form of chocolate but also through many great acts of philanthropy. Also in 1907, Milton opened Hershey Park in Spring Creek, PA—adding to community life with a recreational site for baseball, picnicking, and boating. It later became home to the Hersheypark amusement park with roller coasters and other fast-paced attractions. Unable to have children of their own, Hershey and his wife Catherine created the Milton Hershey School for orphaned boys in 1909.

Hot Dogs

Franks, wieners, red hots—call them what you will. The stories behind the coining of the term "hot dog" are as diverse as the nicknames that have evolved for America's quintessential pig-in-a-blanket. Pork sausages were purveyed in the German city of Frankfurt-am-Main as early as the fifteenth century. The term "frankfurter" was used by a butchers' guild in 1852 to describe a smoked sausage that was slightly curved, rumored to have been coaxed into this shape in honor of one butcher's pet dachshund. The term "wiener" originates from the city of Vienna, Austria, where sausages of beef and pork were the gold standard. German immigrants bought the sausage to the United States in the mid-nineteenth century, selling frankfurters and sauerkraut from pushcarts on New York City's Bowery, while German butcher Charles Feltman introduced the idea of the frank inside a warm roll at his Coney Island concession stand in 1867. St. Louis, MO, peddler Antoine Feuchtwanger claims to have done one better and placed the frankfurter inside a slit, slender bun, thus inventing the hot dog bun. He called his creation a "red hot." During the 1893 Columbian Exposition in Chicago, hungry crowds consumed a multitude of sausages couched in rolls—the perfectly convenient portable snack for strolling and viewing the exhibits. But the term "hot dog" is still couched in as much mystery as the source of meat used in said sausages. According to Dr. Gerald Cohen, professor of foreign languages at the University of Missouri-Rolla, and amateur linguists Barry Popik and David Shulman, the term originated well before 1900. Vendors would sell sausages around the dorms of eastern universities in carts called "dog wagons." The urban legend at the time was that the meat used was dog meat. A poem appeared in the October 5, 1895 edition of the *Yale Record* that hints at the term "hot dog."

"Echoes from the Lunch Wagon"

"'Tis dogs' delight to bark and bite,"
Thus does the adage run.
But I delight to bite the dog
When placed inside a bun.

A popular myth debunked by Cohen, Popik, and Shulman purports that "hot dog" was first coined by hawkers at a Giants baseball game on the New York Polo Grounds in 1902. It was a cold April day, and concession stand owner Harry Mozley Stevens was not selling much ice cream or cold soda as a result. He supposedly sent a vendor to buy some dachshund sausages and some rolls to spice up sales. Upon his triumphant return, the vendor

Patrons wait for hot dogs at the hot dog stand outside Luna Park at Coney Island, New York, ca. 1904. (Library of Congress)

started yelling "They're red hot! Get your dachshund sausages while they're red hot!" T.A. "Tad" Dorgan, a sports cartoonist for the *New York Evening Journal*, was present at the game. Upon hearing the bellowing vendors, he drew a cartoon of a frankfurter with a tail, legs, and head. Not knowing the proper spelling of "dachshund," he used the words "hot dog" in the cartoon panel. But that myth was tanked when Harry Stevens admitted in a 1926 interview that it was his son Frank who first convinced him to sell hot dogs, instead of ham and cheese sandwiches, in front of Madison Square Garden during a six-day bicycle race in 1906. Nor was Tad Dorgan even employed by the *New York Evening Journal* at the time! The only indisputable fact about hot dogs is their lasting popularity, with 7-Eleven selling approximately 100 million grilled hot dogs a year.

Ice Cream Cones

Although they've been around for centuries, ice cream cones were popularized in the United States at the St. Louis World's Fair Exposition of 1904, where more than 50 ice cream vendors scooped ice cream onto cones for hungry fair-goers. The certainty of the American progenitor, however, is still debatable. Italo Marchiony, an Italian immigrant from New York, was reputedly the first American to receive a patent for a " . . . molding apparatus as is used in the manufacture of ice cream cups and the like" in 1903. Marchiony had been selling homemade lemon ices from his pushcart on Wall Street since 1896. The custom was to serve ice cream scoops in liquor glasses, which was not cost effective, as customers would routinely wander off with the glasses. Additionally, this practice was somewhat unsanitary, as the ice cream was licked straight from the glass, which was washed in water, and handed to the next customer. What was Marchiony's solution? He created a baked, edible waffle to contain the scoop. While the waffle was still hot, Marchiony folded it into the shape of a cup. Marchiony's waffle cups made him the hottest ice cream vendor on Wall Street. His empire grew to 45 pushcarts, operated by men working under Marchiony's careful watch. His patent, however, was undercut as a result of the explosion of ice cream cone vendors at the St. Louis World's Fair. Since Marchiony's patent only specified one particular method of waffle mold construction, numerous aspiring ice cream cone entrepreneurs jumped on the bandwagon and created their own patents for waffle molds. But Marchiony still ran a successful Hoboken, NJ-based ice cream and wafer-making company until 1934, when the business unfortunately burned down. Another story purports that at the 1904 St. Louis World's Fair, pastry maker Ernest Hamwi rolled ice cream in crisp wafers, called Zalabia. The International Association of Ice Cream Manufacturers credits Hamwi as being the father of the modern ice cream cone. Hamwi traveled throughout the country for various manufacturers promoting the waffle cone before he opened the Missouri Cone Company in 1910.

Jell-O

"America's Most Favorite Dessert" rose to fame as *the* preeminent after-dinner treat during the first decade of the twentieth century. The quivering gelatin was originally patented in 1845 as a packaged dessert with instructions by American inventor, philanthropist, and industrialist Peter Cooper. However, he never actively marketed the sweet, shimmering stuff. Gelatin itself has a lengthy culinary past. Extracted from animal bones through the process of boiling, "geletine," as coined by the French, leaves a tasteless, colorless, and odorless gel in its wake. The jiggling, translucent gelatin eventually benefited from the addition of some flavorful fruit syrup by

---

Jell-O Art

Throughout the years, renowned artists such as Norman Rockwell, Rose O'Neill, and Maxfield Parrish illustrated Jell-O cookbooks and advertisements, sealing the deal on the brand name's legendary status. Some of these artful advertisements portrayed apple-cheeked, cherubic-looking children, surrounded by hearts, doilies, and other Art Nouveau embellishments, usually on the cusp of consuming a delicious slice of quivering Jell-O mold or dreaming about eating one. Fruit desserts were popular during the early years of the twentieth century; thus, the fruit-flavored gelatin was a natural companion to the 1900s dinner table.

---

former carpenter Pearl B. Wait of LeRoy, NY, who bought the patent from Cooper in 1895. Pearl was originally dabbling in cough remedy formulations, which led him to experiment with gelatin. Wait's wife, May David, is the one credited with coining the phrase Jell-O, which would soon be emblazoned not only on the infamous small cardboard boxes but eventually the American psyche. The Waits trotted out four Jell-O flavors: strawberry, raspberry, orange, and lemon. Jell-O was not an immediate success, and the Waits sold their patent to local townsman and medicinal salesman Frank Woodward for the sum of $450 in 1899. Woodward had some prior success and notoriety from the marketing of a product that eliminated chicken lice, as well as a roasted coffee product called Grain-O. Sales were still gelatinously slow at first, and by 1900, Woodward tried to sell the business to his manufacturer Sam Nico for $35, but even he wouldn't touch the quaking lump of a business! A rigorous advertising campaign carried out by dapperly dressed salesmen, in concert with some positive press by cooking "experts," who claimed that Jell-O was the perfect accompaniment to end an elegant meal, saved Woodward's burgeoning Jell-O brand in the end. Sales reached $250,000 by 1902 and nearly $1 million by 1906. The first printed Jell-O ad debuted in *Ladies Home Journal* in 1904, in addition to printed Jell-O recipe booklets.

Muffuletta Sandwich

The great wave of emigration from Sicily to New Orleans brought about the creation of the tasty sandwich known as the "muffuletta" (also spelled "muffoletta" or "muffolata") and inadvertently, a new way of doing business. The word "muffoletta" translates literally as "small, fingerless mitten." Sicilian bakers working from pushcarts sold various kinds of breads directly to customers, including the round Sicilian loaf known as muffoletta. Sicilian American workers would traditionally buy and eat all the ingredients for their lunch separately, the bread from a pushcart, the meat, cheese, and vegetables from the grocer and other vendors. Eventually, a crafty grocer named Salvatore Lupo of Central Grocery decided to strike up a deal with the local baker, buying up his supply of bread and reselling it to customers, thus turning the bread vendors into wholesalers. In 1906, Lupo came up with yet another brilliant lunchtime innovation. About 10 inches in diameter with sesame seeds sprinkled on top, muffoletta bread has a crisp crust and chewy center, perfect for sandwich making. He combined all the ingredients workers usually bought for lunch into one handheld, convenient sandwich. Muffoletta bread proved its mettle and could hold the contents without leakage. Salvatore stuffed the bread with olive salad, cheese, and meats. Spelling, however, was not his forte, and the name of the sandwich was changed to "muffuletta." The sandwich was so easy to carry that it became an instant lunchtime hit, and Central Grocery was the go-to destination for muffuletta. Today there are many variations on the sandwich, but in essence, the muffuletta bread at its heart contains marinated olive salad, capicola, salami, emmentaller, mortadella, and provolone. The olive salad comprises olives, carrots, celery, and cauliflower, seasoned and marinated for 24 hours before serving. Visitors to New Orleans today can still visit the Central Grocery for a slice of the original muffuletta sandwich.

New York–Style Pizza

New York City is considered to be the birthplace of pizza in America. In 1905, Antonio "Totonno" Pero began making tomato pies, fired out of a coal oven at Generro Lombardi's grocery store, a popular lunch spot in Little Italy at 53 ½ Spring Street. The pies would be wrapped in paper and tied up with string, so workers, mainly of Italian descent, could transport them back to their worksites. An entire pie in those days would cost 5 cents, but not everyone could afford it, so Lombardi would carve the pie into slices according to what customers could pay. Thus began the tradition of New York–style pizza by the slice. Totonno eventually left Lombardi's in 1924 to start his own pizzeria in Coney Island. Generally speaking, New York–style pizza is characterized by wide, flat, thin, foldable slices. Tomato sauce and mozzarella cheese are the foundation, often topped with accoutrements

---

Regional Cookbooks

Much can be learned about Americans' eclectic palates from regional cookbooks published during the first decade of the twentieth century. Written in both Finnish and English, *The Finnish-American Cookbook*, published in Kaleva, Michigan, in 1905, utilizes American fish and vegetables prepared with Scandinavian flair. Minnie Fox's 1906 *Blue Grass Cookbook* is an authentic Kentucky recipe collection, including directions on how to cure your own ham ("Kill your hogs when the wind is from the Northwest," the book advises). *One Hundred and One Mexican Dishes*, compiled by May Southworth in San Francisco in 1909, had home cooks dishing out enchiladas, tortillas, and tamales well before Taco Bell appeared on the market.

---

such as sausage, pepperoni, or mushrooms, and a splash of oregano flakes. The high-gluten dough is hand-tossed, and many think the minerals that are present in New York tap water are responsible for the unique taste of its crust that is rarely duplicated outside New York City. The original Lombardi's shuttered its doors in 1984, but a childhood friend of Jerry Lombardi, Generro's grandson, reopened it at 32 Spring Street in 1994. The cult of Lombardi lives on.

Peanut Butter

J. H. Kellogg, of Corn Flakes fame, received a patent in 1897 for "Process of Preparing Nutmeal," which he originally developed as a vegetarian source of protein for his Battle Creek Sanitarium. The first published reference to a peanut butter and jelly sandwich in the United States was rumored to be by Julia Davis Chandler in 1901. The winning flavor and texture combination of gooey sweetness became an immediate hit with young children. However, peanut butter was still considered a delicacy in the early 1900s, and what today would be considered a down-home lunchbox staple was to be found at some of New York's haughtiest tearooms. Peanut butter at the turn of the century was paired with pimento, watercress, and other seemingly odd ingredients, often on crackers or toast triangles. The clinging quality and nutty taste of peanut butter made it a natural, spreadable companion to both sweet and savory flavors. On Valentine's Day of 1903, St. Louis physician Dr. Ambrose W. Straub received a patent for his peanut-inspired invention—a mill for grinding peanuts into a buttery paste. He invented this machine in order to create a steady supply of nut paste to use as a palatable food for geriatric patients who could not chew easily. Straub convinced George Bayle, of Bayle Food Products, Inc., to mechanize the process and package his peanut butter, which was then sold out of barrels for roughly 6 cents a pound. Dr. George Washington Carver, an agricultural chemist at the Tuskegee Institute in Alabama, also revolutionized the peanut industry with his discovery of more than 300 uses for peanuts, including peanut butter, in the early twentieth century. The popularity of peanut butter gained even more momentum at the St. Louis Universal Exposition in 1904, where C. H. Sumner sold more than $700 worth of the spread at his concession stand, touted as a health food. The oldest peanut butter company in the United States was founded in 1908, Krema Products of Columbus, Ohio. Founder Benton Black used the slogan "I refuse to sell outside Ohio," a strong selling point during an age when barreled peanut butter would spoil quickly if transported long distances, and where interstate roads did not exist. Americans are still nuts about peanut butter, as half the peanut production in the United States is used toward making peanut butter.

Pepsi-Cola

The motivation behind the invention of one of America's greatest colas, Pepsi-Cola, was to create a thirst-quenching beverage as respite from a hot, humid North Carolina summer. Caleb Bradham, a New Bern, NC, pharmacist and drugstore owner, wiled away the summer of 1898 experimenting with various combinations of spices, syrups, and juices in search of a refreshing soft drink to serve parched customers. He settled on an elixir of kola nut extract, vanilla, and other rare oils that his customers called "Brad's Drink." Theories abound on the origin of the word Pepsi. It could be from the Greek word "pepse," which means to digest, as Bradham promoted the soft drink as a cure for dyspepsia. It could also have come from the feeling of "pep" that Caleb's customers experienced when they drank the beverage. Some think it comes from the popping sound made from the can opening. Caleb Bradham originally bought the name "Pep Cola" from a bankrupt Newark, NJ, competitor for $100 and renamed the soft drink Pepsi-Cola. In 1902, Bradham founded the Pepsi-Cola Company, then just a room in the back of his New Bern pharmacy. At first Bradham mixed his own syrup, which was sold only through soda fountains, but he soon realized a greater market was to be had in bottling Pepsi, which people could drink and transport anywhere. His idea was a hit, and business began booming. Pepsi was trademarked by the U.S. Patents Office in 1903. An artist and neighbor of Bradham designed the first

Pepsi advertisement, and Bradham was able to move his business into a larger warehouse. By 1904, Pepsi was being sold in 6-ounce bottles, and Bradham began to franchise the syrup to local bottling plants. In just six years, Pepsi was franchised in 24 states. As with many businesses, World War I had a devastating effect on Bradham's hold on Pepsi-Cola. Sugar prices fluctuated wildly, and Bradham was forced to speculate on this key ingredient. His gamble did not pay off, and by 1923, he was forced into bankruptcy. Bradham returned to his humble beginnings at the pharmacy. Pepsi-Cola changed hands several times throughout the 1920s and 1930s, being salvaged in 1931 by Loft Candy manufacturer Charles Guth. Loft Candy maintained retail candy stores with soda fountains and promoted Pepsi as a result of Coca-Cola refusing to give him a discount on syrup. Pepsi regained its prominence once again in 1940 with the first Pepsi broadcast advertising jingle, "Nickel Nickel," which lampooned the higher cost and smaller bottle size of competing Coca-Cola. Pepsi began targeting an African American demographic in the 1940s, which resulted in threats to Pepsi-Cola employees by the Ku Klux Klan. Other notable events in Pepsi history include the 1959 meeting between Soviet Premier Nikita Khrushchev and the U.S. Vice President Richard Nixon over a bottle of Pepsi. Ensuring its long-term success, Pepsi advertising campaigns have always changed to suit the signs of the times over the years, such as "Join the Pepsi People, Feelin' Free" in the 1970s and "Pepsi. The Choice of a New Generation" in the 1980s.

Planter's Peanuts

Roasted peanuts were first popularized as a portable snack food in the United States by Amedeo Obici, who founded Planter's Peanuts in 1906. Obici was born in Oderzo, Italy, and emigrated to the United States in 1889, where he worked at Musante's fruit store in Wilkes-Barre, PA. The Musante's had a peanut roaster and used a fan to blow the scent of roasted peanuts out into the street to lure customers inside the store. After learning the ins and outs of grocery, Obici was eventually inspired to break out on his own, fashioning a peanut roaster from local scrap parts for $4.50. In a few years, Obici, with his horse and wagon, became a peanut legend, calling himself "The Peanut Specialist." One of his gimmicks was to put each letter of his last name into the bags of peanuts. Only one in fifty bags contained the "O." If a customer was lucky enough to capture the bag with the "O," the customer would receive a "gold watch" (worth about $1). Obici had the foresight to understand the allure of the prize in the package, and with his newfound money, he was able to bring the rest of his family to the United States in 1895, as well as open his own fruit stand. In 1897, Obici opened an eatery in downtown Wilkes-Barre with Mario Peruzzi. The restaurant served oyster stew and, of course, roasted peanuts. The pair founded the Planter's Peanuts Company in 1906, which roasted and salted Virginia peanuts. The business was incorporated as Planters Nut and Chocolate Company in 1908. Obici's innovation in blanching the red skins from shelled peanuts, so that the skins came off cleanly, contributed to the success of his snack peanut business. His business philosophy revolved around garnering repeat business and building the brand name rather than pocketing steep profits at the beginning. The mascot Mr. Peanut debuted in 1916, and that unmistakable peanut dressed in top hat, monocle, and cane created the classy hallmark one associates with snack peanuts. The icon came about from a contest Obici held to develop a trademark. The iconic Mr. Peanut was inspired by a drawing submitted by 14-year-old Anthony Gentile of a "little peanut person." Mr. Peanut prizes are now expensive collectible items, particularly those produced prior to 1961.

Sweethearts Candy

What says "Be My Valentine" more than a fistful of Necco Sweethearts Conversation Hearts? Sweethearts debuted in 1902 from the Necco Wafer Company, and some of the original sayings such as "Be Mine" and "Kiss Me" are still in existence today. Necco emerged as a candy powerhouse after Bird, Wright and Company and Chase and Company combined forces in 1901 to form the largest confectionary company in the United States, based out of Boston. The tradition of branding candy with coy sayings actually started in the 1860s with the brother of Necco's founder, Daniel Chase. These prototypes would be passed around at weddings with adages such as "Married in pink, he will take to drink" and "Married in white, you have chosen right." The 1902 Sweethearts Conversation Hearts were also produced in the shape of postcards, baseballs, horseshoes, and watches, in addition to the hearts. The recipe for Sweethearts has never veered from its original formula: sugar, corn syrup, gelatin, gum, food coloring, and artificial flavoring. Dough is fashioned and rolled out, imprinted with a saying, stamped into a heart shape, and then dried for 45 minutes. In the 1990s, Necco Vice President Walter Marshall gained considerable notoriety for unraveling a new Sweetheart saying, "Fax me."

Necco still sells more than 8 billion hearts a year and produces about 100,000 pounds of hearts a day.

Further Reading

Anderson, Jean. *The American Century Cookbook*. New York: Clarkson N. Potter, 1997.

Crowley, Carolyn Hughes. "Meet Me at the Automat." *Smithsonian*, August 2001. http://www.smithsonianmag.com/history-archaeology/object_aug01.html.

Levenstein, Harvey. *Revolution at the Table: The Transformation of the American Diet*. Los Angeles: University of California Press, 2003.

Wold, Burt and Smith, Andrew F. *Authentic Regional Cuisine: Real American Food*. New York: Rizzoli Books, 2006.

Food and Drink at the Pan-American Exhibition

http://ublib.buffalo.edu/libraries/exhibits/panam/food/culture.html

2

1910s

Sherri Liberman

One often associates the decade of the 1910s with the outbreak of World War I, although American involvement in this conflict lasted only from 1917 to 1918. This brief window had a staggering impact on how Americans lived, worked, shopped, and consumed. The first real draft in U.S. history dramatically changed the American diet. Food riots erupted in the streets of New York as the cost of wheat skyrocketed. Sugar rationing was federally mandated. Even after Armistice was declared, rations were encouraged to make food available for the reconstruction efforts in Europe. People were urged to cut down on white bread, butter, and sugar consumption, as these restricted food items were earmarked for U.S. and Allied troops. The U.S. Food Administration, created by Herbert Hoover during the war effort, stated that wheat, beef, dairy, and sugar offered the greatest nutritive value while taking up the least shipping space. The rations were a great success in part because of decades of public debate regarding the safety of food supply, the virtue of a healthy diet, and an emphasis on more economical cooking.

Rations were also capitalized upon as a financial market by food processors that seized the opportunity to promote baking powders as substitutes for eggs and vegetable and cottonseed oil as replacements for lard and butter. Molasses and corn syrup were touted for use as sweeteners in place of sugar. Canneries had a chance to push their canned salmon and tuna as meat substitutes as other meat became more and more unobtainable. Health gurus promoted the consumption of peanuts and legumes. Door-to-door campaigns asked householders to sign cards to promote the sacrifice of wheat and red meat for the war cause and operated with methods similar

to those of the Temperance movement. By the end of 1917, more
than half of U.S. families signed
the ration cards. The cards urged
families to give up red meat on
Tuesdays, eat no wheat on Wednesdays, do without pork on Satur-
days, and commit to one meatless
meal per day. Butter became "war
butter," which was butter cut with
gelatin or milk. It was not a stable
substance and could not be used in
baking or cooking.

Almost one-tenth of the U.S.
population were German immigrants or from the Austro-
Hungarian Empire. German was
the most commonly spoken second
tongue in the United States in the
1890s, and bilingual schools were
common. Unfortunately, World
War I led to the suppression and
persecution of German culture and
ethnic foods in the United States.

United States Food Administration poster
encourages Americans to "save the food" during
U.S. involvement in World War I. (National
Archives)

The anti-German sentiment was so strong that H. L. Mencken called sauerkraut "liberty cabbage" in his book, *The American Language.* The Liberty Bread
Company initiated this campaign in 1918: "Better eat war bread now than the
black bread of Germany later." And the *Official Recipe Book by The State Council
of Defense of Illinois* states that the United States must not run out of wheat,
meat, or fats, lest the Germans win the war.

Other "ethnic" cuisine thrived during and after World War I. Chili
became a mainstream staple of the American diet after World War I,
although the chili fad did not fully blossom until the 1960s and 1970s.
The first commercially produced chili powder was introduced in 1902 by
German immigrant William Gebhard in Texas. Army chili did not contain
the traditional beans until 1910. Before that, chili was strictly *con carne,*
popularized in the West during the Mexican-American War, and first
appeared as a written recipe in the *Manual of Army Cooks* in 1896. Chili
con carne was referred to as American Chop Suey by the army during
World War I, and canned chili became available at grocery stores.

President Wilson's declaration of war on April 16, 1917, delayed passage of Prohibition legislation, but teetotalers from the Anti-Saloon League urged that wheat should be conserved for food, not distilled into liquor. The fact that most beer brewers were German also added fuel to the Prohibitionist movement's fire.

The nutritional value of food became a subject of great interest to researchers during the 1910s, when vitamins A, the B's, C, D, and E were identified and classified. Vitamins were discovered to be healthful components of food, and a diet without them was responsible for diseases such as scurvy and rickets. In 1911, author Upton Sinclair published *The Fasting Cure*, extolling the health virtues of fasting. He documents 277 cases where fasting had improved health, including his own.

Wealthy mining engineer Herbert Hoover became the U.S. Food Administrator under President Wilson in 1916 and organized food relief in Belgium and other war-ravaged countries. Herbert Hoover also hired food writers to promote alternatives to consuming meat, sugar, and butter. Cookbooks were published to promote recipes using the substitutes based on the *Manual for Army Cooks*, compiled by Captain L. L. Deitrick. Many veterans became short-order cooks after gaining cooking experience overseas in the war. Wartime cooking techniques carried into postwar cuisine. Bakers continued to use barley flour in their cakes, as it held moisture well. Bran muffins were introduced in 1912, when Fannie Farmer published the recipe in her *A New Book of Cookery*. Heavier muffins were later promoted by Kellogg's cereal company using All-Bran and raisins in 1919.

The suffrage movement was in full swing in the 1910s. Suffrage cookbooks were profitable tools for fundraising and showed that feminist politics were not incompatible with cooking. Home bread baking dropped to 70 percent, while packaged cereals, pancakes, and the Aunt Jemima brand began to flourish. Pancakes, once considered only a cold-weather food, were now elevated to the status of breakfast treat and eaten all year round. Improved refrigeration meant that national ice cream consumption skyrocketed, from 30 million gallons in 1909 to 150 million gallons in 1919. In 1914, New York fur trader Clarence Birdseye noticed that fish that had been frozen rock hard for months defrosted fresh, eventually inspiring his line of Birds Eye frozen foods. In 1912, the first cellophane was produced, which did wonders for food preservation.

Urbanization and immigration popularized ethnic cuisines and glamorized gustatory excess. On the other end of the spectrum, popular all-American icons such as the Quaker Oats man appeared on the scene, with the debut of Quaker Puffed Rice in 1913. Patented in 1916, processed cheese became known as American cheese. Kraft eventually won the contract to supply the armed services with 6 million pounds of its yellow-orange-tinged cheese. Despite the growing focus on packaged foods, tripe, heart, sweetbreads, kidneys, brains, turtle, frog's legs, pig's trotters, and calf's head were the meats of choice during the 1910s.

The postwar economy may have even spurred on the invention of the fortune cookie. One popular legend posits that David Jung, founder of the Hong Kong Noodle Company, invented the fortune cookie in 1918 to lift the spirits of unemployed men who gathered on the streets, presenting the skid rowers with a sweet treat and an encouraging word. In addition, after the war-chop suey, key lime pie, red flannel hash, and Swedish meatballs all became mainstream American dishes.

Housework became much easier throughout the 1910s thanks to several innovations in home appliances, freeing up housewives to do more than chores during the days. More households than ever had access to electricity and running water. The invention of the vacuum cleaner in 1908 sped the process of tidying up considerably. Refrigerators reduced the necessary number of trips to the grocery store per week, as the shelf life of food could be extended much longer. Kitchen cabinets replaced the home food pantry. The era of the combination stove began, using gas plus wood or coal as fuel. Grocery stores themselves began to evolve into the self-service entities they are today, with the opening of the Piggly Wiggly supermarket chain in 1916 in Memphis, Tennessee. Grocery stores also began carrying thousands more items to make creative cooking easier. A&P grew to more than 1,726 grocery stores during this decade. Electric toasters popped onto the scene in 1919, making bread warming a snap. The Electric Exhibition, which took place in New York in 1911, introduced chafing dishes, skillets, grills, percolators, toasters, and waffle irons to a beguiled audience. Despite these burgeoning luxuries, new appliances were prohibitively expensive for the majority of householders. A new refrigerator cost around $600, about half the annual income of most American households at the time.

Many new innovations in packaging were introduced during the 1910s as well, including Campbell's condensed soup, which debuted in 1911. Condensed soups simply required adding water to make an instantly delicious meal. By 1920, more than one million cans of 20 varieties of soup were sold. In 1916, Campbell's published *Helps for the Hostess* to show women how to use canned soups in recipes, using the brand name as a powerful marketing tool. Oreo cookies became America's most popular packaged cookie. Advertising played a major role in the success of both these brands. The tradition of finding a prize in the Cracker Jack box began in 1913, a clever ploy on the part of advertisers to encourage brand loyalty.

The gestation of major social changes that began during the decade of the 1910s evolved the culture of cuisine and home economics in the United States. The last great wave of immigration from southern and eastern Europe permanently changed the population makeup of American cities, and thus their dietary and restaurant offerings. The growing exodus of African Americans from the U.S. South introduced soul food to northern U.S. cities. The improved mechanization of chores lent a helping hand to women as the women's suffrage movement grew, and the perception of women's roles in and out of the home became more flexible. On the cusp of modernity, with many vestiges of the industrial age still intact, the 1910s created a bridge between an old-fashioned era of penny candy and home cooking on the stove and a speedier dynamic of branded food and self-service.

Entries

California Associated Raisin (Sun-Maid)

Although it is likely that the Phoenicians and Egyptians were among the earliest consumers of dried fruits more than 3 millennia ago, their debut in the United States began roughly around the time of the Gold Rush in California. The soil, climate, and California sun were amenable to raisin cultivation. By the late 1800s, raisin grape acreage had flourished, and attempts to form a raisin growers' cooperative began in 1898. However, not until 1912 did the California Associated Raisin Company became an officially

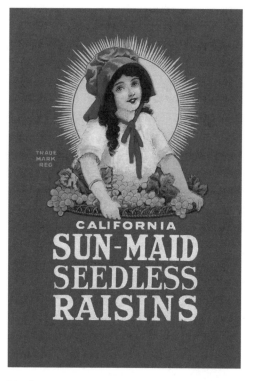

The Sun-Maid raisin trademark was created after a Sun-Maid raisin executive spotted employee Lorraine Collett Petersen wearing her mother's red sun bonnet in 1915. (Courtesy of Sun-Maid Growers of California)

established entity. In 1915, the brand name Sun-Maid Raisins was adopted by the association to promote and identify its product. The inspiration for the iconic red-bonneted maid was a teenager named Lorraine Collett Petersen. Originally from Kansas City, Missouri, Ms. Petersen came to Fresno, California, with her family to work as a seeder and packer while attending high school. Sun-Maid executive Leroy Paine spotted Lorraine in her backyard drying her long brown hair and then donning her mother's bright red bonnet. It was this vision of Ms. Petersen that inspired the image of the Sun-Maid raisin maiden. Lorraine wore her quintessential red bonnet, her smiling face with grape tray perched upon her waist. She, the sun maid in all her glory, became the symbol of California raisins and remains so to this day. The original likeness was painted by watercolor artist Fanny Scafford and was trademarked in 1916. Lorraine also worked as a spokesmodel for California Associated Raisin, promoting the dried fruit at the Panama Pacific International Exposition. One of the more unusual campaigns involved dropping packs of raisins from an airplane flying over San Francisco. The campaign was so successful, Sun-Maid needed to expand its headquarters in 1918, and the headquarters was soon recognized as "the finest building west of Detroit." The company prospers to this day, with the USDA recognizing raisins as an important part of a healthy lifestyle.

Pineapple, Canned

Canned pineapple went through a major spike in popularity around 1911, when more than 95 percent of Hawaii's pineapples were being canned and sent to the mainland United States for consumption. Jim Dole founded the Hawaiian Pineapple Company in 1901, later to become the Dole Food Company, single-handedly creating the modern pineapple industry in Hawaii. Running a series of successful magazine ads in 1907, Dole created a demand for canned pineapple. The desire for sweet, chunky pineapple also grew with the release of a pineapple-themed cookbook by the Pineapple Growers Association of Hawaii. The increased demand for canned pineapple resulted in lower prices so that pineapple was an affordable treat for most Americans. In 1913, Dole purchased a Ginaca machine, which could peel and core up to 35 pineapples per minute. By 1921, pineapple was Hawaii's largest crop and industry. In 1925, the Hawaiian Pineapple Company, now known as Dole, solicited creative recipes from cooks using canned pineapple. They received more than 60,000 entries, and 100 were selected for the publication in "Pineapple as 100 good cooks serve it," which included the winning recipe for Pineapple Upside Down Cake. Hawaii's control of the pineapple market began to wane after the 1960s as local labor costs soared, causing Dole to seek production facilities elsewhere, such as the Philippines, Costa Rica, and Thailand.

Commercial Mayonnaise, Commercial

Delicatessens began experimenting with preserving easy-to-spoil mayonnaise in the early twentieth century. A Philadelphia deli owner named Schlorer added preservatives to his wife's mayonnaise and sold it under the label "Mrs. Schlorer's Mayonnaise." He trademarked the mayonnaise in 1911. Meanwhile, in New York City, Richard Hellmann began selling his ready-made mayonnaise at his delicatessen in 1905, based on his wife Nina's original German recipe. The spread was a hit, first sold by the scoop in house, then sold in bulk to other stores. In 1912, he began mass marketing the sandwich spread in wooden containers. Later, Hellmann sold the mayo in glass jars and slapped a blue ribbon on one. This became the famous Hellman's Blue Ribbon Mayonnaise, later, trademarked in 1926. Both Schlorer and Hellmann also produced a mayonnaise cookbook in the 1920s, encouraging readers to explore the possibilities of adding mayo, and it is thought that preserved commercial mayonnaise accounts for the increased popularity of coleslaw as an accompaniment in American cookery.

Crème Vichyssoise

Emblematic of French elegance, the cold, cream-based, potato leek soup bedecked with chopped chives known as Vichyssoise was never actually popular in France. Vichyssoise was, in fact, invented in the United States, albeit by a French national. The creator was Luis Diat, Chef de Cuisine of the Ritz-Carlton Hotel in New York City for 41 years. Most accounts attribute the debut of Vichyssoise to the June 1917 opening of the Ritz-Carlton rooftop restaurant. Based on *potage bonne-femme*, the hearty potato leek soup popular among French housewives, Chef Diat made the recipe amenable for summer and high-end palates by chilling the mixture. He pureed it, added rich cream, and served the soup over ice. Diat's inspiration sprang from the hearth of his mother's kitchen, as recounted in his autobiographical cookbook *Cooking à la Ritz* (1941). He and his siblings wanted a heat-friendly version of their mother's soup, so they urged her to add some milk to the potage. The soup was named after the town where Diat was born, just outside of Vichy. Although there were nefarious connotations associated with the French region of Vichy after World War II, the soup remained a popular American dinner party standby. Irma and Marion Rombauer's *Joy of Cooking* (1975) adds the modern twist of using a blender to puree the potage. If Campbell's Soup is the icon of packaged convenience soup, crème Vichyssoise is its long-lost upper-crust cousin.

Crisco

Crisco, the first shortening to be made entirely of hydrogenated vegetable oil rather than animal fat, made its public debut in 1911. This was at the height of an era when home baking with butter and lard was commonplace. The origin of the substance that became known and trademarked as Crisco dates back to the pre—Civil War era, when Cincinnati candlemaker William Proctor Procter got together with his brother-in-law, the soap-maker James Gamble, to enter the shortening business after bearing the brunt of too much competition in the candle- and soap-making field. In the late nineteenth century, the meat packers controlled the candle- and soap-making enterprise and were the primary suppliers of the lard and tallow used in the manufacture of soap and candles. Proctor and Gamble set out to gain control of cottonseed oil production from farm to factory to use as an alternative to lard. In 1905 P&G owned eight cottonseed plants, and by 1907 the duo hired a chemist who developed two processes for hydrogenation, which entailed adding hydrogen chains to fatty acid chains. The result of this process turns a liquid into a solid. This solidified form of cottonseed oil was again first marketed for soap and candle making. But electric lighting was making a real dent in the candle business, and demand for candles began to drop. Procter and Gamble needed to find other uses for their hydrogenated cottonseed oil. The duo noticed that the product looked like lard; so, why not sell it as such? The name Crisco was decided upon as an acronym derived from crystallized cottonseed oil. Procter and Gamble then had to devise a way of convincing savvy housewives to switch to their new product from tried-and-true lard. The two-pronged angle proposed that Crisco was "a healthier alternative to cooking with animal fats . . . and more economical than butter." They supported their attack on cooking with animal fat by publishing and distributing a free cookbook called *The Story of Crisco*, using Crisco in all 615 recipes. The cookbook is considered a landmark in the art of subtle commercial manipulation. *The Story of Crisco* strongly implied that Crisco was a not only a cleaner and more digestible alternative to animal fat and butter but a more modern and enlightened product as well. They also appealed to Jewish housewives, as Crisco could be considered a Kosher product that could be used as a substitute for butter and therefore used with meats. Current nutritional research reveals, however, that Crisco's claims to be a healthy alternative to animal fat are false. Partially hydrogenated oils, such as the cottonseed oil contained in Crisco, contain trans-fatty acids, which can raise LDL levels (the harmful form of cholesterol) while lowering HDL levels (the helpful form of cholesterol). Excessive consumption of trans-fatty acids can lead to heart disease.

Frigidaire

Food preservation at home became substantially easier with the advent of home refrigeration. The first documentation of home refrigeration was the debut of Fred W. Wolf's Dolmere in 1913. The Dolmere contained an air-cooled refrigeration unit mounted atop an icebox. In 1915, Alfred Mellowes did one better with his home refrigeration unit. It was distinct from the Dolmere in that it was an electric refrigeration unit attached to a wooden cabinet. With a group of investors, Mellowes founded Guardian Refrigerator Company in Fort Wayne, Indiana, and began manufacturing the Mellowes refrigerator in 1916. He set up a small Guardian factory, but production was sluggish, with fewer than 40 units manufactured in the first two years of operations, because Mellowes chose to hand-assemble the appliances. The company lost more than $30,000 in the first two years of production. The president of General Motors, William C. Durant, recognized the importance of Guardian refrigerators and personally bought the company with his own funds, rescuing the brand from imminent financial collapse. He then renamed the company and all its affiliate products Frigidaire. Durant resold the business to General Motors in 1919. Using the assembly-line methods employed in car manufacture, this heralded the era of mass-produced appliances. Production time was reduced dramatically, but the hefty price tag of $775 per unit was well out of reach for most home consumers. Eventually, improvements in the refrigeration technology and company restructuring at Frigidaire produced a better product at a lower price. Frigidaires dropped to $468. The wooden ice cabinet of yore was replaced by a porcelain-coated, steel, insulated product. Other improved features included ice cream cabinets in 1923, soda fountain equipment in 1924, and water and milk coolers in 1927. By 1929, more than 1 million refrigerators were manufactured, a marked improvement from about 10 years earlier.

Hush Puppies

What's in a name? While fritters have existed since the time of the ancients, the term "hush puppies" is theorized to have first appeared in print between the years 1915 and 1920. The phrase was coined in the Deep South, and the recipe may have evolved during the days of scarcity following the Civil War. Using scraps of catfish, battered and deep fried in cornmeal, hunters supposedly tossed an occasional fritter to their dogs to keep them quiet, so, "Hush, Puppy!"

Fried Clams

The first batch of modern, batter-fried clams was prepared by Lawrence Henry "Chubby" Woodman on July 3, 1916. He and wife Bessie opened the Woodman's concession stand in 1914 on Main Street in Essex, MA, selling groceries, fresh clams, and homemade potato chips on the weekend. Fried clams and oysters were already a well-established culinary tradition in the Northeast, dating back to the Parker House hotel's restaurant in Boston, MA, in 1865. A fisherman named Tarr complained to Chubby about poor business one day, saying: "Business was slower than a couple of snails headed uphill." He pointed at the bucket of clams and suggested Chubby fry them up the same way he did his potato chips. Customers who were within earshot scoffed at this proposal, but Bessie and Chubby thought long about the idea. Why not try frying the shucked clams? Bessie fired up some lard, experimented with batters, and invited the locals for a taste test. The overall response was positive, and on the Fourth of July 1916, Chubby and Bessy dished up the debut of their fried clams at the Essex Independence Day parade. A year later, the Boston fish market devised its own fried clams, as did the Howard Johnson restaurant chain. Proud of their fishy innovation, Chubby and Bessie wrote on the back of their marriage certificate: "We fried the first fried clam—in the town of Essex, July 3, 1916."

Girl Scout Cookies

The sale of cookies as a way of funding Girl Scout troop activities originated about five years after Juliette Gordon Low founded the Girl Scouts organization in 1912. The first documented Girl Scout cookies were baked by the Mistletoe Troop of Muskegee, Oklahoma, who sold them as a service project in a high school cafeteria in December 1917. In 1922, *American Girl* magazine ran a cookie recipe by Chicago troop director Florence E. Neil. Neil urged the 2,000-odd scouts to sell the cookies for 25 to 30 cents a dozen. The pace quickened in the 1930s, when the Girl Scouts of Greater

First Lady Grace Coolidge eats a cookie presented to her by a New York Girl Scout troop on October 17, 1923. (Library of Congress)

Philadelphia began their march toward marketing the first commercially produced cookies of their kind. They sold their baked goods in the windows of the gas and electric company, using the funds for their local Girl Scout council programs. In 1935, the Girl Scout Foundation of Greater New York cast a die to emblazon the trefoil symbol on its boxes of cookies, the recognizable emblem of Girl Scout cookies to this day. The organization consolidated its cookie trade in 1936, when the Girl Scout councils banded together and bought a license to hire the first commercial baker to sell a uniform product nationwide. Production slowed during World War II, when there were sugar and flour shortages, and calendars were sold to collect revenue instead. The popular Thin Mints made their debut in the 1950s, along with two other varieties—sandwich and shortbread. The 1960s saw an increase in cookie sales from the burgeoning Baby Boomer generation, as well as the introduction of using foil-wrapped packages for freshness. Girl Scout cookie boxes sported one uniform design, focusing on scenes of Girl Scouts in action. Low-fat and sugar-free options became available in the 1990s. The message of happy, strong, active scouting comes through in the distinctive Girl Scout packaging and in the nearly century-long commitment to cookie excellence.

Life Savers

Ohio candymaker Clarence Crane, father of famous American poet Hart Crane, was looking for a sweet alternative to chocolate that could withstand the summer heat when he came up with the idea for Life Savers candy. Chocolate, prone to melting, was not a big money maker in the hot summer months, and Crane thought that cooling, soothing mints might be more appealing treats in the heat. While at the pharmacy purchasing flavoring agents, Crane observed the druggist using a pill-making machine. Crane realized he could fashion the mint out of this machine. The machine he purchased had a malfunction that could be rectified by punching a hole in the middle of the candy, which created a ring effect. Crane observed the candy's similarity to life preservers, which were only then becoming commonplace on ships after the sinking of the *Titanic*, and Crane took inspiration from their round shape and used it as the namesake for the mint. In addition, the shape was a distinctive alternative to the mints that were being produced in Europe at the time, which were mainly square. In 1912, Clarence rolled out Crane's Peppermint Life Savers. Crane sold the trademark to Edward Noble in 1913 for the sum of $2,900. Noble's innovation was to wrap the opaque white mints in a roll of tinfoil, which kept the contents fresher than in the cardboard cartons they were formerly packaged in. He called the candy Pep-O-Mint Life Savers. This process was not automated until 1919, the same year that several other flavors were rolled out, Wint-O-Green, Cl-O-ve, Lic-O-Rice, Cinn-O-Mon, Vi-O-Let, and Choc-O-Late, which remained the standard lineup until the late 1920s. Aluminum foil replaced tinfoil in 1925. Fruit Life Savers made their debut in 1921, the rainbow-colored package representing lemon, lime, grape, and

Cracker Jack Prizes

In 1912, the first Cracker Jack prizes were buried in the ubiquitous box with the saluting sailor. The exquisite joy of unearthing a tiny spinning top, a bird whistle, or a presidential trading card was among the reasons for the company's longevity and success. Sold primarily at baseball games, these days the prizes are more likely to be a Pokemon character or a fake tattoo, but the tradition, now nearly a century strong, is still a draw.

orange fruit drops. Cherry- and pineapple-flavored Life Savers debuted in 1931, and the traditional five-flavor pack of lemon, lime, orange, cherry, and pineapple emerged, which remained the formula until 2003. Although never truly successful, Life Savers were produced in anise, root beer, and cola flavors in the late 1920s as well. Besides being a stimulating treat, Life Savers are sometimes recommended to diabetics by doctors as a quick jolt of glucose to the system during a hypoglycemic event.

Lobster Palaces

After the turn of the century, New York emerged as a glitzy nightlife capital centered around Broadway shows, ragtime, and vaudeville performances. A typical night out included cocktails, a show, and dinner at one of the many lobster palaces that cropped up in this dazzling entertainment district. A lobster palace is defined as "one of the elegant, expensive new restaurants that emerged in New York City, which specialized in lobsters and attracted the rich and famous"(http://edwardianpromenade.com/amusements/lobster-palace-society/). Pouring out of limousines and theatrical performances, bathed in furs and mink stoles, the elegant upper crust comprised the primary clientele of the lobster palaces. A flashy clientele of chorus girls, newspapermen, wealthy businessmen, and their mistresses frequented these lobster palaces, which became the progenitors of the café society that emerged in New York in the 1920s and 1930s. The co-mingling of classes that took place in lobster palaces challenged the façade of stratifications in society. The granddaddy of all lobster palaces was Café Martin, established in 1899 by French hotelier Louis Martin. Martin introduced the intimate dining booths known as banquettes after Café Martin moved into the space on West 26th Street formerly occupied by Delmonico's restaurant. The combination of comfort and privacy made banquettes a favorite among men who liked to entertain women who were not their wives. The entrances of lobster palaces were often opulent affairs, meant to inspire and impress. Competition among lobster palaces became fierce, especially after the popularity of ragtime music raged. It wasn't until Prohibition took a foothold post-World War I that the lobster palaces faded from their swanky throne among the nighttime elite.

The Mary Frances Cook Book; Or Adventures Among the Kitchen People by Jane Eayre Fryer

The niche genre of children's cookbooks gained popularity during the 1910s. Not merely a collection of recipes, children's cookbooks were aimed at teaching influential lessons of etiquette and behavior to impressionable young women. For little girls, these cookbooks implied that they should start learning in childhood the series of obligations they had to fulfill just around the corner in womanhood. Qualities praised included obedience, kindness, displaying good manners, assuming responsibility, serving the males of the household, and honoring one's parents. This particular tome revolves around the story of an ailing mother who, despite her illness, had feverishly written down her family recipes to be passed on to her children. While mother is away recuperating, Mary Frances utilizes her recipes to feed her family. Unsure of herself as a cook and not knowing how to execute the recipes her mother has handed down, she is delighted to find that utensils in the kitchen come to life to help her out with the home cooking. The utensils contribute to her success in the kitchen, and Mary Frances makes a homecoming dinner to celebrate her mother's return. Her mother is absolutely joyful about Mary Frances's accomplishment and praises her highly. Despite the book's hidden agenda, these books were wonderful because of their charming illustrations and delectable recipes. Here is a recipe culled from the pages of *The Mary Frances Cook Book.*

Boiled Mutton

Yields about three pounds rack of mutton, or "yearling"

- Wipe mutton with a damp cloth.
- Pour three cups of boiling water into a large pot.
- Throw in two peeled onions.
- Place the meat in the pot and cover.
- Boil 10 minutes.
- Draw pot to back of stove where it will simmer, or just bubble, until meat is tender when tried with a fork, which will be about 1 ¼ hours.
- Take out the meat.
- Skim off the fat from the surface of the liquor; or if there is time, cool, and remove the hardened lard.

Moon Pie

The delicious treat known as the moon pie has its lineage in the Chattanooga Bakery, founded in early 1900s, that was a subsidiary of the Mountain City Flour Mill of Chattanooga, Tennessee. First conceived to use the excess products of a flour mill, the bakery offered more than 200 confectionary items for sale by 1910. The first moon pie was developed by the bakery in 1917. The origin of the sweet was never documented. A North Carolina historian, Ronald Dickson, authored *The Great American Moon Pie Handbook*, a document outlining the history of the moon pie. Not long after its publication, Dickson was contacted by Earl Mitchell, Jr., who claimed to be the son of moon pie inventor Earl Mitchell, Sr. Earl Mitchell of Chattanooga Bakery was surveying his territory of Kentucky, West Virginia, and Tennessee when he stopped in for a snack at a company store that catered mainly to coal miners. He asked the miners what their idea of a good snack was. Solid and filling were two qualities mentioned; size was another concern. "About how big?" Mitchell asked the miners. At the time he asked that question, the moon was rising in the sky, so one of the miners raised his hands round and wide and replied "About that big!" With this image in his mind, Mitchell headed back to his bakery with a new snack vision. Other ideas were percolating at the home bakery, too. Workers were dipping graham crackers in marshmallow and allowing them to harden on the window sill. Adding another layer of cookie and a generous coating of chocolate made the moon-shaped cookie even more delicious. Mitchell sent the prototype around for taste tests with sales representatives. The response was overwhelmingly positive. Moon pies became a quick staple at the bakery, and by the 1950s, moonies were the only product the bakery ever needed to sell.

Morton Table Salt

The hand-drawn young girl in the pert yellow dress was first branded on blue cylinders of Morton Table Salt in 1914. The Morton Umbrella Girl sprang to life in order to illustrate a national consumer campaign for Morton Table Salt. The campaign was launched to tout the benefits of salt that could pour out of a spout, freely flowing, even in damp weather. Hidden beneath an umbrella on a rainy day, scattering a trail of salt in her wake, the coy Morton salt girl appeared on the pages of *Good Housekeeping* in 1911 alongside the motto "When it rains, it pours." This claim to fame was possible only after Morton added the compound magnesium carbonate to ordinary table salt, allowing it to pour easily and not clump in damp weather. Calcium silicate is currently the agent used in Morton Table Salt for this same purpose. Joy and Mark Morton established the Morton Salt Company as a corporate entity in 1902. Their father, J. Sterling Morton, was also the founding father of Arbor Day, the national holiday celebrating trees. The Morton umbrella girl went through numerous permutations, always changing with the style and etiquette of the times. In 1924, Morton Salt Company became the first producer of iodized salt for the home to help prevent the onset of goiter, which was a serious health problem in the United States at the time. During the boom of highway construction in the 1950s, the company built the world's deepest salt mine in Fairport, Ohio, to meet the demand for ice salt. Morton Salt Company is still the leading producer of consumer salt in the nation today.

Nathan's Hot Dogs

Nathan Handwerker, a Polish immigrant by way of Belgium, began his famous career in hot dogs at Charles Feltman's Coney Island hot dog concession in 1915. Feltman opened up the first hot-dog stand on Coney Island in 1874 and is credited with the idea of bunning the hot dog, turning it into a portable sandwich. Feltman's stand eventually became a full-fledged restaurant, serving more than 2 million customers a year by the end of the second decade of the twentieth century. Feltman's was a great training ground for Handwerker, where the budding hot dog restaurateur honed his trade splitting rolls and making deliveries. With $300 in savings from the job at Feltman's, Handwerker rented a building at the corner of Surf and Stillwell Avenues, where Nathan and his wife Ida opened Nathan's Famous Hot Dogs in 1916. They sold the dogs for 5 cents apiece, served up fresh from the grill. A hint of garlic set them apart from other hot dogs. Although the product was cheaper than Feltman's, this actually made people wary. Why were the Nathan's hot dogs so cheap? So Nathan came up with a series of incentives to draw new customers in. First he hired unemployed men to stand around and make Nathan's look busy. But the disheveled men only dissuaded passersby from approaching the venue. Then Handwerker got the notion to dress students in white coats, as if they were doctors, in order to make it appear that the food was healthy. The first Coney Island Hot Dog Eating Contest took place on Independence Day 1916, which brought more notoriety and name recognition to Nathan's Famous. It has since become an annual Fourth of July tradition on Coney Island. With the opening of the Coney Island subway station in 1920, thousands shuttled in by the carload, cementing Nathan's Famous as a legendary Coney Island landmark. When Feltman's finally shuttered its doors in 1954, Nathan's Famous expanded, opening chains in other cities. Nathan's Famous hot dogs can now be found in supermarkets, airports, hotels, and sports arenas; however, nothing can beat the taste of a Handwerker hot dog in the hot summer sun.

Oreo Cookies

Oreos have been America's top-selling cookie since their inception in 1912. Originally produced at the Nabisco factory in New York City, Oreo Biscuits were thought to have been launched by Nabisco in order to compete with Hydrox Biscuit Bonbons, another nearly identical chocolate sandwich cookie stuffed with vanilla cream, which had been selling since 1908. Another theory posits that Oreos were invented to capture the taste buds of the British market by spicing up the ordinary biscuit. Oreos were packaged in tins with glass tops for easy viewing and sold for 25 cents a pound. The first Oreos came filled with two different flavors—lemon meringue and cream—and the cream was mound-shaped. Rumors abound on how Oreos got their name. Some posit that the mound-shaped cream inspired the name Oreo, from *oros*, the Greek word for mountain. Another theory states that the name came from the French word for the color gold, *or*, which was the color of the first Oreo packages. Also considered was the thought that the "re" in Oreo came from the word cream, surrounded by the "o's" in the word chocolate. Cream proved to be the breadwinner for Nabisco, so the lemon meringue filling was discontinued in 1924. The name was changed several times, first to Oreo Sandwich in 1921, then to Oreo Cream Sandwich in 1948, and yet again to Oreo Chocolate Sandwich in 1974. New varieties of Oreos occasionally emerged, with the Double Stuff premiering in 1917. Touted as "Milk's Favorite Cookie," it was featured in the "Got Milk?" campaign of the early 1990s. Sales were only slightly hindered by the low-carb diet craze of 2003, and Oreos became the best-selling cookie in China in 2006 after an aggressive marketing campaign in that country led by Kraft. With the seal of Nabisco emblazoned at the center of each cookie and with minute fluting around the chocolate edges, 362 billion Oreo cookies have been sold since 1912. Oreos are still considered the best-selling cookie in the world.

Ovaltine

The chocolate beverage known as Ovaltine began production in the United States in Villa Park, Illinois, in 1915. It was originally developed in Switzerland by chemist Dr. George Wander. Wander was experimenting with barley malt as a nutritional supplement when it dawned on him to combine the complex carbohydrate-rich barley malt with milk, eggs, and finally, cocoa flavoring, to make the mixture more palatable to children. The beverage, called Ovomaltine, was "prescribed" to malnourished children, breastfeeding mothers, and the ill and infirm as a fortified, high-nutrient, yet tasty chocolate milk product. The drink was first exported to England in 1909 under the moniker Ovomaltine. The most basic ingredients in Ovaltine are malt, milk, eggs, and cocoa flavoring, formulated into a powdery substance that can be dissolved in hot or cold milk. Sponsor to such classic radio programs as *Little Orphan Annie* and *Captain Midnight* in the 1930s and 1940s, Ovaltine began marketing premiums during these shows to attract the attention of children, and the secret decoder rings became coveted items.

Piggly Wiggly Stores

Former general store clerk Clarence Saunders proposed a radical new concept in grocery shopping when he opened the first Piggly Wiggly market in 1916 in Memphis, Tennessee—the self-service grocery store. Until that time, clerks had to pull items from shelves behind the counter, resulting in longer lines and requiring more hired employees. Saunders was first mocked for his idea. Open shelves for browsing, providing customers with baskets to gather items, and scaling back on store staff were unheard of at

With stores opening first in Tennessee, ca. 1917, Piggly Wiggly grocery stores offered self-service shopping with a turnstile for entering, four aisles of merchandise, and a cash register to finalize purchases.

the time. But eventually, Saunders became, in effect, the godfather of the modern retail sales model of self-service, pioneering an era of hundreds of independent franchises. Theories surrounding the invention of the name Piggly Wiggly abound. One theory proposes that Saunders saw from a train three pigs struggling to get under a fence, wiggling about. Another theory purports that when someone asked him directly why he selected the name, he replied, "So someone would ask exactly that question." The concept was patented in 1917. Each store featured a turnstile, which would lead to four self-service aisles. Customers would wend their ways through the aisles, organized by departments, to the end point of a cashier. Branding and packaging became tantamount, as customers themselves were making consumer choices from among an array of products. Piggly Wiggly was the first among firsts. It was the first grocery store to price-mark all the items keep produce refrigerated for longer shelf life, have employees wear uniforms for a clean image and work environment, and create an atmosphere of uniform design in all franchises. Today there are still more than 600 Piggly Wiggly stores located throughout the Midwest and Southeast.

Pop-Up Toaster

The seeds of invention often lie in frustration. In 1919, Charles P. Strite, a master mechanic at a Stillwater, Minnesota, factory, got sick of eating burnt toast from the company cafeteria. Whereas other employees complained that nothing was done about the complaints, Strite went one step further. He experimented with designs for an improved toaster, and during the course of this undertaking, he invented the pop-up toaster. Eliminating the need for human intervention, Strite's toaster incorporated a spring and a variable timer. It took advantage of electrically heated wire coils to toast the bread. With the success of the patent of his invention in 1919, Strite quit his job at the factory and began manufacturing his own product. The Waters Genter company of Minnesota began marketing its Toastmaster model based on Strite's prototype, the first commercial model of its kind. It could hold down the pieces of bread while they were browning and then eject browned pieces based on a timer. This shows that complaining about a problem will not bring about a solution, and rewards await those who dare to invent.

Pyrex Dishware

The Corning Glass Works introduced Pyrex bakeware in 1915, but its circuitous route from lantern glass to window display in a Boston department store is a fascinating tale. Corning started producing globes of glass that were weatherproof after railroad companies complained about easy-to-shatter lanterns frequently bursting. This sturdy, low-expansion, shatter-proof glassware, called *fire glass*, was so efficient that Pyrex began losing money because replacements were needed less frequently! Resistant to heat, breakage, and chemical corrosion, Pyrex found new life thanks to Bessie Littleton, wife of the company's newest scientist. Disappointed that her Guernsey casserole shattered after only two uses, Bessie asked her husband to craft a dish that would not shatter in the oven, similar in character to the fire glass. She tested out the dish with a sponge cake and noticed the following: the cooking time was shorter; the cake was easy to remove from the dish; the glass remained odorless after cooking; and one could watch the cake baking through the clear glass. Bessie's cake was so impressive that scientists at Corning worked an additional two years before Pyrex made its commercial debut. In the early 1920s, many wealthy families still hired servants to cook meals. Sturdy, easy-to-clean, and virtually unbreakable, Pyrex dishes were instantly successful with such families, who often feared that the hired help would "ruin the dishes." When Sarah Tyson Rorer, editor for *Ladies Home Journal* as well as a columnist for *Good Housekeeping*, got behind the product, the nonstick properties of Pyrex began to stick with the public. Advertising was especially effective during World War I, as Pyrex glassware was a labor-, metal-, and fuel-saving device; the dishes could be used to bake and serve. So baking in Pyrex became not only technically superior but an act of patriotism during wartime as well. By 1919, more than 4 ½ million pieces of Pyrex bakeware were in American homes, and this number soared to more than 30 million by 1927. The versatile, durable, stain-proof power of Pyrex still makes it the best-selling bakeware in the United States today.

Streit's

Aron Streit, Inc., known under the moniker of Streit's, was founded on the Lower East Side of New York City by Austrian immigrant Aron Streit in 1916. It was and remains the only family-owned and-operated matzoh factory in the United States with international distribution. Although the Streits manufacture other types of kosher foodstuffs, it is their matzoh that is world renowned. Aron and his wife Nettie emigrated to the United States in 1890s. They operated a matzoh-baking enterprise in Austria, and they brought their handmade matzoh tradition with them upon the opening of their first factory on Pitt Street. At this factory, Streit, alongside his associate Rabbi Weinberger, handmade each of the matzohs. As the Jewish immigrant population began to soar in the Lower East Side, Streit, with his two sons, moved into a larger space on Rivington Street. The neighborhood, which once served the thriving Jewish immigrant community, lost much of its clientele once the residents were affluent enough to move out of the tenements and into wealthier neighborhoods. Aron Streit died in 1937, but his family carried on the matzoh business, as the company has always prided itself on its commitment to traditional values and customs. This manifests itself in the production of Passover matzohs. Passover matzoh has changed little in thousands of years. The basic components of matzoh are flour and water that are mixed and baked no longer than 18 minutes. The process begins as early as October in preparation for the April holiday. The factory shuts down for a week for a thorough cleaning, and all production of year-round matzoh comes to a halt. During the shutdown, products that are non-kosher for Passover, such as malt, shortening, and salt, are removed from the premises. Currently, Streit's manufactures up to 16,000 pounds of matzoh each day. Gentrification in the Lower East Side has caused the Streit family to put the factory up for sale at a price of $25 million, with plans to permanently relocate to a New Jersey facility.

The U.S. Food Administration

Wartime austerity measures were the impetus for the creation of the United States Food Administration. Its first great task was to manage the intake and distribution of the U.S. food supply during World War I. Spearheaded by its first director, Herbert Hoover, the USFA significantly impacted American food norms, causing Americans to eat less and thereby feel better. Influential health movements already promoted more conservative food intake before the United States entered the war in April 1917, but the creation of the USFA spread this food ethic primarily to the moneyed and better-fed middle and upper classes. Fighting in Europe had already disrupted the production and distribution of foodstuffs, and President Wilson was confronted with the reality of controlling food riots, shortages, and hoarding. Food was a powerful weapon during wartime, as the United States was one of the major world food producers. An agency was needed to regulate food production and distribution. The natural candidate to head such an agency was Herbert Hoover, who had already developed his reputation in this field while overseeing the distribution of a million dollars in foodstuffs to Belgium. Hoover initiated a program of voluntary restriction of white flour, meat, sugar, and butter, but he did not want to institute a mandatory requirement. Through an advertising campaign that promoted "meatless Mondays" and "wheatless Wednesdays," Hoover utilized the principles behind the new nutrition movements that encouraged both less wasteful and more healthful cooking methods. The USFA also drew from the burgeoning Prohibition and advertising movements, encouraging housewives to sign cards pledging to observe the rules of the USFA. The American Home Economics Association set up an emergency wartime committee to churn out recipes that worked within the framework of USFA wartime restrictions. Social pressure from the USFA was wielded by certain, predominantly middle-class, standbys such as Protestant church groups, women's clubs, the Boy Scouts, and fraternal organizations. Although appeals for better health were one motivation for enforcing USFA initiatives, the primary objective was to inspire a sense of patriotism. With articles like "Recipes for Menus that Serve Your Country" appearing in women's magazines, there was no question that food had become a political issue. Signs and posters appeared with the slogan "Food Will Win the War." Hoover's propaganda campaign managed to reduce food consumption by 15 percent without rationing. This not only helped feed the Allied troops overseas but prevented postwar famine in Europe as well.

Further Reading

"A Few Choice Morsels: Children's Cookbooks." http://gherkinstomatoes .com/2010/04/21/17471/.

Jackson, Donald Dale. "Hot Dogs Are Us." *Smithsonian*. June 1999, Vol. 30, Issue 3, p. 104.

Levenstein, Harvey. *Paradox of Plenty: A Social History of Eating in Modern America*. Berkeley: University of California Press, 2003.

Richman, Adam. *America the Edible: A Hungry History from Sea to Dining Sea*. Emmaus, PA: Rodale Books, 2010.

Shephard, Sue. *Pickled, Potted, and Canned. How the Art and Science of Food Preserving Changed the World*. New York: Simon and Schuster, 2001.

Smith, Andrew F. *Eating History: 30 Turning Points in the Making of American Cuisine*. New York: Columbia University Press, 2009.

3

1920s

Sherri Liberman

During the 1920s, food production and storage options improved dramatically, allowing the transport of foodstuffs over longer distances and providing a wider array of food choices available to consumers. Refrigerators became more affordable, which extended the shelf life of perishables, saving American families both time and money. Gas ranges replaced wood- and coal-burning stoves. Data from 1920 reveal that nearly 44 hours per week were spent preparing and cleaning up after meals. Food was cheap and plentiful during most of the decade, thanks to a surplus in production from American farms. Meat and potatoes were still staples of the American diet, though research from the previous decade on the benefits of consuming vitamins spurred more interest in consuming milk, fruits, and vegetables. For the first time, Americans could drink orange juice year-round due to the improvements in storage and food transport. After years of influence by home economists and nutrition scientists, the American diet was becoming healthier. In 1928, Americans ate less in terms of quantity (about 5 percent fewer calories per capita) but consumed a wider array of nutrients than in 1890. Fruit consumption, especially citrus fruits, green vegetables, milk, and cheese were on the rise in the American diet. By the end of the decade, white flour and cornmeal consumption were down. Beef consumption fell from 72.4 pounds per capita in 1899 to 55.3 pounds by 1930. The change in diet showed measurable health gains. A study of upper-middle-class Boston schoolboys in 1926 found that they averaged three inches taller than their counterparts of 1876. The importance of nutrition in the American diet

A woman demonstrates the features of a new gas cooker, December 2, 1926. Appliances to make food preservation and preparation more convenient reduced the time housewives needed for kitchen tasks. (Hulton Archive/Getty Images)

became more legitimate through the establishment of the American Society for Nutritional Sciences in 1928.

As the decade progressed, American housewives began to embrace the shift toward processed foods. Instead of spending their time plucking chickens, shelling peas, and grinding coffee beans, Americans steadily began to prefer the ready–to-cook options that frozen and canned foods offered. Why spend the day chopping and peeling when it could conveniently be done by food processing plants? Some of the more prominent brands to emerge during the 1920s were Wonder Bread, Welch's Grape Jelly, Wheaties, Popsicles, Peter Pan Peanut Butter, and Velveeta Cheese. The first White Castle opened in 1921, spurring the fast-food chain movement. Women's magazines featured ads that revealed the most popular foods of the time were timesavers, such as Campbell's Tomato Soup, Aunt Jemima Pancake Flour, and 3 Minute Oat Flakes. This growth in processed foods inspired corporate consolidation. Postum cereals acquired Jell-O, Minute Tapioca, and Birds Eye, renaming itself General Foods in 1929.

When Prohibition went into effect on January 16, 1920, it profoundly changed consumer drinking and even eating habits. It increased the production of soft drinks, which was a boon to soda manufacturers. Nehi sodas and Yoo-Hoo brands were introduced. Numerous restaurants and hotels collapsed financially due to the inability to profit from alcohol sales. Soft drinks stabilized these losses somewhat. Cafeterias and tearooms opened, with creative menus designed to attract customers with fine dining rather than liquor. The fruit cocktail was a popular Prohibition-era creation in place of the more potent variety. Bedecked with marshmallows and powdered sugar, fruit cocktails soon replaced oysters on the half shell as appetizers at well-heeled establishments during slim times. There may also be a link to the increase in cocoa and chocolate consumption during the era. During Prohibition, speakeasies, named for the soft voice required for entry to

New York City Deputy Police Commissioner John A. Leach (right) watches agents pour confiscated liquor into a sewer following a raid during the height of Prohibition. (Library of Congress)

under-the-radar establishments serving alcohol, spawned their own cuisine and dining atmosphere. Many speakeasies were located on the wrong side of the tracks, but others, such as the 21 Club, were cleverly disguised as fine dining venues. Sporting two bars, an orchestra, and dining rooms on two floors, New York City's 21 Club, known as Jack and Charlie's during that time, was the high end of the speakeasy scale.

Since public alcohol consumption was swept under the rug in the 1920s, there was an increase in home entertaining during this decade. John Mariani, author of the *Dictionary of American Food and Drink*, surmises that Prohibition encouraged the home cocktail party, spurring on the popularity of hors d'oeuvres, such as deviled eggs and gelatin-based salads. Other unusual and dainty salads emerged, such as banana balls with French dressing in a peel, banana and popcorn salad, and crushed tomatoes and pineapple encased in lettuce cups.

A fascination with exotic cuisine was a hallmark of the Jazz Age during the 1920s. Silent film stars like Anna Mae Wong and on–screen "Sheik" Rudolph Valentino were glossy Hollywood- projections of a nationwide fascination with faraway cultures. Although Italian American, eastern European, and Germanic cuisines were already well established in the United States through decades-long waves of immigration, new generations, particularly from China and Mexico, began boosting the population and infusing American palates with new flavors. However, much of what was considered foreign cuisine in America would barely be recognizable in said native countries. For example, American-Arabian recipes from the 1920s were made with pork, which shows total disregard for Muslim halal food restrictions. Chop suey was the darling of Chinese American cuisine but was strictly an American invention, rarely eaten by native Chinese. Spanish-Mexican-American cuisine in the 1920s was considered any dish that contained tomatoes, hot peppers, rice, garlic, or California olives. Mildly seasoned Spanish rice and beans was the most popular Mexican dish, with few takers on more adventurous recipes, such as mole poblano. Tamale pie was an American invention, based on the traditional Aztec dish. Tamales were made of corn dough stuffed with spices, meats, and cheese, generally steamed in cornhusks. Tamale pie did away with the messy dough and cornhusks and combined ground beef, canned tomatoes, cornmeal, onions, bell peppers, garlic, and chili powder in a baking dish to make the traditional Meso-American delicacy appealing to American audiences. Regardless of authenticity, ethnic cuisine provided a refreshing break from the predominantly bland and predictable American fare. The ethnic food movement was not embraced by all Americans by any stretch of the imagination. School dieticians dissuaded children from eating meals containing pasta, garlic, and other spices, asserting that meat and potatoes were a great formula for muscle building.

Prior to the 1920s, Italian food was a bland shadow of its authentic self. Pizza was not yet known in most American homes. There was a growing proliferation of small family-owned Italian restaurants during the 1880s to 1920s in New York, San Francisco, and Chicago, primarily opened by immigrants from Sicily and southern Italy, but non-Italian Americans rarely dined in them. Prohibition provided a great boon to these Italian eateries, which often doubled as speakeasies. Hordes of new crowds who had never before set foot in Italian restaurants were being served carbohydrate-laden plates of pasta, a vast improvement over American "macaroni," which was often crafted from potato flour. Italian speakeasy fare consisted of whatever Mama was cooking up in the kitchen, and glasses of wine that Papa made in the basement. While traditional Sicilian cuisine was often Mediterranean in character, with fresh vegetables, olive oil, and lemon pervading, Sicilian American cuisine capitalized on the bounty of American meat and produce—meatballs, shellfish, veal cutlets dressed in parmesan, rich tomato sauces, and hunks of mozzarella eaten as appetizers.

Although Americans were adopting foreign dishes, they were often watered-down versions created by housewives and restaurant cooks who strove to Americanize them. French cuisine nearly disappeared because of Prohibition, because the time, money, wine, and spirits necessary for fine French food were no longer available. Upscale restaurants closed as the economy faltered; many of them turned into cafeterias. It was not until the gourmet trend began in the 1940s and 1950s that French cooking reappeared on the American culinary scene. Fine dining was a low priority after the stock market crash of October 24, 1929. Toward the end of the raucous Roaring '20s, Americans returned their focus to the home kitchen out of necessity.

Entries

American Culinary Federation

With the founding of the American Culinary Federation in 1929, the social status of the cooking profession was upgraded from being considered low-end drudge work, or merely a housewife's duty, to a respectable occupation. Before this time, Americans were rarely trained to become restaurant-grade chefs. German and French immigrants with previous training through European apprenticeships ran most of America's fine dining establishments. But the advent of Prohibition during the 1920s shifted the focus from alcoholic beverages to culinary talent in many of America's top restaurants and hotels, which created a need for more formalized chefs' training. The American Culinary Federation (ACF) grew out of that need. Now considered the authority on cookery in America, the ACF was originally formed from the combined forces of three existing chefs' organizations: the Societe Culinaire Philanthropique, the Vatel Club, and the Chef de Cuisines Club of America. The organization promoted the adoption of apprenticeship systems similar to those already in place in Europe that would blend hands-on experience with theoretical classroom instruction. That goal was squelched with the advent of World War II, but the organization flourished in the postwar era with many GIs returning and taking advantage of the GI Bill's benefits for educating returning veterans. Through arduous campaigning, the ACF became responsible for the U.S. Department of Labor's upgrading the category of executive chef from service to professional status in 1976.

Blimp Cuisine and Dining

Travel by large airships such as blimps and zeppelins was commonplace among the wealthiest of jet setters during the 1920s. The slow, leisurely pace of blimp travel was perfect for people with lots of time and money on their hands. A trip from Europe to Brazil by blimp could take as long as three days in the air. Firsthand accounts of the period reveal that kitchens and dining facilities aboard dirigibles were on a par with cruise ships of the time. But weight restrictions on airships were a major factor in deciding what foodstuffs and crockery could be taken aboard. Lightweight aluminum utensils fit the bill. An account was made of the dining details of the trans-Atlantic flight of the American dirigible ZR-2 from Germany to Lakehurst, NJ, later the site of the Hindenburg disaster. The account appeared in the fall of 1924 in *the New York Times*. Meal times were set in accordance with schedules of ships at sea; breakfast at 8:00 a.m., lunch at noon, tea at 4:00 p.m., and dinner at 8:00 p.m. Coffee was offered during mornings; otherwise cocoa was served, for its "nourishing" properties. Drinking water was shipped in the form of ice and then chipped off and melted for drink. According to another article that appeared in *the New York Times* in October 1928, "In order not to overload the dirigible and yet serve the passengers adequate meals, it was decided after careful

Wait staff stand in the luxurious dining room aboard the R100 *Airship* in 1929. First-class dining facilities were part of the appeal for wealthy travelers. (Hulton Archive/Getty Images)

calculation to allow 7 ½ pounds of victuals per capita daily, including food and drink, with an additional meal for the night watch."

Bubblegum

Walter E. Diemer, an accountant, invented bubblegum in 1928. "It was an accident," he says. "I was doing something else." While working for the Fleer Chewing Gum Company in Philadelphia, Diemer wound up playing around with different gum recipes in his spare time. At the age of 23, Diemer concocted a chewing gum that was less sticky than ordinary gum and stretchier as well. This unique stretch factor sparked the idea of bubblegum. Diemer delivered five pounds of this material to a local grocery store, and it sold out that very afternoon. Fleer agreed to market his creation and taught his coworkers how to make the gum and blow bubbles. Bubblegum is primarily pink, because pink was the only available food coloring at Fleer. Fleer President Gilbert Mustin named the chewy product Double Bubble, and the gum remained unchallenged by competitors for years, until Bazooka entered the picture. And Walter Diemer remained at Fleer for decades, eventually making his way up the ladder to senior vice president. He never patented his creation or received any royalties. The only glory he received was when his wife informed the newspapers. Diemer simply enjoyed inviting children to his house, telling them the tale of the invention of bubblegum, and hosting bubble-blowing contests.

Caesar Salad

The legendary salad named Caesar was not a product of the Roman Empire but the creation of a border-town Mexico hotelier. Caesar Cardini ran a small hotel in Tijuana in the 1920s, where Hollywood- types would come to party and escape Prohibition just across the California border. They often ended their soirees with a bite to eat at Caesar's restaurant. Legend has it that on July 4, 1924, Cardini was overwhelmed with a dinner crowd. There were few fresh vegetables on hand at the time, and salads were not considered popular with many Americans. With limited options, Caesar thought he could win over the audience by preparing a simple salad at tableside, adding a little entertainment to the mix. Using ingredients commonly found in an Italian kitchen, he mixed romaine lettuce, garlic-infused oil, salt and pepper, lemon juice, parmesan cheese, croutons, Worcestershire sauce, and a coddled egg. The salad looked as fresh and good as it tasted. Driving to Tijuana for a Caesar salad became the "in" thing to do among celebrities ranging from Clark Gable to W.C. Fields. By 1948, Prohibition was long over, and the Cardinis moved to Los Angeles to be closer to his patronage. He bottled the Caesar salad dressing to sell to customers, inadvertently spawning the bottled salad dressing industry, and sold his packaged product worldwide. Many variants on the Caesar salad have emerged over the decades, such as adding chicken or seafood though anchovy vinaigrette is the most frequent addition to the original Cardini recipe.

Candy

Many of our nation's sweetest, most endearing treats came into being during the 1920s, and many originated in the Midwest. The Curtiss Candy Company first pitched Baby Ruth bars in 1921, a refashioning of their product originally called Kandy Kake. Baby Ruth is a candy bar comprised of chocolate-covered peanuts, caramel, and nougat. Was it merely coincidence that the fame of baseball legend Babe Ruth was on the rise at that time? The Curtiss Candy Company claims that the bar was named Ruth

---

Marshmallow Fluff

Since 2006, Marshmallow Fluff enthusiasts gather in Somerville's Union Square to celebrate the sweet spread at the What the Fluff? Festival. Archibald Query, who first invented fluff in 1917, sold the recipe to confectioners H. Allen Durkee and Fred L. Mower in 1920. Durkee and Mower originally marketed the stuff under the Toot Sweet Marshmallow Fluff label. The annual What the Fluff? Festival includes cooking contests, burlesque dancers, and performances by The Flufferettes, modeled after radio performances sponsored by Marshmallow Fluff during the 1930s.

---

after the daughter of ex-U.S. President Grover Cleveland, but that seems to have been a ploy to avoid paying the baseball star any royalties. Oh Henry was another chocolate bar with peanuts, caramel, and fudge that debuted in 1920 from the Williamson Candy Company of Chicago, Illinois. However, the candy bar was first crafted by Tom Henry of Arkansas City, Kansas. He originally called it a Tom Henry bar. The lightly sugar-coated fruit-flavored jellies known as Chuckles first appeared in 1921. Each package always contains all five flavors—cherry, lemon, lime, orange, and licorice. In 1923, the Mars confectionary company of Minneapolis, Minnesota, founded by Frank C. Mars, introduced the Milky Way bar. It was the first commercially distributed filled chocolate bar. The name and the flavor were inspired by malted milkshakes. Milk Duds were supposedly a happy accident. In 1923, the Curtiss Candy Company launched another innovation, Butterfinger. The flaky, orange-colored center covered in compound chocolate needed a name, and the company launched a contest to choose the title. "Butterfingers" was a slang term that described a clumsy person who couldn't hold onto a ball at sporting events. As a publicity stunt, planes dropped Baby Ruth bars and Butterfingers from airplanes on various cities to increase their profile. In 1926, the F. Hoffman and Company in Chicago tried to produce a perfectly round, milk chocolate-covered, caramel candy, but the shape that came out was far from ideal, thus the "dud" moniker.

Gelatin-Based Salads

The 1920s were the heydey of fruits and vegetables suspended in gelatin and aspic. The intersection of these two unlikely partners on the plate happened for a variety of sociological, biological, and technological reasons. During this time, domestic scientists promoted the consumption of roughage, vegetables, and fruits for being rich in vitamins and minerals, but the dainty and delicate sensibilities of the Jazz Age encouraged chefs to hide these oft dirt-covered products of the earth in lettuce cups, fruit skins, and other less raw arrangements. Meanwhile, gelatin desserts and dishes were already quite popular in the late nineteenth and early twentieth centuries, but the amount of labor required to make gelatin at home from calf's foot did not make it an ideal candidate for easy-to-whip-up use. As home refrigeration became more popular, chilling items such as packaged Jell-O became easier than ever. Postum Cereal, later General Foods Corp., acquired Jell-O, and by 1925, Jell-O sales made up a substantial portion of its new parent company's profits. With the intention of simplifying the housewife's cooking preparations, home economists

Gelatin is a great medium for preserving and serving delicate fruits and vegetables. Jell-O brand made preparing gelatin at home easy in the 1920s. (Akross/Dreamstime.com)

were quick to realize the potential of embalming messy fruits and vegetables in gelatin. Whether fresh or canned, cubed or sliced, jellied fruits and vegetables were the way to go. The two most popular preparations were tomato aspic and a concoction called perfection salad (also known as jellied coleslaw).

Gerber Baby Food

Daniel Gerber, a proud new father and owner of a canning business in Fremont, Michigan, invented Gerber Baby Food. Encouraged by their pediatrician, Daniel and Dorothy Gerber started straining by hand vegetables for their seven-month-old daughter, Sally. Workers at the Freemont Canning Company plant began asking Gerber for baby-food samples regularly, and at the behest of his wife Dorothy, he decided to can their strained fruit and vegetable products commercially. Peas, prunes, carrots, and spinach were among the first Gerber baby foods available, and they were

American parents quickly adopted them. Conditions in the 1920s were ripe for Gerber's success. The products sold cheaply, were easily available at grocery stores, and more American physicians were starting to promote a diet rich in fruits and vegetables for children. But Gerber's popularity was also due to its marketing and advertising strategy. An ad in *Child's Life* magazine offered six cans of Gerber for a dollar, which was less than half the pharmacy price. And the timeless image of the Gerber baby quickly became an American icon. The Gerbers ran a competition for the best drawing to represent the Gerber baby. A simple charcoal sketch by Dorothy Hope Smith of baby Ann Turner Cook stood out among many portraits, including oil paintings. The simple, half-drawn sketch of cherubic Ann captured the hearts of the Gerbers, and it became the official emblem of Gerber Baby Food in 1931. Ann Turner Cook's curious expression and sparkling eyes made her the most famous baby in the world and personified Gerber's image of commitment to raising happy and healthy babies. Gerber was acquired by Nestle Foods in 2007.

Good Humor

Good Humor is credited with being the first company to put an ice cream snack on a stick. The story began in 1920 when Harry Burt, an Ohio confectioner, invented the Jolly Boy Sucker, a lollipop on a stick. Later that year, Burt invented a chocolate coating in his ice cream parlor. Burt's son, Harry Jr., suggested adding ice cream with the chocolate coating to a frozen Jolly Boy Sucker stick. The result was the very first ice cream treat on a stick! Burt named his new treat a Good Humor bar. The legend behind the name is that Burt believed that a person's sense of humor, or temperament, was related to one's humor of the palate, or sense of taste. His slogan for the novelty was "the new clean convenient way to eat ice cream." Burt filed for a patent on January 30, 1920, but the patent officials were tied up among competing ice cream confections at the time (such as Eskimo Pie). It took three years and a trip to Washington, D.C., with a bucket full of Good Humor ice cream bars to be granted exclusive rights to patent Good Humor ice cream. With his patent in hand, Burt rolled out his marketing strategy. He bought a line of 12 chauffeur-driven trucks fashioned with ringing bells, which made a circuit around neighborhoods rather than remaining at fixed locations. Youngstown, Ohio, welcomed Good Humor ice cream with great enthusiasm. Good Humor ice cream men wore white uniforms to promote a clean-cut, wholesome image, which contributed to their success. Burt strove to create a national brand that would retain the same ingredients and flavors in a nationwide market. Good Humor ice cream tasted the same no matter where it was purchased. Harry Burt passed away in 1926, and his wife Cora took over the business. She was responsible for making Good Humor a public entity, and franchises were available for just $100. The business expanded into other parts of the Midwest, and by 1930, a New York businessman and investor named M.J. Meeham acquired the company. The Meeham family controlled the business until 1961, when it was acquired by Unilever, a division of the Lipton Company. Good Humor trucks were sent on their last mission in 1976, when Lipton decided to focus its efforts on grocery store freezer cabinets. Individual and independent ice cream distributors kept the neighborhood Good Humor ice cream trucks rolling.

Hot Brown

Although the gooey sandwich known as a Hot Brown sports earthy hues from the bread and gravy it contains, the Brown referred to in its moniker comes from where the sandwich was invented. In 1926 Fred K. Schmidt created the Hot Brown at Louisville, Kentucky's, Brown Hotel, and it became one of two signature sandwiches crafted by chefs shortly after the hotel's opening in 1923. The Hot Brown was offered as a creative twist on the ham-and-egg late-night meal, typically served to guests at their hotel restaurant after nightly dinner dances. The classic Hot Brown is an open-faced sandwich on white bread piled with slices of turkey, chicken, or ham. It is drizzled with a generous helping of hot Mornay sauce and a sprinkle of Parmesan cheese, and then baked or broiled until the sauce begins to bubble and brown. Crispy bacon, pimentos, or sliced tomatoes then top the sauce. Sometimes a melted cheddar or American cheese sauce is substituted for the Mornay, but purists would argue against that choice. When the sandwich was first invented in the 1920s, sliced turkey was a rarity in everyday cookery. It was usually used only in extravagant holiday meals, adding a layer of swank to the down-home hearty sandwich. Hot Browns soon became the top choice among 95 percent of diners visiting the Brown Hotel restaurant. The hoteliers saw a wider market for the dish and added Hot Browns to their lunch menu and even countered with the Cold Brown. The cold version featured chicken or turkey with lettuce and tomato on rye bread with hard-boiled egg, covered in Thousand Island Dressing. It is rarely served commercially anymore. Hot Browns were briefly out of rotation as its originating course when the Brown Hotel was shuttered between 1971 and 1985. Beyond the Brown Hotel, the Hot has grown into an affectionate signature dish of the upper South and can be found on menus both regionally and throughout the United States.

Howard Johnson

Howard Deering Johnson, a newsstand and soda fountain operator from Quincy, Massachusetts, pioneered new concepts in American chain restaurant management and hospitality that remain cornerstones of food business practice to this day. His first innovations involved already popular snack foods such as ice cream and hot dogs. Johnson developed the first commercial premium ice cream in 1925. His ice cream boasted natural flavorings and twice the butterfat content of other ice creams on the market. Rumors abound on whether Johnson borrowed the ice cream recipe from his mother or purchased the formula from a local German immigrant. Nevertheless, Johnson scooped larger portions of ice cream for his clients than his competitors with the help of a specially designed larger ice cream scoop, instituting the popular American dining concept of "bigger equals better." Johnson expanded his newsstand enterprise, selling soda pop, ice cream cones, and hot dogs from beachfront wooden stands during the summers in Massachusetts. He grossed $240,000 in sales by 1928, and the original vanilla, chocolate, and strawberry flavors expanded to 28 flavors, with the number "28" becoming his trademark. Howard Johnson put his own twist on hot dogs as well. His "Frankfort" involved a wiener clipped at both ends and notched lengthwise down the middle, nestled in a butter-toasted roll. His stands grew in popularity and credibility, so he was able to borrow money from local bankers to open his first sit-down Howard Johnson's restaurant in 1929 in downtown Quincy, Massachusetts. It was situated in a brand-new 10-story building, and the menu featured New England specialties such as fried clams, baked beans, and chicken potpie, in addition to the Howard Johnson classics like large fountain sodas, hot dogs, and ice cream topped with a cookie bearing the HJ logo. Through happenstance, a theater performance of Eugene O'Neill's play *Strange Interlude* was relocated to Quincy, MA, after Mayor Malcolm Nichols banned performances of the show in Boston. Howard Johnson captured the attention and palates of hungry theatergoers and drew crowds of Bostonians going forward. The stock market crash of 1929 halted the expansion of Howard Johnson's for several years, but in 1932, Johnson was able to persuade a friend to open another franchise in Orleans, MA. This was one of America's first franchise restaurants, and by 1939, there were 107 Howard Johnson restaurants, many located strategically along the highways of the East Coast. He outlined procedures of cleanliness and service that were consistent from location to location, a unique quality in the food industry during this time. Johnson bid successfully for exclusive rights to serve drivers at turnoffs along the Pennsylvania, New Jersey, and Ohio turnpikes. Unfortunately, World War II put a grinding halt to American motor leisure travel, and many of the franchises withered away. Only 12 restaurants remained in 1944. Howard Johnson's company survived wartime by serving meals to war workers and U.S. Army recruits. But the business bounced back robustly as the postwar United States rolled out new cars, suburban highway infrastructure, and the beginnings of the Baby Boom. Howard Johnson's became the "Landmark for Hungry Americans" under the moniker HoJo's. Food was produced centrally and shipped out to franchises, ensuring uniformity among restaurants. Road travel flourished, spawning the first Howard Johnson's Motor Lodge in 1954.

Kool-Aid

The punchy fruit drink known as Kool-Aid was invented by patent medicine chemist Edwin E. Perkins and his wife Kitty in 1927, in Hastings, Nebraska. Originally known as Fruit Smack, Perkins formulated a powdered version of the drink to reduce shipping costs. He called this powder Kool-Ade. It was renamed Kool-Aid several years later, and this change is rumored to have been instigated by a government requirement that only products containing fruit juice were allowed to contain the suffix "ade." Perkins moved his operation to Chicago in 1931 and sold the company to General Foods in 1953. The Kool-Aid Man mascot was introduced not long after the General Foods acquisition, a man-sized frosty pitcher of Kool-Aid, often cherry flavored. He is known for suddenly bursting through walls and shouting "Oh, yeah!" when instigated by children stirring up a fresh batch of the drink. Some of Kool-Aid's more unusual flavors included Eerie Orange, Incrediberry, Purplesaurus Rex, and the Great Bluedini. Every year during the second weekend of August, Hastings, Nebraska, hosts Kool-Aid Days—a fun-filled family weekend of activities and antics.

La Choy

La Choy is the oldest and most successful commercial Asian American food producer in the United States. The company is the brainchild of two college pals who met at the University of Michigan—Wally Smith, an

American grocer from Detroit, and Ilhan New, a Korean American businessman who was managing a company called La Choy, which meant "Good Vegetables" in a Chinese dialect. Smith wanted to add a line of bean sprouts at his grocery store, and New was well acquainted with methods of growing them. So while most of the United States was busy brewing illegal spirits in their bathtubs during Prohibition, Smith and New were growing bean sprouts in theirs. The idea was so successful that the pair decided to incorporate their business in 1922 as La Choy Food Products Company. They quickly switched from selling the sprouts in glass jars to metal cans and added a variety of Oriental vegetables to their line. New eventually left the company, and Smith was unfortunately killed by lightning in 1937. However, the company thrived under new management, expanding to include soy sauce, kumquats, water chestnuts, bamboo shoots, and chow mein noodles. The company faced dire times during World War II, when the federal government declared Chinese food production nonessential to the U.S. war effort, and canning was curtailed. The company was further hindered by the conflict between the United States and Japan, severely restricting its ability to import ingredients from other regions of Asia. La Choy sold its Detroit factory to the government for munitions production and relocated to Archbold, Ohio. The company never recuperated from the financial sting of the war and was acquired by Beatrice Foods of Chicago, IL, in 1943. During the 1950s, the company invested in academic research that revealed a method for growing mung beans hydroponically in an indoor gardening facility. From then on, the company was able to produce stable mung bean crops. The Archbold plant doubled in size and began producing and canning chow mein noodles in 1958. The company peaked in the 1960s and has been experiencing a slow and steady decline with many corporate handovers as a result of the popularity and ease of acquiring Chinese take-out food just about anywhere throughout the United States.

Lender's Bagel Bakery

The popularity of bagels spread beyond urban centers when Polish baker Harry Lender opened the first bagel plant outside of New York City in 1928 in New Haven, Connecticut. Lender, an immigrant from Lublin, Poland, first worked in a bagel bakery in Passaic, NJ, when he arrived in the United States in 1927. For $600, he purchased the bakery in New Haven, which he named the New York Bagel Bakery, and his family joined him on New Year's Eve, 1929. The timing was perfect as it was a time of peak population growth for New Haven, as well as increasing diversity, with immigrants flooding in from eastern Europe, Russia, Italy, and the American South. Jews in particular were a large percentage of the new-comers, accounting for almost one-sixth of the population. The center of the Jewish community in New Haven was on Oak Street, a boon for Lender's burgeoning bagel business. Lender sold not only to individuals but to bakeries in restaurants in New Haven as well. Sunday mornings were the biggest bagel-buying day of the week, and the fresh bagels were prepared Saturday nights, with crowds from in and out of town swarming the store to scoop up the freshly baked bagels. By the 1950s, the ability to produce up to 6,000 bagels for Sunday morning consumption began to become problematic. In 1954, Lender developed a method for freezing bagels throughout the week so that Saturdays would not be so labor inten-sive. This secret of the frozen bagels fooled customers for a while, until one day the bagels were delivered frozen without being thawed first. Although customers were initially angry that what they thought were fresh-baked bagels were actually frozen, they were soon won over by the convenience of frozen bagels, which were marketed as far away as the Catskills. Murray Lender, son of Harry, took over part of the business after Harry passed away and traveled throughout the country on a campaign to tout the ben-efits of frozen bagels to a market that was both disdainful of frozen foods and unfamiliar with bagels. He organized the frozen food industry and declared March Frozen Foods Month. Now a long way from New Haven, Lender's bagels can still be found today in the frozen food aisle at many national supermarket chains.

Orange Julius

Natural, fresh-squeezed orange juice was first converted into the shake-like refreshment marketed as Orange Julius in Los Angeles, California. The drink emerged from Julius Freed's fresh-squeezed orange juice stand, relocated to a downtown Los Angeles storefront location with the help of his real-estate agent friend Willard Hamlin in 1926. Hamlin had a back-ground in chemistry and suspected there was a market for more interest-ing orange-flavored drinks for sale at Freed's stand. Experimenting with orange juice, crushed ice, and various food powders, Hamlin came upon a frothy mixture that was orange kismet. In many ways the precursor to the smoothie, Orange Julius tamed the acidic nature of fruit juice into a creamy, more palatable beverage, which was also less irritating to sensitive stomachs. With the addition of the drink to Freed's juice repertoire, sales increased. People shouting "Give me an Orange, Julius!" provided the inspiration for the chain's eventual name. The drink was so successful that Hamlin left real estate to focus on marketing and franchising the Orange Julius operation. There were about 100 stands between Los Angeles and Boston by 1929. Prohibition may have also contributed to Orange Julius's great success, with a public thirsting for more innovative drink options without the alcohol. Times Square was even referred to as Orange Juice Gulch during the 1920s, with a proliferation of juice joints such as Nedick's and Orange Julius, often paired with hot dogs, in that urban area. Expansion of the chain was curtailed by the Depression and the outbreak of World War II, but Orange Julius's popularity experienced resurgence during the 1950s. It was named the official drink of the 1964 New York's World Fair. In 1987, International Dairy Queen acquired the chain, and Orange Julius is often seen paired with Dairy Queen stands in mall centers throughout the United States. Today, the chain faces stiff competition from more modern smoothie outlets, such as Jamba Juice, but there are still about 300-odd Orange Julius establishments scattered throughout the United States, Canada, and around the world.

Pineapple Upside-Down Cake

Food historians quibble over the exact date of the first published recipe of the pineapple upside-down cake, but many agree it appeared sometime during the 1920s. One tasty result of tropical fruits becoming more commercially available in the United States was the popularity of this unusually shaped fruit cake. The comely pineapple, considered one of the most fashionable of the exotic fruits during the 1920s, dressed up what was essentially a solid core of sponge cake. Hot, fruited skillet cakes, often using apples, cherries, or apricots, date back even further to the turn of the century and were cooked on the stove top in cast-iron skillets. Maraschino cherries were also often featured in pineapple upside-down cake recipes that sought to develop a new role for the cherries in cuisine after their favored position as cocktail embellishment came to a halt during Prohibition. The classic pineapple upside-down cake is a simple skillet cake poured over butter, brown sugar, and fruit. Variations on the pineapple upside-down cake included a recipe called pineapple glace, featured in a Seattle charity cookbook in 1924, and caramel pineapple-cake, chosen as the best new recipe of 1927 in *Pictoral Review* magazine. In 1925, the Hawaiian Pineapple Company (later Dole) ran ads in women's magazines soliciting recipes involving pineapple, particularly of the canned variety, and a prizewinning pineapple upside-down cake recipe was plucked from among 2,500 entries. The winning recipe by Mrs. Robert Davis of Norfolk, VA, was later published in the Hawaiian Pineapple Company cookbook.

Po-Boy

The Po-Boy, or Poor Boy, sandwich is a legendary staple of New Orleans cuisine. The filling can vary, but the thick, crusty loaves of French bread are what make the Po-Boy such a unique Southern comfort food. Rarely found outside New Orleans bakeries, the bread is notable for its extremely light interior, contrasted with its crusty, crunchy exterior. Fillings run the gamut from deep-fried seafood common to the Gulf such as shrimp and oysters, to Creole hot sausage or roast beef bathed in a rich gravy called "debris." The invention of the Po-Boy is credited to Bennie and Clovis Martin. The duo worked for years as streetcar operators before opening the Martin Brothers Coffee Stand and Restaurant in the French Market in 1922. During a streetcar motormen and conductors strike in 1929, more than 10,000 people gathered in downtown New Orleans to protest. Rumor has it that the Martins handed out free or inexpensive sandwiches to any striker who was hungry and couldn't afford to pay. Whenever they saw another striker coming, they apparently said, "Here comes another poor boy," and the moniker stuck. Their generosity also extended to poor children, who would frequent the stand. The Martins would cut the sandwiches into thirds and hand the pieces out to poor, hungry children. In those days, the sandwiches likely also contained French fries and gravy in addition to one of the regular fillings. To avoid wasting precious bread at the tapered end of a loaf, the Martins consulted baker John Gendusa to craft a 40-inch loaf that was a uniform rectangle from end to end. This could be easily cut into 20-inch halves, perfect for sharing, and they offered a 15-inch size as well. The strike ended at the start of the Great Depression, and many streetcar men lost their jobs. But the unflagging support of the Martins left them with a fleet of loyal customers that benefitted business for years to come. Clovis branched out and started his own franchise called Martin and Son Po-Boy Bar and Restaurant during the 1930s. By then, the popularity of the Po-Boy had already spread beyond the original stand on St. Claude Avenue. Today Po-Boys can be found on menus near and far afield from New Orleans, but the experience and history of the sandwich are best enjoyed in its hometown with locally made bread and regionally caught seafood.

Popsicles

There is great speculation, debate, and mystery surrounding the origin of the Popsicle. Lore has it that as a youth, Frank W. Epperson left a mixture of powdered soda and water with a stirring stick stuck in it out on a night of record low temperatures in San Francisco, California, in 1905. By morning, the drink had frozen itself to the stick, much like a lollipop. As an adult, Epperson tried again to recreate his accidental invention in earnest. He called the invention an "Epsicle" but his children referred to it as "Pop's sicle." Epperson dreamed that Pop's Popsicle had the potential to appeal to a wide audience. In 1923, while working at a lemonade stand at an amusement park in Oakland, CA, he realized the Popsicle's commercial possibilities. With fellow employees of the Loews Movie Company, he formed the Popsicle Company in 1923. The concession was sold for the first time at amusement parks and beaches during the summer of 1923. One stand at Coney Island is rumored to have sold as many as 8,000 Popsicles during one hot summer day. The Popsicle Corporation of the United States was founded in 1924, taking over operating rights from the Loews group. Sales topped $6.5 million that year. Epperson filed for a patent of his Popsicle design in 1924. In 1925, Epperson sold the rights to the brand name Popsicle to the Joe Lowe Company of New York, and by 1928 earned more than $60,000 in royalties. As more families moved to the suburbs in the 1950s and owned home refrigerator or freezer units, Popsicle introduced its supermarket multipack, which contained an array of Popsicle flavors individually wrapped and boxed for the home freezer. Today, Popsicle is still the number-one brand among children's frozen novelties.

Soda

Soft drinks gained much popularity during the supposedly alcohol-free 1920s. In the earlier part of the century, people believed that carbonated beverages could cure common ailments, and soft drinks were mainly marketed as a fun, refreshing beverage during the era of Prohibition. Two carbonated beverages emblematic of the United States' new taste for carbonated refreshment came to fruition during the 1920s—Nehi and 7Up. In 1924 the Chero-Cola Company introduced Nehi soda (pronounced "knee-high") in an effort to add more flavors to this soda manufacturer's repertoire. Nehi soda was offered in grape, orange, root beer, and peach flavors and soon surpassed Chero-Cola's cola drink in popularity, so much so that the company changed its name to the Nehi Corporation in 1928. Nehi soda had a wide-ranging advertising campaign that included placement on the back of matchbook covers. Somewhat suggestive, the Nehi logo sported a picture of a woman in black pumps, wearing a skirt, with her legs exposed up to her knees, with the text "Drink Nehi, Quality Beverages." Nehi was acquired by Royal Crown Cola, also known as RC Cola, in 1935, and RC Cola went on to eclipse Nehi's popularity eventually. The formula for the lemon-lime soda later called 7Up was invented by Charles Leiper Grigg of the Howdy Corporation in St. Louis, MO. The product was originally called Bib-Label Lithiated Lemon-Lime Soda and contained lithium citrate, a mood stabilizer. The drink was first sold in St. Louis in 1928 and was then granted a federal patent under the name Seven Up in 1929. It was advertised as 7Up Lithiated Lemon Soda and touted as a Prohibition-era hangover cure. In 1931, probably due to lithium's ability to counteract cluster headaches, a Pennsylvania newspaper claimed the beverage as a cure for "Morning After Toxicity." The ingredient was abandoned in the drink in 1950, as lithium was found to cause side effects such as dizziness, nausea, and thyroid problems.

Supermarkets

It was not until the 1920s that chain stores, particularly those that sold groceries, became commonplace and a truly all-American concept. Small regional chains, such as Kroger's, began expanding their domain. A&P gained national representation, with more than 10,000 stores throughout the United States by the end of the decade. At the time, the stores were economical because they were typically staffed by only two to three employees at a time and did not offer meat or produce, which were common perishables. The "cash-n-carry" concept was first pioneered by the grocery store Safeway, founded in 1925. The supermarket was named by way of a contest sponsored by the W.H.R. Weldon firm, which had just purchased the ailing chain from Los Angeles grocer Sam Selig. The slogan was "Drive the Safeway, Buy the Safeway." Paying for groceries by credit was customary at the time, but Safeway discouraged shoppers from accumulating debt by allowing only cash purchases, which was a common scenario during the Great Depression. More than 322 Safeway stores were scattered throughout Southern California by 1926. Eventually Weldon sold his share of the business to Merrill Lynch for $3.5 million. Meanwhile, on the other coast of the United States, more than 100 independent retailers in Poughkeepsie, NY, and Sharon, CT, joined forces in 1926 to form IGA, the Independent Grocers Alliance. It was formed to integrate wholesalers, retailers, and manufacturers of grocery items, strengthening the role of all three. The group expanded to 150 retailers by the end of 1926. Mainly located in smaller cities, IGA sports the motto "Home Proud." Today, it is the world's largest voluntary supermarket, with more than 4,000 stores in more than 41 different countries.

Texas Hot Wieners

Ironically, Texas Hot Wieners were *not* invented in Texas. Instead, the chili-laden hot dog was created by a Greek entrepreneur and hot dog stand operator on Paterson Street in downtown Paterson, New Jersey. Back then, a hot dog stand was considered a small sit-down operation hosting small stools at a countertop. The owner was dabbling with several different kinds of chili sauces to top his hot dogs when he settled on a mixture that paid homage to his culinary heritage. The original Texas Hot Wiener featured a topping that resembled a Greek spaghetti sauce of tomatoes, meat, and spices. In its classic form, the Texas Hot Wiener is an all-beef hot dog blanched in boiling vegetable oil in a deep fryer, followed by another hot oil bath in a tilted steel pan. Next, the item is embedded in a bun, topped with spicy mustard, chopped onions, and a chili sauce containing tomatoes, more onions, and a mélange of spices including cayenne, cinnamon, allspice, and cumin. The name of the Greek inventor of the Texas Hot Wiener, as well as his choice of "Texas" in the naming of the snack, remain elusive. Speculation is that the spicy taste of the hot dog and faraway locale of Texas (to native New Jersey residents) added an exotic zest to the appeal of the product. Chili engenders visions of cowboys, Latino culture, and the West, and the "Texas" denomination sums up much of this chili image. In 1936, Paterson Street hot dog stand employee William Papas left to open his own establishment, called Libby's Hot Grille, which carried on the Texas Hot Wiener tradition. It is still in business today. It is considered among the most authentic of the establishments serving Texas Hot Wieners in Paterson, NJ, and is widely imitated.

Wheaties

The Breakfast of Champions was conceived quite by accident. A Minnesota clinician working at the Washburn-Crosby Company, later known as General Mills, spilled hot bran flakes onto a hot stove. It took more than 36 attempts to make the flakes strong enough to withstand packaging. The head miller, George Cormack, perfected the flake in 1924. The first run of the product went under the name of Washburn's Gold Medal Whole Wheat Flakes. An employee contest sponsored by Washburn-Crosby to brand the cereal resulted in the winning entry of Wheaties. Other potential entries included Nutties and Gold Medal Wheat Flakes. The tie-in with sports and athleticism began in 1933 with an advertising campaign at a minor league baseball game in Minnesota. One of the most popular slogans in advertising history was created that year. General Mills's contract for sponsorship of the broadcasts of the Minneapolis Millers games on WCCO radio included a large billboard at the ball park. Knox Reeves, an advertising executive for Wheaties, was asked what to print on the sign. He came up with the famed phrase "Breakfast of Champions," which has secured Wheaties as an image for healthy, wholesome breakfast ever since.

White Castle

Hamburgers were not quite the American obsession that they are today back in the early twentieth century until a Wichita, Kansas, cook named Walter Anderson created a new style of hamburger in 1916. He jazzed up the beef patty by grilling a thick, small ball of ground meat slowly with onions on a griddle. The formula was such a success that he opened three hamburger stands in Wichita between 1916 and 1920, selling the mini-burgers on a bun for 5 cents apiece. In 1921, Edgar Ingram, a local Wichita insurance and real estate agent, saw a future in the burger and partnered with Anderson to open a fourth hamburger stand, which was called White Castle, becoming the first fast-food chain in the United States. The business was incorporated in 1924 under the entity White Castle System of Eating Houses. Ingram financed the expansion of the business to 12 major cities throughout the eastern United States. This geographic shift required a move to a more centrally located home office, and Columbus, Ohio, became the center of White Castle operations, which it remains to this day. Ingram eventually bought out Anderson's share of the company and became the sole proprietor in 1933. Part of White Castle's success as the country's first chain restaurant involved having a written set of standards for operations, food preparations, and employee appearance, encouraging sanitary restaurants with friendly employees. The White Castle building structure was modeled after Chicago's Old Water Tower and designed by a White Castle employee, Lord Ray. He designed a portable hamburger stand with a five-stool, steel-framed structure, with enamel porcelain panels that were easy to erect and break down. White Castle also made strides in the marketing of hamburgers, which did not have a great reputation before 1920. They reached out through offering a newspaper coupon. The first coupon was offered in a St. Louis newspaper in 1932 and was good

---

Sliced Bread

While many things may claim to be the greatest thing since sliced bread, Otto Frederick Rohwedder of Davenport, Iowa, perfected the invention of sliced bread itself. Rohwedder had been working since 1912 on the prototype of a bread-slicing machine and sold his first model to the M.F. Bench's Chillicothe Bakery in Missouri in 1928. They marketed the product as Kleen Maid Sliced Bread. Sandwiches have never been the same since.

---

for a take-out order of five hamburgers for the cost of 10 cents, thereby expanding the hamburger-eating audience. White Castle also offered tours to local housewives and gave away hamburger recipe books in the 1930s in an attempt to market the business to a wider demographic. The beef and sugar rations that hit during World War II curtailed the expansion of White Castle restaurants during wartime. The shortage of working males also led to the first hiring of White Castle female employees in the 1940s. After the 1950s and through the 1970s, the size of White Castle buildings expanded, and drive-through service was introduced. In the 1980s, White Castle forged into the frozen microwave hamburger arena. White Castle is the first fast-food chain to sell both one million and then one billion hamburgers. The Ingram family still owns the business and its subsidiaries, and there are White Castles everywhere now from Maryland to Malaysia, but ironically, there are no more White Castles in Wichita, Kansas, where it all began.

Wonder Bread

One of the most wonderful things about Wonder Bread is its delightful packaging. Enveloped in plastic, bedecked with bright yellow, red, and blue circles, Wonder Bread owes much of its popularity to its peppy image. Taggart, an Indianapolis baking company, was the first to pack Wonder Bread into its recognizable package in 1921. In 1925, the Continental Baking Company purchased Taggart, and Wonder Bread became the first packaged sliced bread in the United States, inspiring the well-known phrase "the best thing since sliced bread." In the 1940s, with the metal shortages of World War II, Wonder Bread cut back on slicing and sold unsliced bread. But the decade also proved to be an enriching one for Wonder Bread, and the company became one of the first to fortify its product with vitamins and minerals. In 1941, it also became the first packaged bread to eliminate holes in the bread. Nutritional information became available on the package in the 1970s, and a reduced-calorie version debuted in 1986.

Yoo-hoo

Yoo-hoo came hollering into existence in the 1920s when the Olivieri family started thinking about adding a new flavor to its Tru-Fruit soft drink repertoire in its small New Jersey store. Proprietor Natale Olivieri discovered a method to produce a chocolate-flavored beverage that would not spoil. He discovered a steam sterilization method that, when used after the beverage was bottled and capped, would result in a long shelf life. As long as Yoo-hoo was sealed, the chocolate drink would not go sour. The name Yoo-hoo was already being used for some of Olivieri's other fruit-flavored beverages. Speculation exists that the name Yoo-hoo was chosen from the popular expressions of the day. For example, competing beverages at the time had names such as Whoopee, Vigor, and Moxie. In any case, Yoo-hoo was such a smash that a major bottler began distributing the drink to local supermarkets. Sales soared, and distribution spread beyond the bounds of New Jersey. The efforts of Yogi Berra and the Yankees during the 1950s resulted in the most successful ad campaign in Yoo-hoo's history. The slogans "Mee-Hee for Yoo-Hoo" and "The Drink of Champions" were popularized by the championship Yankees team, as was the image of Berra drinking Yoo-hoo while wearing a classy suit. B.B.C. Industries owned Yoo-hoo at this time of great success in the 1950s and for the next two decades, until 1976, when Iroquois Brands acquired it. Ownership of Yoo-hoo changed hands through the years many times. Dr Pepper Snapple Group of Plano, Texas currently owns and operates the brand. Besides the classic chocolate flavor, other flavors of Yoo-hoo include lite chocolate, double fudge, and strawberry. Former flavors that did not stand the test of time were chocolate-pomegranate, dyna-mocha, eggnog, and vampires & cream (Halloween edition).

Further Reading

1920s Wedding Menus. http://www.associatedcontent.com/article/3019434/1920s_wedding_menus.html?cat=23.

Coe, Andrew. *Chop Suey, A Cultural History of Chinese Food in the United States*. New York: Oxford University Press, 2009.

Hogan, David Gerald. *Selling 'Em by the Sack: White Castle and the Creation of American Food*. New York: New York University Press, 1997.

Lovett, Laura. "The Popeye Principle, Selling Child Health in the First Nutrition Crisis." *Journal of Health, Politics, and Law* 30, Issue 5, October 2005, 803–838.

Shapiro, Laura. *Perfection Salad: Women and Cooking at the Turn of the Century.* Los Angeles, UCLA Press, 1986.

Skilnik, Bob. *Beer and Food: An American History.* Lookout Mountain, TN: Jefferson Press, 2007.

4

1930s

Sherri Liberman

The bleak economic landscape of the Great Depression dominated the 1930s. The American dream had become a nightmare. What was once the land of opportunity was now the land of desperation in the wake of the stock market crash. Americans were questioning all the maxims on which they had based their lives—democracy, capitalism, and individualism. Farmers affected by the Dust Bowl packed their families into cars and sought work in the agricultural fields or cities of the West. Their role as independent landowners had evaporated. In 1932, the average American family income was $1,500 per year, nearly 40 percent less than when the stock market crashed in 1929. Fortunately, the United States remained a democratic nation despite the troubled times, whereas European nations such as Germany and Italy turned into dictatorships as a means to solve their economic problems. The Hooverville shanties that began the decade, along with a political philosophy that aid to the poor should come from private agencies, ended with Franklin Delano Roosevelt's array of government-funded social programs. In 1935, the Social Security Administration was created to assist the elderly, and the Wagner Act was passed to allow workers to legally unionize. This type of federal intervention was a key part of the nation's economic recovery.

Bread lines and soup kitchens were common sights in the United States, and the need for subsidized meals grew dramatically when the Great Depression swept across the nation in the early 1930s. The first soup kitchens emerged around 1929 from churches and local charities. By the mid-1930s, state and local governments were involved in operating soup

Unemployed men eat the free meals they receive at the Works Progress Administration/Volunteers of American soup kitchen in Washington, D.C., in 1936. (Franklin D. Roosevelt Library)

kitchens. Serving mainly soup and bread, this was an economical choice, requiring mostly water. Chicago's most famous gangster, Al Capone, even started a soup kitchen, ensuring that Chicago's unemployed were served three meals a day.

By 1932, 12 million Americans, nearly 25 percent of the population, were out of work. Despite this staggering statistic, people did what they could to make their lives more enjoyable during the 1930s. Hollywood movies provided a temporary escape, as did board games, gambling, and baseball. Parker Brothers debuted the board game Monopoly in 1935, based on an old Quaker game called The Landlord's Game and designed to demonstrate how money and power tend to end up in the hands of the few at the expense of the many. By 1939, nearly 80 percent of the population had radios, and families gathered round to listen to the big-band sounds of Benny Goodman, follow the Yankees and their stars like Jo DiMaggio, or laugh with comedians like George Burns and Gracie Allen.

Despite the economic poverty that characterized the 1930s, for those who could afford it, the age of labor-saving devices was in full force and nowhere more pertinent than in the kitchen. Electric refrigerators, gas and electric stoves, pop-up toasters, waffle irons, and coffee percolators were commonplace, timesaving devices. Easy-to-mop linoleum flooring replaced wood floors scrubbed on hands and knees. By the late 1930s, electric grills were being sold for home use, and chafing dishes were popular for home entertaining. In 1936, Sylvan Goldman and Fred Young invented the first shopping cart. The 1930s were the dawn of the age of the diner, designed with the look of modern train dining cars. Utilizing sleek stainless steel, chrome, and glass, barrel-roofed diners of the 1930s embodied the Art Deco aesthetic. Refrigeration methods improved, and synthetic materials such as nylon and cellophane became more commonplace in the home.

Several key technological advances were applied to modernize restaurants and home kitchens during the 1930s. In 1931, the Wilcox's Pier Restaurant of New Haven, CT, boasted the first automatic swinging doors between kitchen and dining room, thanks to the addition of a photoelectric cell. Coca-Cola introduced its first automated soda fountain dispenser in May 1933 at the Century of Progress Exposition in Chicago. And Teflon was accidently discovered in 1938 by Roy J. Plunkett of DuPont Laboratories, who was working on chlorofluorocarbon refrigerants at the time.

However important these advances, there were still more rural families than urban dwellers in the United States, who were getting by with "grandma's kitchen," an enamel-topped wood stove, a free-standing sink, an ice box, and a "Welsh dresser" for dishes rather than the premade built-in cabinets showing up in more modern kitchens. Packaged baking became evermore popular during the 1930s. Bisquick was invented as a result of a General Mills sales executive observing a railroad dining car chef mixing the lard and dry ingredients for biscuits ahead of time. The recipe was altered using hydrogenated oil, eliminating the need for refrigeration. At first, sesame oil was used as the preservative, known for years as Ingredient S on the box. Bisquick debuted on grocery store shelves in 1931 and was originally intended for a quick way to make biscuits, but other uses for the powdered mix include pizza dough, pancakes, and even dumplings.

Although the Great Depression certainly impacted the way families cooked, shopped for food, dined out, and entertained, the popular magazines of the day did not provide much evidence of the economic scarcity that was prevalent among readers. Americans dined out less during the 1930s, and when they did, it was mainly at restaurants serving American food. Chipped beef was a prevalent and economical meal often served in the 1930s kitchen, requiring only dried beef, water, flour, butter, and half and half. Dinner parties and home entertaining in the 1930s certainly still existed, but with some adjustments. Most families did not have maids, and grand, formal dinner parties were a rarity. Instead, hostesses were more likely to hold luncheons, teas, and Sunday night suppers offering up mixed fare on the chafing dish. Biscuits, waffles, and other starchy foods often were comforting menu items of Sunday night dinners, as was chili con carne. Women's clubs proliferated, gatherings focused around bridge or charitable activities, in contrast to the more individualistic trends of the 1920s. Often served were "women's foods," which were usually dainty, light, sweet, and creamy. Marshmallows appeared in any number of dishes, including fruit salads and vegetable dishes. Topiary salads provided an opportunity for creative expression, such as Indian salad modeled after a Native American chief's headdress.

The Dust Bowl, or the Dirty Thirties, as they were known, was a period of severe dust storms that caused major ecological, agricultural, and economic damage to the American and Canadian prairie from 1930 through 1936. Severe draught in addition to excessive farming without crop rotation caused soil erosion that led to this tragedy. The farmland became useless, causing "Okies" to leave home, many for California. John Steinbeck's *The Grapes of Wrath* chronicled the life of a displaced Oklahoma family that had lost its farm to the drought of the Dust Bowl. The Dust Bowl inspired a nostalgic revival for country cooking, evident in the publication of *Country Cookbook* in 1937 by Cora, Rose, and Bob Brown. The text focused on a fondness for country picnics, filled with such American classics as fried chicken, buttermilk biscuits, and flakey-crusted pies.

The end of Prohibition in 1933 might have begun a new golden age in fine dining had the Depression not intervened. The pressure to end Prohibition primarily came from hotels, restaurants, and the wine and liquor industry, which were suffering financially due to the pressure from both the Depression and Prohibition. In 1933, Prohibition was repealed when Utah and Nevada voted for the 21st Amendment, which repealed the 18th Amendment prohibiting the sale and consumption of alcohol in the United States. It heralded an economic boom to hotels and with the repeal of Prohibition, the 1930s revived the life of the cocktail, which from then on saw the invention of many drinks such as the Bloody Mary, the Zombie, and the non alcoholic Shirley Temple. The martini was the drink of choice above all. Art Deco–style chrome cocktail shakers were fashionable, and built-in bars were popular among those who could afford them. Cocktail parties were all the rage. Not at all ironically, in 1938, the Harger Drunkometer, the first alcohol breath-testing device, was introduced in Indiana.

The onset of World War II impacted American food choices, as did the requisite influx of women in the workplace. These were prime conditions for marketing new packaged food products, such as Kraft Dinner, later called Kraft Macaroni & Cheese. In 1937, Kraft Dinner was first introduced in the United States and Canada. Milk and dairy products were already being rationed, with an increased dependence on meatless entrees. Kraft Dinner was easy to prepare and required fewer dairy products and no meat. Made of dry macaroni pasta and powdered, processed cheese, the

Kraft Dinner required only that you boil and drain the pasta and, add milk, butter, and the cheese powder to enjoy this hearty meal.

Despite all the novelty and packaged goods that were introduced in the 1930s, alongside the resurgence in drinking, health was still a priority concern for the American diet. By the 1930s, the culmination of years of research into vitamins elicited serious public interest in nutrition. In 1932, C. Glen King at the University of Pittsburgh first isolated vitamin C from lemon juice. Food and drug companies began bombarding the public with ads for vitamins and nutritional supplements. Vitamin sales increased from $12 million in 1931 to more than $82 million in 1939.

Choice of produce was still fairly limited by seasonality despite improvements in shipping and refrigeration. Fruits were dried and canned in the fall for winter consumption. Salads were common in spring and summer, with squash, turnips, and other hardy root vegetables more commonplace in winter. Exotic tropical fruits such as grapefruit and oranges were available in winter, but at an expensive premium. In 1931, the tangelo, a hybrid of a tangerine and a grapefruit, was developed. In 1937, spinach growers in the United States erected a statue in honor of Popeye the comic strip sailor. And in 1939, the seedless watermelon was developed. Receiving fruits and nuts for Christmas in the 1930s was considered an expensive and rare treat for those on a limited budget. Rural areas might see an orange perhaps once a year. In the 1930s, chicken was not the affordable, commonplace meat it is today. When it did appear on the dinner table, it was usually a tough, older bird, to be used in chicken and dumplings recipes. Hens old enough to lay eggs were too valuable to be sold for meat. Pork was cheap and plentiful, and beef for stew and organ meat was the more affordable option for meat-eating Americans. In the South, ham was

Popeye statue stands in Crystal City, Texas, in honor of the spinach-loving comic hero, ca. 1939. (Library of Congress)

the meat of choice, either smoked or sugar-cured for longer storage. And anyone with a shotgun could easily acquire squirrel, rabbit, pheasant, pigeon, and venison for the table. Turkey or goose were holiday specialties that required a year of family saving.

The 1930s were rife with many critical agricultural and labor issues. The first sit-down strike occurred at the Hormel meat-packing plant in Austin, Minnesota, in 1933. Angry, unionized workers armed with clubs removed CEO Jay Hormel from the company's headquarters. The laborers shut down the plant's refrigeration system for three days, until a compromise was reached. Since then, Hormel has been known for its generous labor policies, including weekly paychecks and more secure long-term employment.

The 1930s were a decade of both high-brow and low-brow food firsts. These years saw the invention of peach melba and melba toast, named after the late operatic soprano Helen Porter Mitchell, also known by her stage name Nellie Melba, in 1931. The dishes were reportedly invented by her chef George Auguste Escoffier, known as "the King of Chefs and the Chef of Kings." The rich dessert Anna Pavlova, a meringue of whipped cream and fruit, was named for the famous Russian ballerina after her death in 1931. Also in 1931, Harry MacElhone of Harry's Bar in Paris invented the elegant Sidecar cocktail, the same year the canned rattlesnake first appeared on the market, packaged by George K. End of Arcadia, Florida. In 1933, a California packer started what is now the famous Skippy Churned Peanut Butter, and Kraft Miracle Whip Salad Dressing debuted. Miracle Whip combined the best properties of mayo and boiled salad dressing and quickly began to outsell jarred mayonnaise in the United States. It is claimed that cheeseburgers were first served at Kaelin's restaurant in Louisville, Kentucky, in 1934. Also in 1934, Campbell's Chicken Noodle Soup and Cream of Mushroom Soup were introduced, both some of Campbell's best-selling varieties of all times. These soups could stand alone as soups or be added as ingredients in everything from dips to beef Stroganoff. Louis Ballast of Denver, Colorado, was given a trademark for the name "cheeseburger" in 1936. He never enforced it, though. The illustrious beer can was first created by the American Can Co. and introduced in Richmond, Virginia, in 1935 by the Gottfried Krueger Brewing Company of Newark, New Jersey. The products were Krueger's Finest Beer and Krueger's Cream Ale, served in enamel cans. The Cobb salad was invented in 1936 by none other than Robert Cobb at his Brown Derby Restaurant in Hollywood, California. Felix Frederickson founded the first American blue cheese plant in 1936, in Faribault, Minnesota. The same year, the Oscar Mayer Wienermobile, a giant hot dog on wheels, made its first run. Carl Mayer, nephew of packaged pork product founder Oscar

Mayer, invented the Wienermobile, which was built by General Body Company at Chicago, Illinois. There is now a fleet of six Wienermobiles. George A. Hormel & Co. developed Spam and first marketed it in 1937. Kix corn puff cereal was introduced in 1937, as was Pepperidge Farm bread. The first Krispy Kreme doughnut was sold in Salem, North Carolina, in 1938, while on the West Coast, Lawry's Seasoned Salt was created by Lawrence L. Frank for use in his new restaurant, The Prime Rib, in Los Angeles. And last but not least, in 1939, President Franklin D. Roosevelt served hot dogs to King George VI and Queen Elizabeth of England during their 1939 visit to the United States. It was the first time they had tried this American gourmet treat.

Entries

1939 New York World's Fair

In 1935, during the worst of the Great Depression, a group of retired New York City policemen came up with the idea of hosting an international exposition to lift both the spirits and the economy of the nation out of the doldrums. The World's Fair took four years in planning and opened its first exhibits to the public on April 30, 1939, which coincided with the anniversary of George Washington's inauguration as president. The largest world's fair of all time took place in the 1,216-acre space of Flushing Meadows-Corona Park in Queens, NY. The fair encompassed a wide array of innovations, including but not limited to transportation, color photography, nylon, air conditioning, and fluorescent light. There was an entire area of the World's Fair devoted to food called the Food Zone. The Borden's exhibit included a space for 150 cows, including the famous Elsie attached to a "roto-lactator" that mechanically milked them. The Wonder Bread exhibit had an authentic wheat field growing adjacent to it, from which wheat was harvested and baked. A sign pointed out that it was the first time in 100 years that wheat had been cultivated in New York City. Many countries were housed within the Food Zone, including the Italian pavilion, the French pavilion, and a miniature Sweden and Turkey. The Schaefer center, sponsored by Schaefer Beer, "America's Oldest Lager Beer," contained a circular restaurant that could seat 1,600 visitors. A mural showing the history of beer and brewing was a unique feature of the fair's largest open-air bar. Many dishes, such as Welsh rarebit, which was much in vogue at the time, contained beer as one of the ingredients. The Beech-Nut exhibit contained dioramas about the growing, harvesting, and roasting of coffee and provided an entertaining circus with more than 500 acrobats, aerialists, and clowns. The ultra-futuristic-looking Heinz Dome housed a theater that dramatized the story of strained baby food and where the Aristocrat Tomato Man sang, nodded his tomato head, and smacked his lips. The unique blend of outlandish architecture and brand marketing gimmicks made the 1939 World's Fair a unique bookmark in American food history.

Bloody Mary

The origins of the Bloody Mary cocktail are somewhat murky, but what is clear is that the Bloody Mary and its many variants are among the most popular vodka cocktails in America. It was purportedly originated by the American bartender Fernand "Pete" Petiot at Harry's Bar in 1921 in Paris, frequented by famous writers of the day such as Ernest Hemingway. Petiot served the drink with equal parts vodka and tomato juice but spiced up the drink with Tabasco, black pepper, Worcestershire sauce, and lemon when he returned to New York as bartender of the St. Regis hotel in 1934. The other arch-competitor for the title of inventor of the Bloody Mary is George Jessel, an American songwriter and producer. It was touted in New York gossip columns in 1939 that Jessel's "newest pick-me-up which is receiving attention from the town's paragraphers is called a Bloody Mary: half tomato juice, half vodka." Another legend suggests that the drink was named after a waitress at a Chicago watering hole called The Bucket 'o Blood. Regardless of who came first, today's classic drink involves 2 ounces vodka, 3 ounces tomato juice, ½ ounce lemon juice, a few dashes of Worcestershire sauce and Tabasco sauce, salt, and black pepper, garnished with a crisp celery stalk. Today the innumerable varieties of the cocktail include the Ruddy Mary, which replaces vodka with gin, and the Bloody Maria, where tequila is the libation.

Booyah

Likely a play on the word bouillabaisse or bouillon, the stew-like soup known as booyah is traditionally served at church fund raisers, at Belgian-American ethnic festivals, and at Green Bay Packer football week-ends. Traditionally a dish of clear chicken bouillon served with rice intro-duced by Belgian Walloon settlers to the Green Bay, Wisconsin, region during the 1850s, the dish was usurped by men participating in the Belgian American kermis (or church) harvest festival during the 1930s. They turned the dish into a thick soup containing boned chicken meat and vegetables served with saltines at the kermis festival. They made the dish in pots large enough to require canoe paddles for stirring. The Belgian-American festival itself was called Booyah after the featured dish. The event has become something of a male-bonding ritual, complete with a chosen Booyah King, and is celebrated in much the same way as barbecue, burgoo, and chili con carne events. The dish has transformed from a thin soup traditionally made by women at home to a thick stew made by men at communal events.

Candy

The 1930s were a banner decade for sweets. Perhaps the sour times of the Depression were prime territory for introducing the sweetest small pleasures of life. The Mars corporation debuted Snickers bars in 1930, which to date are still the best-selling candy bar of all time, grossing more than $2 billion annually. At its core, Snickers is a candy bar comprising peanut nougat topped with peanuts, covered in caramel, and finally encased with a sheath of milk chocolate. Snickers bars were named after the favorite horse of the Mars family, a family already well established in the confectionary trade after the success of their Milky Way bar. Two years later, Mars introduced the 3 Musketeers bar. Originally it had three flavor varieties in one package: chocolate, vanilla, and strawberry. Rising costs for sugar and wartime restrictions phased out the less popular vanilla and strawberry pieces, and 3 Musketeers became just nougat with whipped chocolate. It was one of the largest candy bars available and was marketed as one that could be shared by friends. In the mid-1930s, the Ferrara Pan Candy Company created fiery Red Hots, using the cold pan candy-making method. The cold pan process involves building pieces from candy centers and tossing them in revolving pans while adding flavor, color, and other ingredients until the candy reaches the desirable size. Cough drop magnate William H. Luden broke from tradition when he introduced the candy bar 5th Avenue in 1936, a crunchy peanut butter bar with milk chocolate coating, which was eventually acquired by Hershey's. And last but not least, Hershey's miniature bars were launched in 1939 as an assorted packaged chocolate bar selection, featuring the most popular Hershey's bars of the time in miniature form. The original line up included Hershey bars, Mr. Goodbar, Hershey's Special Dark, and Krackel.

Carvel Ice Cream

In 1929, after borrowing $15 from his future wife, Agnes Stewart, Athanassios Karvelas, later known as Tom Carvel, built and began operating a truck to sell frozen custard to vacationers. Several years later, the intervention of fate led to the founding of the first national retail ice cream chain, Carvel. Tom Carvel's vending truck suffered a flat tire in Hartsdale, NY, during Memorial Day weekend of 1934. However, Carvel was not deterred. He simply started selling the frozen custard in the parking lot of the pottery store where he broke down. In two days, most of Carvel's custard sold, although much of it was partially melted. This provided Carvel with the inspiration to sell frozen custard at a fixed location and to sell soft, as opposed to hard, frozen desserts. Carvel grossed more than $3,500 his first year. By 1937, he had a permanent custard stand in Hartsdale, which had a freezer, so he could produce the frozen custard on site. Profits rose to $6,000 by 1939. During the 1940s, Tom Carvel sold frozen custard around the carnival circuit while Agnes manned the Hartsdale stand. Carvel spent time in Fort Bragg, NC, during World War II, where he gained knowledge of more advanced refrigeration technology. With this, he designed and patented the Custard King freezer, selling 71 freezers at $2,900 each by 1947. Carvel also pioneered the concept of the ice cream novelty. The custard stand remained in Hartsdale until 2008.

Dinner Parties

As the Depression wore on, people continued to host dinner parties, but they needed to cut financial corners. Tight purse strings were no excuse to curtail an active social life; thus the popularity of the Dutch treat party during the 1930s. Each guest brought one course of the meal, and labor and expenses were shared by all the guests. Games were a prominent feature of dinner parties in the 1930s. Charades, limericks, and 20 questions were inexpensive and fun entertainment that lightened the mood during dark times. The wealthy elite continued to hold formal dinners with maids and butlers, though some of the dishes traditionally served at these exclusive dinners contained canned soup. Boula, also known as boula-boula, was one of the more popular menu items served at high-end dinner parties. It consisted of a can of condensed pea soup, a can of condensed green turtle soup, water, heavy cream, dry sherry, and salt. This soup has effectively disappeared from modern menus but was heralded at the time at banquets and exclusive clubs. Table fashions included gold and silver lame tablecloths, with rock-crystal candlesticks, for those who could afford them. Popular cocktails of the time included a clam juice cocktail—non-alcoholic of course.

Don the Beachcomber

The trend of Tiki bars can trace its faux Polynesian roots to the restaurant Don the Beachcomber on McCadden Place in Hollywood, CA. Its proprietor, Ernest Raymond Beaumont Gantt, was originally from Limestone County, TX. He changed his name to Don Beach after leaving Texas and traveling around the world to exotic locales in the Caribbean and the South Pacific. After a brief career as a bootlegger during Prohibition, Beach settled in Hollywood in the 1930s, where he opened a bar called Don's Beachcomber. In 1937, he opened a restaurant across the street with a tropical theme called Don the Beachcomber. Don served what appeared to be exotic cuisine but was in actuality typical Cantonese fare done up with fancy presentation. It is likely one of the first pu pu platters was served at Don the Beachcomber, an appetizer plate brimming with egg rolls, spare ribs, chicken wings, and other Chinese American delights. The signature drink at Don's was the Zombie, a rum cocktail served in a shapely glass with a folding umbrella. It featured four different kinds of rum, apricot brandy, pineapple and papaya juice, and a splash of grenadine. Don Beach originally crafted the Zombie for a friend bound for San Francisco. The friend drank three of them and returned to tell Beach that he was walking around like a zombie for his entire trip, as the drink is known for its extremely high alcohol content, intensified by the presence of fruit juice. As a result, Don the Beachcomber limited the number of Zombies to two per customer. The Tiki-bar fad continued to expand after World War II. Don divorced his wife and business partner, Sunny Lund, who gained control of the chain of restaurants. Don relocated from California to Hawaii, where he lived the rest of his life.

Tropical Flavors

A taste of the tropics was in fashion during the 1930s, especially in California. In 1934, A.W. Leo, Tom Yates, and Ralph Harrison crafted a tropical fruit-flavored syrup called "Leo's Hawaiian Punch" to add to their line of ice cream toppings. Sold to local Fullerton, CA, restaurants, soda fountains, and ice cream manufacturers, it soon became known without Leo's moniker. Hawaiian Punch is still sold today by the Dr Pepper-Seven-Up group. Victor Bergeron transformed his Oakland, CA, bar, Hinky Dinks, into the first Trader Vic's in 1936, with Polynesian-inspired food and beverages. And Ernest Gantt patented more than 80 drinks throughout his life as first owner and proprietor of Hollywood's Don the Beachcomber's, most famously the rum-soaked Zombie cocktail.

Elsie the Cow

Elsie the Cow was created in the 1930s as the fictitious and unofficial mascot of the Borden Company. Gail Borden, founder of the Borden Company, was the first to develop a commercial method of condensing milk during the mid-1800s. In 1930, Borden Company invented the Rotolactor, a glass-enclosed, automated cow-milking system. Cows were washed and then herded onto a giant turntable, where they were milked by an automated machine. Borden envisioned Elsie as the perfect dairy representative, sporting a big smile and necklace of daisies. She soon began appearing as a sketch in print ads during the 1930s. The story has it that the Borden family approached a farmer for the big eyed-Jersey cow named You'll Do Lobelia, purchased her, renamed her Elsie, and set her official public debut at the 1939 New York World's Fair along with the Rotolactor. Elsie soon became the prime attraction. Between runs of the Rotolactor, Elsie was paraded around to curious and adoring audiences. Since then, she has remained one of the most recognizable product mascots in the United States and Canada. After the fair, Elsie went on tour and was often the guest of honor at swanky New York press dinners. Her "mate" was Elmer the Bull, later used as the mascot for Elmer's Glue, a product from Borden's chemical division. Elsie was put to sleep after unfortunately suffering from spine and neck injuries when her vehicle, the Cowdillac, was hit from behind by another truck while stopped at a stop light in 1941. Elsie the Cow is buried at Walker-Gordon Farm in Plainsboro Township, New Jersey.

Ernest and Julio Gallo Winery

The E. & J. Gallo winery was founded in 1933 by brothers Ernest and Julio Gallo in Modesto, California. The family grew up in the foothills of the Sierra Madres, sons of Italian immigrants. Their father Joe was in the grape-growing business, which they helped with until their father's tragic death in 1933. Ernest became head of the business, and Julio oversaw the production. They initially faced stiff competition, as more than 800 wineries sprouted up in California in the years following Prohibition. Although novices to the field, the brothers learned the craft from reading old pamphlets on winemaking published by the University of California that were stored in the basement of the Modesto Public Library. Ernest worked so hard to expand the business to a broad national market that he suffered a stay in the hospital after a bout with exhaustion in 1936. He aimed to make Gallo the "Campbell's Soup of the wine industry." Their secret to initial success was marketing their product to inner-city communities. Ernest made cheap, fortified (20 percent alcohol content) wines, such as White Port and Thunderbird. The largest exporter of California wines in the world, the winery played a key role in establishing Sonoma County, California, as one of the premier wine regions of the world. As the company became more successful, it struggled to shed its low-rent image. The Gallos became generous supporters of both the Republican and Democratic parties, courting each when it came to local, state, and national liquor regulations. Despite family squabbles over sharing the Gallo fortune that led Ernest to court with his brother Joe, E. & J. Gallo remains the largest family-owned winery in the United States.

Fritos

Charles Elmer Doolin, the father of Fritos, owned a confectionary in San Antonio during the Depression. Not content to sell just ice cream, Doolin wanted to place a corn chip snack strategically at the point of purchase in his shop. He noticed that tortilla chips went stale far too easily, so he embarked on a mission to perfect a corn snack chip recipe. While at a gas station, Doolin noticed a Mexican man making fried corn chips out of masa, a dough made from ground corn that's been soaked in a lime-and-water solution. These were "fritos," little fried corn chips commonly sold on the beaches of Mexico. He tracked down the man who made the chips and bought the recipe for $100. In 1932, Fritos were born, with Doolin's mother tweaking the recipe. He first sold them out of the back of his Model T and made $2 a day, but eventually C.E. Doolin and his brother Earl took up the manufacturing principles of Henry Ford and began producing the chips assembly-line-style on a conveyor belt. Doolin set up test kitchens everywhere—in his factory, in his house, bedecked with beakers and test tubes, It was during this phase of experimentation that the Cheeto was invented as well. Doolin's children were his steadfast test audience, says his daughter, Kaleta. Doolin went so far as to start hybridizing his own corn. He hired farmers throughout Texas to grow different varieties until he found the exact taste he was looking for. Doolin dreamed big and launched Casa de Frito in Disneyland and in Dallas, a precursor to the fast-food restaurant that blended hamburgers and Mexican cuisine. However, Doolin, a vegetarian and health nut, imagined Fritos as a light accompaniment to soups and sandwiches and would be shocked at the casual consumption of entire bags of the product that is commonplace today. The heart of Fritos' success was the strong family spirit that kept the business thriving. Doolin's wife Katherine invented such novelties as the Frito pie, and the recipe was printed on the back of Frito bags. Before his death in 1959, Doolin teamed up with potato chip mogul Herman W. Lay to form the snack chip entity Frito-Lay.

Goya Foods

Goya Foods was founded by Don Prudencio Unanue and his wife Carolina in 1936 in a storefront in Lower Manhattan. Originally from Spain, Unanue moved to Puerto Rico in 1903 to establish a small food business. He later moved to the New York metropolitan area, where he became a broker of Spanish food products. When the Spanish Civil War broke out in 1936, most food supplies from Spain were suddenly cut off. Unanue was in a real bind. All he could obtain were Moroccan sardines, olives, and olive oil from a Spanish company, which he packaged with his wife in a small warehouse and sold to local grocery stores. The brand name of the sardines was Goya, which is the name he kept when he repackaged them. The Goya brand began to shine with the influx of Puerto Rican immigrants to New York City immediately after World War II. Unanue built two canneries in Bayamon, Puerto Rico, to package food that was not common in U.S. supermarkets, such as beef tripe stew, tropical juices, pigeon peas, and a variety of other beans. Goya salesmen pitched the canned goods to bodega owners who catered to New York's Hispanic population. Goya formed its own Inter-American Advertising Agency in the 1950s to fill the niche in ethnic advertising. By 1969, Goya expanded its reach up and down the East Coast from Boston to Miami and throughout the Midwest. Goya is still the largest Hispanic-owned food company in the United States. Its motto, "If it's Goya, it's got to be good," encapsulates Goya's commitment to authentic Latino cuisine, which now includes Spanish, Caribbean, Mexican, and Central and South American food products. The Unanues are the second wealthiest Hispanic family in America, with a net worth of more than $750 million.

Krispy Kreme

What secret sets Krispy Kreme doughnuts apart from dozens of other doughnut shops? There are several key ingredients to the company's sweet success. Foremost is the recipe itself; the yeast-raised doughnuts were first credited to New Orleans-based chef Joe LeBeau during the 1920s. LeBeau sold his doughnut shop and his secret recipe to Vernon Rudolph and family in 1933. Rudolph originally sold the doughnuts at grocery stores in Nashville, TN. With $25 in cash, Rudolph later rented a building in what is now historic Old Salem, North Carolina. He convinced a local grocer to lend him the doughnut ingredients on credit in return for payment when his first doughnuts sold. The first doughnuts from this new shop—called Krispy Kreme Doughnuts—were made on July 13, 1937. He first delivered the doughnuts to clients in the back of his Pontiac, but people were so fond of them that he soon had a crowd of customers clamoring at the brick-and-mortar shop to ask for hot doughnuts from the oven. The first doughnuts available at the Krispy Kreme retail store sold for 25 cents a dozen. The store's distinctively vintage style and logo contribute to the brand's current appeal. The franchise is often a red-bricked building topped with a green roof, outfitted with a clearly visible conveyor belt inside displaying the hot doughnuts speeding by to mouthwatering customers. Keeping repeat customers and encouraging positive community relations are key to the company philosophy, promoting a wholesome, if not sugar-coated, image of the Krispy Kreme family of franchises.

Mott's

The 1930s were a decade of great change and diversification for the Duffy-Mott family of apple cider and vinegar products, beginning in 1930 with the introduction of Mott's Applesauce. The 1929 acquisition of the Standard Apple Products Company and its processing plant in Hamlin, NY, allowed Duffy-Mott to expand into new product territory that had not been possible during previous decades. Seeking to expand into other food markets during the non-apple-growing season, Duffy-Mott formed a partnership with the California Prune and Apricot growers (now Sunsweet) and introduced a bottled consumer prune juice beverage. Mott branched into jarred jellies in 1936. Flavors included pure apple jelly, marmalade, and fruited blends such as apple-raspberry and apple-grape. These jellies were popular during the Depression but were later dropped from the Mott roster for faster-selling items. In 1938, Mott's introduced its classic Mott's Apple Juice to the public. Since cider was seen as a seasonal product, they sought to introduce a beverage that could be warehoused year-round. Food scientists were able to engineer a product that captured the natural bouquet and flavor of apples and could be quickly manufactured and pasteurized.

Nescafé

Instant coffee was originally invented by a Japanese scientist from Chicago named Satori Kato. He exhibited his invention at the Pan-American

Exposition in Buffalo, NY, in 1901. After eight years of tinkering in the lab, Nestlé introduced its commercial instant coffee product called Nescafé in 1938. Nestlé, a Swiss firm founded in 1867 by Henri Nestlé, was already famous around the world for its chocolate products. The word Nescafé was a mélange of the company name Nestlé and the Italian word for coffee, *cafe*. The idea was to create a romantic, European image for the instant coffee product. Nescafé targeted primarily American housewives with its expensive ad campaign, emphasizing the classiness of a café product combined with the ease of instantly brewed coffee. The ad campaign was enormously successful for Nescafé, and established the brand's popularity both in the United States and worldwide. World War II was the catalyst for popularizing the powdered coffee product in America, as the U.S. military purchased it in bulk to keep the troops well caffeinated. However, Nescafé sales tanked in the postwar United States after an unsuccessful ad campaign that touted the "no coffee grounds" benefits. Today, Nescafé is second only to Coca-Cola in terms of brand recognition worldwide.

Papaya King

The seemingly unfamiliar bedfellows of tropical fruit drinks and hot dogs mingled first at the popular urban fast-food and drink chain the Papaya King. The Papaya King was founded by Gus Poulos, a Greek émigré to New York who worked his way up from deli counter helper in 1923 to owner within three years. Now a business owner with more money and leisure time on his hands, Gus took a vacation to Miami Beach, Florida. Here he saw tropical fruits that ignited his imagination and set off to concocting various fruit shakes. When Gus returned to New York, he sought out papaya and other tropical fruits. After years of research and making connections with tropical fruit distributors, Gus sold the deli and opened a juice store in 1931 called Hawaiian Tropical Drinks, Inc. It was not successful, and Gus was loaded with perishable, costly tropical fruits. Deciding that he would rather give the fruit away than let it go to waste, Gus hired women to dress up in Hawaiian skirts and hand out free glasses of blended fruit drinks on the street corner. The trick worked. He soon had customers lining up, and word of the papaya drink spread. By 1935, he opened a second store in Brooklyn, and in 1937, it expanded to Philadelphia. Although successful, Gus felt that the business could be improved upon. The original store, located in the Yorkville section of Manhattan, was home to many German and Polish immigrants. It was no coincidence that Gus had recently married a German-American woman named Birdie when he introduced the frankfurter to the juice stand repertoire. Thus the marriage of papaya drinks and hot dogs was consummated in 1939. The name Papaya King caught on by way of customers declaring Gus "the Papaya King," and he officially changed the name in the early 1960s. The Beatles are rumored to have stopped at the Papaya King before their stint on the *Ed Sullivan Show* 1965. Now listed in many New York tourist guides, Papaya King is still the king of the best inexpensive lunch in town.

Philly Cheesesteaks

Pat and Harry Olivieri are the Philadelphians behind the tasty and nationally famous Philly cheesesteak sandwich. Quite by accident, the Olivieris began serving grilled chopped steak on a hoagie roll with sautéed onions at their humble hot dog stand near the Italian Market in South Philadelphia in 1933. The original steak sandwich had no cheese. Pat sent Harry to the market for some inexpensive steak for lunch one day. They sliced it and grilled it with some onions, which attracted the attention of one of their regular customers, a cabbie who ate hot dogs at the stand every day. The cab driver insisted on having steak and onions, too. After devouring the sandwich, the cabbie convinced Pat that it might be worth selling every day. Rumors spread among cab drivers and other clientele. The new steak sandwich was so popular that the brothers eventually opened a restaurant called Pat's King of Steaks. The cheese was first added to the sandwich by "Cocky" Joe Lorenza, the manager of a Pat's King of Steaks, at the Ridge Avenue location. The cheese first used was provolone. The cheesesteak in its current incarnation is defined as thinly sliced sautéed rib eye beef with melted cheese in a long crusty roll. Cheez Whiz has become the most common cheese of choice, and fried onions and sautéed mushrooms are also popular accompaniments

Rink-Tum-Tiddy or Rumtum Tiddy

This recipe is a variation on Welsh rarebit, a popular dish during the 1930s. Neither Welsh in origin nor involving a rabbit, Welsh rarebit is a savory sauce of melted cheese, often cheddar, served over hot toasted bread. During the Great Depression, the popularity of variants on Welsh rarebit made sense. With meat being scarce and eventually rationed due to the outbreak of World War II, a hearty cheese concoction provided the necessary protein. The origin of the name Welsh rarebit, or rabbit, was a pejorative term for the poor. In Wales of the 1700s, most people could not afford meat, so cheese was the poor man's meat. It is no surprise that this

---

Depression-Era Cookery

The era of the Great Depression forced Americans to be strict and resourceful about their diets, and recipes often depended on what was available regionally. For example, families who lived on farms often had animals on hand for milk, eggs, and meat and grew their own vegetables, while many city dwellers were not so fortunate. Dust Bowl victims who stayed behind were forced to subsist on locusts and weeds after the great winds destroyed most of the tillable land. Rations on dairy products resulted in baked goods void of eggs, milk, and butter. *Stories and Recipes of the Great Depression of the 1930s* by Rita Van Amber is a multi-volume series of cookbooks compiled from people's memories and first-hand accounts of growing up during the Great Depression. It is a comprehensive account on what it was like to survive during those grim economic times.

---

dish experienced a spike in popularity during the trying economic times of the 1930s in the United States. A typical recipe follows:

2 tablespoons butter
1 onion, thinly sliced
1 ½ pounds Cheddar cheese, cut into small cubes
2 cups canned tomatoes, drained and chopped
1 teaspoon dry mustard
1/2 teaspoon paprika
1 teaspoon Worcestershire sauce
2 large eggs, slightly beaten
Salt and pepper

Melt the butter in a chafing dish or heavy saucepan. Add the onion and cook over low heat until the onions soften. Then add the tomatoes, mustard, paprika, and Worcestershire sauce. Cook over low heat for about 15 minutes. Add the cheese, stirring until it melts. Stir a little of the warm mixture into the eggs, then turn the warmed eggs into the saucepan and cook, stirring constantly for 5 minutes or until the eggs thicken slightly. Correct the seasoning and serve on toasted crackers or warm toast.

Ritz Crackers

Ritz Crackers were introduced in 1934 to be eaten either as a stand-alone cracker or with a topping. Developed during the Depression as a classy yet inexpensive snack, the crackers were named Ritz after the Ritz-Carlton hotel to conjure up an image for the cracker associated with wealth and class. During that dire age, Nabisco attempted to cheer the public psyche with its crunchy, buttery cracker. Unlike the real Ritz-Carleton, a luxury out of reach for most people during the 1930s, Ritz crackers were affordable at 19 cents a box. The crackers are round, lightly salted on one side, provide a hint of buttery taste, and feature scalloped edges. Nabisco had been toying with the formula for many years, looking for a recipe strong enough to compete with the other crackers on the market. The butter crackers had a different, richer taste than the soda crackers that existed at the time. The Ritz cracker contained more shortening and less yeast, which made the cracker crispier yet less fluffy. More than 5 million crackers were produced by Nabisco during the first year,

Ritz crackers, named after the Ritz-Carlton Hotel, offer a rich buttery taste not available in most crackers in the 1930s. (Thoun Kheang/ Dreamstime.com)

supported by an appealing ad campaign that assured "Anytime Is the Right Time to Serve Ritz" and "Today's Tomorrow's Cracker—Today." In just three years, Ritz became the most popular and best-selling cracker in the world, with more than 29 million crackers produced daily. Today, Ritz crackers have morphed into several varieties, such as Original, Low-Sodium, Reduced-Fat, Whole Wheat, Roasted Vegetable, and Honey Butter.

Shirley Temple

Named after the adorable child star of the 1930s, Shirley Temple, this alcohol-free cocktail is also known as Grenadine Lemonade. Made with either lemon-lime soda or seltzer, it is mixed with grenadine syrup and garnished with a maraschino cherry and an orange slice. In Canada, orange juice is often added. It was designed so that children could partake in the experience of drinking cocktails with adults, without the added alcohol. The Royal Hawaiian Hotel in Waikiki claims to have invented the drink, as the actress herself visited this hotel frequently, but there is consensus that the drink originated during the late 1930s.

Spam

Although more commonly the namesake of junk e-mail these days, the versatile meat product known as Spam first got its can on the market in 1937. First advertised as "the miracle meat," Spam was promoted as a meat that could be consumed with any meal. What exactly is Spam? It's a blend of chopped pork shoulder and ham. Predating Spam, Hormel Foods produced its first canned ham in 1926, called Hormel Flavor-Sealed Ham. Eleven years later, Hormel came up with the first canned meat product that did not require refrigeration. Initially given the rather uninspired name Hormel Spiced Ham, the product was invented by Jay C. Hormel, son of Hormel founder George A. Hormel. The cans were soon left to sit on the shelf in obscurity, as other canned lunchmeat products began to crowd them out. So Hormel embarked on a search for a catchy name that would set this product apart from its competition. Hormel offered $100 for the catchiest name. Spam was the winning entry, and a legend was born. Spam was one of the first food products to feature a singing jingle. Hormel sponsored the *The Burns and Allen Show* (on radio), which included a character called Spammy the Pig. World War II was a banner time for Spam, and sales skyrocketed, as the product lasted indefinitely without refrigeration. All-American Spam was not subject to the wartime rationing that limited beef supplies.

Toll House Chocolate Chip Cookies

Ruth Wakefield never would have guessed it, but she began an American revolution in baking straight from her colonial Massachusetts kitchen. Wakefield and her husband Kenneth owned and operated an inn located halfway between Boston and New Bedford, MA. The structure was built in 1709 and originally served as a tollhouse for weary travelers, where they could change horses, eat a home-cooked meal, and lodge for the night. The Wakefields opened their home to the public as the Toll House Inn in 1930. Ruth recreated many traditional colonial recipes at the inn and always baked for guests. Her desserts in particular attracted much attention, and people from all over New England began flocking to the Toll House Inn to sample her legendary treats. One day while she was preparing a batch of Butter Drop Do cookies, she decided to add chopped bits of a Nestle Semi-Sweet Chocolate Bar to the batter, expecting them to melt during baking. Surprisingly, the chocolate held its shape, softening to a creamy consistency. The cookies were a hit with the Wakefields' guests. Soon Ruth's recipe was published in several local newspapers, as well as in Boston. This improved sales of Nestle's Semi-Sweet Chocolate Bars immensely. Ruth negotiated with Nestle for an agreement that would allow the company to publish her recipe on the wrapper of Nestle Semi-Sweet Chocolate Bars. She was also granted a lifetime supply of the bars for her own recipe-making purposes. Nestle began packaging the chocolate bar in scored portions, enclosed with a special chopper for cookie making soon afterward. In 1939, Nestle began offering the first chocolate morsels, already in tiny bite-sized pieces. The cookies are still a nationwide favorite today.

Twinkies

The moist, golden cream-filled cakes known as Twinkies were first introduced in Indianapolis, Indiana, by Continental Baking Company, the marketers of Wonder Bread, under the Hostess brand name of snacks. In 1933, James A. Dewar, a baker for Hostess, saw a billboard advertising shoes for the Twinkle Toes Shoe Company while on his delivery route for Hostess cream-filled strawberry shortcakes, which were the original inspiration for Twinkies. As strawberries are only in season during the spring and summer months, the machines that manufactured the strawberry shortcakes sat idle for the rest of the year. Dewar realized that the machines could be useful off season and invented a banana-filled cake. He charged a nickel for the two-cake pack. Money was tight for people during the Great Depression, and Twinkies were a bargain treat. When World War II led to the rationing of bananas, Twinkies had to come up with another cake filling, and this is where the cream comes in. During the 1940s, vanilla cream was such a hit that Hostess never reverted to the banana filling, even after the banana shortage was over. Twinkies gained even more popularity during the 1950s. A mascot was created called Twinkie the Kid, in requisite kerchief and cowboy hat, who appeared as a player on *The Howdy Doody Show*. When fears of nuclear attack started to mushroom during the 1960s, Twinkies were a common item found in bomb shelters due to their unnaturally long shelf life, with claims to "stay fresh forever!" Twinkies are still the best-selling snack cake from Hostess, with more than half a billion per year produced.

Vegetables

The Italian American garden had a profound impact on the types of vegetables that became both mainstream items in American grocery stores and featured in haute cuisine of the 1930s. Asparagus was the stylish vegetable

Artichokes grew in popularity during the 1930s despite the complicated process required for cooking and eating. (Marion429/Dreamstime.com)

of choice at dinner parties in the 1920s and 1930s. Zucchini, also known as courgette, became popular during the 1930s, often featured in ratatouille dishes. Broccoli, which had been grown in the United States since the 1700s, underwent a renaissance during the 1930s and became far more common on American dinner plates than zucchini ever did. The most fashionable vegetable of all during the 1930s was the artichoke. Its complicated method of consumption, which required it be torn "limb from limb" in front of others according to Jeanne Owen in the September 1938 issue of *House and Garden*, made it cumbersome, but it nevertheless made bold appearances on the menus of gourmet clubs specializing in fancy food. Even during the depths of the Great Depression, artichoke recipes included truffles, cognac, parmesan cheese, and chestnut puree.

Waring Blender

The streamlined, Art Deco–inspired Waring blender was popularized by big band leader, Fred Waring, a former engineering student, and inventor Fred Osius. The blender was originally invented by Stephen Poplawski in 1922, who was the first to put a spinning blade at the bottom of a tall, glass container for mixing beverages. Osius, one of the founding fathers of the Hamilton Beach Manufacturing Company, was the powerhouse behind patenting his blending machine in 1933. Rumor has it that Osius, dressed in outlandish attire with a lemon yellow tie, approached Waring after a radio broadcast at the New York Vanderbilt Theater in 1936, seeking a financial backer for his new mixer that would "revolutionize people's eating habits." Waring was intrigued by the product and agreed to finance the endeavor. Unfortunately, six months and $25,000 later, the prototype was unsuccessful. Waring remained supportive, and the engineering problems worked themselves out. The Miracle Mixer debuted at the 1937 National Restaurant Show in Chicago. Waring's connections to radio helped promote the blender, and his singing group, The Waring Blendors, helped. The mixer soon became a fixture in most bars and restaurants, and it wasn't long before consumers began to acquire blenders for home use. Department and specialty stores sold them, and they soon became a staples of the home cook. World War II curtailed blender production, but sales rebounded by 1946. Waring blenders went through innovation during the 1950s and 1960s, picking up attachments that could crush ice and grind coffee. They eventually found useful roles in research laboratories, playing a part in the development of the polio vaccine by Dr. Jonas Salk, who used a Waring blender in tandem with an Aseptic Dispersal Container. Fred Waring died in 1984, but his namesake blender continues to be popular today.

Further Reading

Frederick, J. George. *Cooking as Men Like It*. New York: Business Bourse, 1939.

Great Depression Cooking with Clara. http://www.greatdepressioncooking .com/Depression_Cooking/Blog.html.

Jochnowitz, Eve. "Feasting on the Future: Serving Up the World of Tomorrow at the New York World's Fair of 1939–40." M.A. Thesis, New York University, 1997.

Mullins, Paul R. *Glazed America: A History of the Doughnut*. Gainesville: University of Florida Press, 2008.

Willard, Pat. *America Eats! On the Road with the WPA: The Fish Fries, Box Social Suppers, and Chitlin Feasts That Define Real American Food*. New York: Bloomsbury, 2009.

5

1940s

Margaret Rose Siggillino

The 1940s were a decade of extremes—from Spartan conservation to extravagance. After the Great Depression of the 1930s, the United States was preparing to enter World War II. Just before that, the New York World's Fair took place from 1939 to 1941. Food from 58 countries was sold there, and ordinary citizens got to taste it. This event helped to inspire initial interest in international cuisines. World War II (1941–1945) created jobs with higher wages, so Americans began spending more money on food. Even though food supplies were needed for the war effort, people did not want to stop spending their money on food after it had been denied to them for so long during the Great Depression. Nevertheless, food prices began to rise, and people reacted with fear. When the United States entered the war in 1941, Americans were told to expect major food shortages. In the beginning of 1942, people began hoarding, and goods such as meat and butter disappeared from the shelves. Ironically, real food shortages were actually created because of this. Because of this hysteria, the government began to implement rationing, which included goods such as steel, nylon, tin, wool, cotton, and soap. These resources were needed by factories to produce equipment, ammunition, and weapons. People were encouraged to donate articles such as tin, nylon, and leftover oil and butter from cooking.

The war affected the daily lives of Americans in many ways and required sacrifices on the home front. Since men went off to fight in the war, women worked in the factories in positions previously held by men. This had an effect on the way women fed their families. Since women

Shopkeeper rations canned foods to his customers in a New York City grocery store, December 28, 1942. Ration restrictions were established for food products in 1942 with the intention of lowering food prices and providing more equal distribution of food to Americans. (Library of Congress)

worked outside the home, they had less time to cook, and they also had to cope with rationing. After the Japanese bombed Pearl Harbor in 1941, the U.S. government implemented restrictions on consumer purchases of rubber, tires in particular. In 1942, rationing restrictions were put on food. Rationing helped to keep the food prices down and to ensure an equitable distribution of food to all levels of society—nationally and internationally. It was necessary because more than half of America's food supply was being sent overseas to feed the troops and the Allies, and it wasn't the food people were used to. Examples of items that were rationed include canned vegetables, coffee, high-grade cuts of beef, lamb, mutton and pork. Fats such as butter were rationed. Margarine and seed-based salad oils such as corn oil and sunflower seed oil were easier to obtain. Sugar was also rationed, except for home canning use. Items that were not rationed included poultry, fish, less desirable parts of livestock (e.g., heads, feet, tails), corn syrup, honey, molasses, and flour. Women got around the restrictions of rationing by using cake mixes and other packaged food when available.

Despite the inconvenience of rationing and having to put up with unfamiliar food, many people followed the rules of rationing and did not resort to buying goods on the black market. During that time, the ideal American meal consisted of a large piece of red meat with about two smaller servings of vegetables on the side. The one-pot, meatless meals that women were now forced to serve were seen as inferior, and it was assumed that the meat-and-potatoes meal would be served again. To contradict this theory, cookbook authors, food writers, and dieticians tried to associate food with security and love in their recipes. Women were urged by newspaper articles and cookbook authors to return to the practice of cooking one-pot soups and stews that was common in the 1930s. Because of their work schedules, this was hard to do because the stews had to be made from scratch. As they do today, media, sent contradictory messages, advising women to conserve yet continually promoting the "ideal" meat-dominated meal. Nevertheless, rationing served its purpose of distributing food equitably. Many Americans felt that their food needs were adequately served. Those with lower incomes mentioned that they ate more and better than before.

There was also a great deal of pressure put on women by the media to buy and prepare foods that were patriotically and politically correct. It was implied that if they followed the strictures, they would help the United States win the war. For example, the National Livestock and Meat Board's wartime pamphlet proclaimed, "The U.S. homemaker has an important part to play in the war effort. Her uniform is the kitchen apron and she may wear it proudly; for there is no more important responsibility than hers." The booklet went on to provide an array of recipes women might use when cooking the less appealing cuts of meat. Recipes included French-Fried Liver, Creole Kidney, Jellied Tongue, Tongue Rolls Florentine, and Tripe à la Maryland, the last made with cherries, bay leaf, and lemon. Even stretching meatloaf became part of women's war effort. At the same time, women wanted to provide what they felt was the best food for their families. Home was also portrayed as a refuge and good, nutritious food was said to help families withstand the daily battles of the "outside world." It was challenging for some women to resist the allure of the black markets. M.F.K. Fisher's book *How to Cook a Wolf* reflected the culinary challenges that society faced during this time.

In 1941, the government passed the Recommended Dietary Allowances, which were the first of their kind. Since the allowances were difficult for the consumer to understand, the Food and Nutrition Board developed simpler guidelines. The seven basic food groups were reduced to four basic food groups, which led to the creation of the Food Guide Pyramid. Today the FDA has adopted the symbol of a plate for guidance in healthy eating, dubbed MyPlate (see http://kidshealth.org/kid/stay_healthy/food/pyramid .html). The pyramid was originally developed by the Food and Nutrition Board of the National Research Council to help Americans who were unfamiliar with the basics of good nutrition. Government officials thought that it would be easier for housewives to follow these models without having to spend a lot of time researching particular nutrients, vitamins, and minerals. Daily allowances of nutrients and calories were calculated according to different types of people: men (including factory workers and soldiers), women (including those who were pregnant or nursing), and children of all ages. At this time, vitamins were added to white flour, milk, and bread, and in addition, nutritional plans for institutions were devised.

Victory gardening and canning provided one way for people to provide nutritious vegetables for families, since canned vegetables were rationed. The government encouraged people to grow their own fruits and vegetables by telling them that would help the food industry get more food to the troops and other countries overseas and produce a healthy, more productive workforce at home. Many people began planting victory gardens. At the movement's peak in 1943, roughly 40 percent of vegetables consumed in the United States were grown in victory gardens. A little over 4 billion jars of fruits and vegetables were preserved at home and community canning centers. People associated victory gardening with patriotism and sacrifice, and the gardens helped to strengthen communities and bring people together.

Other food and beverage products that were prominent during World War II included sugarless desserts, soy products, and "variety meats"—the organ meats, feet, and tails of butchered animals. Spam, margarine, and Cola-Cola were also widely consumed. Sugar was rationed, but candy bars were not. During the war, soldiers ate pretty well in terms of food quality and quantity. The type of food that was served was Midwestern farm food with a few variations based on the country that they were in. Because the soldiers were forced to eat this type of food, they got used to it. Many even learned to like it. Soldiers from different parts of the country learned to like new types of food and came home with a taste for them. This had a homogenizing effect on the American palate. In the field, soldiers had to eat C-rations and K-rations, and candy bars were included in those rations.

While the soldiers were away from home, wives who were left behind learned to entertain themselves when they weren't busy working. Entertaining at home was markedly different than before the war, because people no longer had servants. There was no more fancy prewar-style entertaining. People got together for companionship. War was tough.

Entertaining was now more informal, and people began to bring their own food to make it less difficult on the hostess. For potluck suppers, each person brought a dish to the home of the hostess and shared the dish with all of the guests. BBQ gatherings were also popular; people brought their own meat to put on the grill. For victory garden suppers, each family bought the "fruits of its harvest" to the community pot. Since wives worked, they did not have time for fancy cooking anyway. Progressive dinners came into vogue with each course served at a different person's home. For example, appetizers were served at one home, the entrée at another, and the dessert at another. Coffee and dessert parties were also popular. Women enjoyed the companionship and the camaraderie.

This went on until the end of the war in 1945, when the soldiers began to return home. People were happy that the war was over. The economy was good and factories were doing well. If couples were not married before the war, they began getting married and having children, especially in 1946, when the baby boom began. At first, there was not enough housing for everyone, so in response, housing developments such as Levittown were rapidly produced. Masses of people moved from the cities into the new suburbs. People bought factory-built stoves, refrigerators, washing machines, and lawnmowers for these new homes. Veterans had to adjust to civilian life, and most who had gone to war did not have high school diplomas. Some returning veterans got their degrees and then went on to college and technical schools on the GI Bill. This opportunity was unprecedented. Since many took advantage of it, a large, newly educated middle class was created that had more disposable income than previously. This gave the economy even more of a boost. Women were fired from their jobs when the men came home. Consumers living in their new homes were eager for the consumer conveniences that popped up.

Americans temporarily changed their food consumption habits because of rationing, but it was understood that this was temporary, until the war was over. Since the economy after the war was doing well, Americans wanted to return to their normal patterns of eating. Even though they felt deprived during the war, Americans ate more food during the war than before but it was not the food they were used to. So after the war they consumed vast amounts of expensive cuts of red meat such as beef and pork. In 1947, American ate, on average, 155 pounds of meat per person. To meet this new demand, farmers depleted their grain stockpiles to fatten cows and hogs and even killed their breeding stock. Besides meat, Americans consumed in abundance other foods such as ice cream, cheese, eggs, canned frozen fruits, and vegetables. The consumption of butter was down, but the consumption of margarine continued to stay up.

Even though most women no longer worked outside the home, they did not wish to spend more time cooking. Tending to victory gardens, canning, and preserving were activities of the past. Now women used canned and frozen fruits and vegetables because they loved the convenience. Since housewives learned to cook from radio shows and magazines instead of their mothers, they chose nutritionally balanced meals over those that were based on aesthetics and presentation.

Fast foods and cakes made from cake mixes were also popular. Pillsbury and General Mills came out with instant cake mixes in 1947. Other cakes that were popular included chiffon, icebox, upside-down, and pudding. Chocolate chip cookies were still popular. In 1949, McDonald's began to use drive-through windows. Even though more meat was available for consumption, meat prices remained high. Ground beef became a staple and was so popular that it was served even in upscale restaurants. Other convenience-based products and inventions emerged—one of them was aluminum foil in 1947. It was used to line the pan so that cleanup would be easy. KitchenAid produced innovations like the first home dishwasher in 1949.

Coffee consumption dropped after the war because the quality was said to have degraded, perhaps because robusto beans replaced the Arabica beans. People began drinking more soft drinks instead. After the war, candy consumption fell; however, food processers began using corn syrup instead of sugar in their products. Instant food also remained popular. Instant mashed potato flakes joined instant coffee and soup.

Even though many women did not want to spend a lot of time in the kitchen, many made an effort to improve their cooking skills by consulting cookbooks for culinary inspiration. One of the popular cookbooks used from 1945 to 1970 was Irma Rombauer's *The Joy of Cooking*, originally written in 1931. Rombauer, a well-known hostess from St. Louis, Missouri, delivered her eminently practical recipes in a personable, chatty style that resulted in a classic manual destined to sell more than 15 million copies. Since the economy was doing well after the war, Americans began to buy cars and take vacations, and through traveling to other parts of the country, they learned about regional cooking. They became interested in food products from particular areas that could be found nowhere else. Americans were particularly fascinated with California, and many former servicemen were moving there. *The California Cookbook for Indoor and Outdoor Eating,* written by Genevieve Callahan, came out in 1946. The focus of this cookbook was backyard grilling and the use of fresh produce. In 1941, James Beard also wrote about this topic in his book entitled *Cook It Outdoors*.

There were other notable cookbooks published during that time. In 1948, the cookbook *A Date with a Dish: A Cook Book of American Negro Recipes* by Freda DeKnight came out. It was the first cookbook written by an African American about African American cuisine, and it disputed the stereotypical "mammy" in the southern kitchen. DeKnight showcased the accomplishments of African American cooks and how they contributed to American cuisine. When they first came to the United States, they were slaves. After the Civil War, they went on to work in hotels and as caterers and also on railroad dining cars all over the country.

America's tastes expanded beyond its national borders. Some troops developed a taste for foreign cuisines during their time abroad and sought to recreate these dishes at home. Italian spaghetti dinners and Chinese dinners became popular. A cooking school opened up in New York City, and Dione Lucas opened a branch of the Cordon Bleu cooking school. She also wrote *The Cordon Bleu Cookbook* in 1947. At this time, Chinese cuisine also became popular. Buwei Yang Chao published the book *How to Cook and Eat in Chinese* in 1945. It was written in a clear manner and was said to be easy to understand. It taught Americans the basics of stir frying. Food writer M. F. K. Fisher was still active on the culinary scene, but instead of writing about how to survive on very little, she was writing about the sensuous, luxurious aspects on food and drink in *Here Let Us Feast: A Book of Banquets* in 1946. In 1949, she wrote *An Alphabet for Gourmets* in the style of a dictionary. In this book, the connection between food and life is emphasized. Cocktail parties continued to be popular. The 1940s' cookbook author Shelia Hibben, like M.F.K Fisher, was against packaged foods.

Even though cooking with convenience food was common, a group of people was interested in gourmet food. Although many Americans found postwar American fare acceptable, many did not. James Beard said that American soldiers came back with a taste for foreign foods. Not true—according to the food fad authors. The gourmet food fad began in the 1930s. Food writers who travelled abroad came home with appreciation of fine food, and they were appalled at home by weird concoctions developed by home economists. To most Americans, gourmet food meant foreign food. Gourmet clubs began to form, where they cooked and sampled mainly French foods. By the end of the 1940s, the United States separated into two groups: home cooks versus gourmet cooks.

The end of the decade saw a more prosperous America. Starting in 1946, people began to have televisions in their homes—black and white at first and then color. At first, only a few people had them, and then more and more. Advertising helped influence brand loyalty, and this became more prominent in the 1950s.

Entries

Betty Crocker Cake Mix

After four years of research and development, Betty Crocker cake mix began to appear in grocery stores in 1947. The first flavor was Ginger Cake followed by Gingerbread Cake and Cookie Mix, Devil's Food Layer Cake, and Party Layer Cake. These cakes eventually evolved into 130 cooking and baking products. Betty Crocker wasn't the first cake mix ever produced. The first dry baking mixes were produced in England during the Industrial Revolution as convenience foods. Cake mixes came out in the United States during the 1920s. Betty Crocker/General Mills (a grain-product-producing company, producers of Good Medal Flour, Bisquick, Softasilk, Wheaties, and Cherrios) first made them popular. Although the first boxed cake mix came out before World War II, people were skeptical because of the problems of spoilage and inadequate packaging. Other problems included inconsistent results and lack of good flavor. Soap was once added to cake mixes to make them fluffier. At first, powdered eggs were used, and fresh eggs and oil were eliminated from the cake mix instructions. Initially, one just added water to the mix and baked, but the flavor was not satisfactory. Later on, the eggs and oil were added back in, not only for taste, but because people wanted to feel as if they were "home cooking." Betty Crocker cake mix was soon followed by Pillsbury and then Duncan Hines. Although home cooks wanted modern convenience, they had traditional ideals. Convenience foods became popular during World War II with rationing and the fact that women were working and had less time to cook. When soldiers returned home after the war, there was an implicit societal pressure to bring everything back to normal, the way it had been before the war. Betty Crocker represented quality in the minds of many. Betty Crocker was not a real person but rather a persona invented in 1921. The idea for creating Betty Crocker was sparked unexpectedly. The Gold Medal flour company sponsored a contest offering consumers a pin cushion if they completed a jigsaw puzzle of a milling scene. Much to their surprise, the contestants asked many questions about baking, alongside with their entries. Betty Crocker was created to personalize the signatures to the responses. The name was based on the of a recently retired director of the company, William G. Crocker. Employees of the company were asked to create the ideal signature of Betty Crocker. Qualities that were infused into her persona included helpfulness. A radio show spun off of this in 1924, later named *The Betty Crocker Cooking School of the Air.* The growth of consumer demand for information necessitated the hiring of 21 home economists, who were employed to carefully test and demonstrate the company's gold medal-winning flour. This was the beginning of the Betty Crocker Kitchen. In the 1950s, the *Betty Crocker Cookbook* was developed. Although the image of Betty Crocker, with her brown hair and red outfit, underwent many changes throughout the decades to be in sync with the current average American woman she still represented domesticity and harmony.

Cheerios

Under the original name of Cheeriots, General Mills created this cereal in 1941. Cadwallader Washburn founded General Mills in 1866 as a flour mill in Minneapolis, Minnesota with the original name of the Minnesota Milling Company. It was a relative newcomer to the world of cold cereals, which were an American invention that developed because of the health reform of the late 1800s. During that time, many Americans ate a high-protein diet and, as a result, suffered from dyspepsia—a chronic digestion problem. Cold cereals were one of the most modern convenience foods. It all started with Dr. John Harvey Kellogg, who created a cereal called granola while at his sanitarium. It was made of wheat flour, corn flour, and granola. From granola came the development in 1895 of wheat flakes—the first breakfast food in flake form—followed by Shredded Wheat biscuits. General Mills continued to grow. In 1898, Corn Flakes were developed. They were first known as Sanitas Corn Flakes. Will Kellogg, brother of Harvey Kellogg, argued with Harvey over the official recipe for the flaked corn cereal. Will wanted to add sugar to the flakes; Harvey did not. So Will left the Kellogg sanitarium in 1906 and formed the Battle Creek Toasted Corn Flake Company, which become the Kellogg Company in 1925. During that time, Charles W. Post came onto the cereal scene. He opened a sanitarium in Battle Creek in 1897 and created Grape Nuts cereal. Grape Nuts was then a flaked corn cereal called Elijah's Manna. The name was changed in 1908 to Post Toasties because of clergymen upset by the equation of breakfast cereal with religious matters. In the early 1900s, Battle Creek attracted more than 40 breakfast cereal companies and by 1911 produced more than 107 brands of corn flakes. Dr. Alexander P. Anderson spent years perfecting a technique to puff rice from a cannon and in 1905 sold his process to Quaker Oats. Then in 1916 Kellogg introduced All-Bran—(a natural laxative), Rice Crispies in 1928, and then Wheaties by the Washburn Cereal Company in 1921. The number of cereals grew in inverse proportion to the declining number of cereal companies. These brands included Kix, Cheerios in 1941, and Post's Raisin Bran in 1942.

Chiffon Cake

In 1927, Harry Baker, a Los Angeles insurance agent, invented chiffon cake. It is a cross between a butter cake and an angel food cake—light, not dense—because the egg whites and the egg yolks are beaten separately. Baker made the cake with oil instead of butter or shortening—this was a new concept. For 20 years, people loved the cake and asked him for the recipe, but he guarded his secret well. The cake became famous because he made it for parties in Hollywood for film stars and other celebrities. After awhile, he began making it and selling it to Hollywood stars. He also made the cake for the well-known Brown Derby Restaurant, where it soon became a favorite. He sold the recipe to General Mills in 1947. Baker wanted "Betty Crocker to give the secret to the women of America." When the recipe came out, cake flour sales increased by 20 percent. In 1948, *Better Homes and Gardens Magazine* claimed the cake was "the first really new cake in 100 years." In the 1950s, General Mills sponsored chiffon cake contests, and people created many variations on this basic cake recipe.

Colonel Sanders' Secret Recipe

Colonel Harland David Sanders, born in the late 1880s, began cooking early in life. When his father died, his mother had to go out to work. He began cooking for his siblings every night when he was six. Cooking was something that came easily to him. When he was older, he held down a variety of jobs. He was a farmhand, a streetcar conductor, a private in the military in Cuba, and a railroad fireman. Always ambitious, he was also a lawyer, an insurance salesman, and a ferry operator. In 1930, he began operating a service station along a highway in Corbin, Kentucky, and since he noticed that there was nowhere decent to eat in the area, he began cooking Southern food. Fried chicken became his specialty, and the Sanders Café operated out of a small room in the gas station. It did well even during the Depression and was listed in Duncan Hines' *Adventures in*

Good Eating in 1939, a book that listed where one could eat inexpensively on the go. Colonel Sanders wasn't satisfied with his success and wanted to do even better, so he began experimenting with cooking his chicken faster for a better taste with a new device called the pressure cooker. He added his signature 11 herbs and spices a few years later. The base of the secret recipe was eggs, milk, and flour, and this original recipe was completed in 1940. People loved the chicken, and business grew even more successful. In 1949, the governor of Kentucky officially granted Mr. Sanders the title of Colonel to honor his work. After that, Mr. Sanders embraced that identity and began wearing a white suit, a black string tie, and grew a white beard to match his white hair. He became his own brand and his own spokesperson. Sanders went to a National Restaurant Association convention in 1952 in Chicago and met another restaurateur, Pete Harman. They came up with the idea of franchising the chicken recipe, and Harman opened the first Colonel Sanders' Kentucky Fried Chicken eatery. The Colonel gave him a franchise under the condition that Colonel Sanders would get a nickel for each chicken sold. This deal was sealed with a handshake. Although Harman's franchise was successful, the highway was rerouted, and he lost his travelling customers. He sold the place in 1955. Colonel Sanders began to market his own recipe and sold it to other roadside eateries. As a result, by 1960, 200 franchises were selling his chicken. Doing television and radio commercials helped his business to flourish. In the early twenty-first century, KFC was a huge corporation with 12,000 restaurants worldwide. Even though Colonel Sanders died in 1980, his image continues to sell chicken that appears to be home fried.

Concentrated Orange Juice

Before oranges were cultivated in the United States, they came from the West Indies. Since they were imported, orange juice was prohibitively expensive for the average consumer. The orange juice craze began in the late 1920s after the Hungarian scientist Szent-Györgyi discovered the large amount of vitamin C in oranges. The first frozen orange juice from concentrate was developed by the president of the Minute Maid Company, John M. Fox, in the 1940s. At first, Fox intended to create orange juice powder that was inspired by a technique he had seen demonstrated during World War II to dehydrate penicillin and blood plasma. He did not like the flavor of the orange juice powder, so he tried adding water to the reduced concentrate. He discovered that the juice had a fresh-squeezed taste. The basic process for making concentrated orange juice is as follows: Ripe oranges are first tested for the ratio of Brix, the ratio of soluble sugar content to acidity. When the ratio is right, the oranges are picked and sent to a processing plant. They are then washed, graded, and the juice extracted. The peel, pulp, and seeds are removed from this mix. A portion of the juice that is used for concentrate goes into a vacuum evaporator, where most of the water is extracted. The remaining orange juice without the water is chilled and then frozen. It is put into cans and transported to supermarkets or to dairies, where it is reconstituted with fresh water and packaged into cardboard cartons, glass bottles, or plastic jugs. The orange growers in Florida and California advertised the healthful benefits of vitamin C, and people soon began to think that drinking orange juice in the morning was important for maintaining good health. At first, the average consumer drank canned orange juice because freshly squeezed orange juice was so expensive. In the 1930s, frozen orange juice came along, but it did not taste good unless most of the water was removed first and then it was rehydrated. After World War II, frozen foods became big business. Grocers devoted more space to freezers, and appliance makers enlarged the freezer compartments of home refrigerators. By the early 1950s, orange juice accounted for 20 percent of the frozen food market. The largest commercial producers of orange juice in the United States are Minute Maid, owned by Coca-Cola, and Tropicana, owned by PepsiCo. Americans currently consume more than 4 gallons of orange juice a year per person.

Dehydrated Food

Food with its water extracted is dehydrated. The process of dehydration creates food that is lightweight, easy to transport, and virtually imperishable. These products are sometimes called "mummy food" because they can be preserved indefinitely if properly stored. The difference between dried food and dehydrated food is that dried food is normally dried in the sun just enough to preserve it. Examples of dried foods include prunes and apricots. Dehydrated food is made by extracting most of its water, whereas the process of drying the food is more technical. Food is dried in heated rotated drums, similar to clothes dryers. First, sliced fruits and vegetables are put into the rotating drums, which causes the moisture in them to evaporate. These fruits and vegetables come out in a dried, flaked form. When they are rehydrated, the original shape and color are usually restored. Dehydrated foods save a great deal of space because their volume is reduced. Because dehydration was a cost- and time-efficient way of getting more food to more people for less money, dehydrated food gained prominence during World War II. During World War II, 80 million pounds of dehydrated foods were produced, most of which were sent to Europe. The production dwindled to almost nothing during the postwar years. Examples of other successfully dehydrated food include eggs, milk, orange juice, fruit, and vegetables such as potatoes. Other types of prepared meals, such as dried soup mixes, were made from dehydrated foods. Since then, the technology has improved with the introduction of "quick freezing" of vegetables.

Gourmet Magazine

This magazine was founded in 1941 by Earle R. MacAusland after the end of the Great Depression and before the United States formally entered World War II. At this time, people did not have the luxury of being too choosy about what they ate and how they ate it. *Gourmet* magazine was dedicated to the exploration of fine wine and cuisine, entertaining at home, and traveling abroad, with its main focus on French cuisine. This magazine started the beginning of what can be defined as trendy food, or food as fashion. The first issue was published in December 1941. The magazine got off to a shaky start before MacAusland attracted wealthy sponsors. Since wealthy people could no longer travel to Europe because of the war, they could only sample and dream about dishes that they would not get to taste in the countries and restaurants from which they came. As culinary historian Anne Mendelson wrote, "Hardship—and later the war—fostered a taste for images of a happier past and perhaps a happier future." In celebration of its 10-year anniversary, *Gourmet* published its first edition of the *Gourmet Cookbook* in 1951. The magazine was popular in Washington, DC, because of the high population of diplomats. As time went by, the cuisines of other countries besides France were included. The success of this magazine caused similar magazines to sprout. Magazines such as *Bon Appetit* in 1955 were geared towards the middle class rather than the upper class. Food magazines geared toward different target audiences soon followed. *Food & Wine* magazine, which made its debut in 1978, targeted both men and women. Newspapers began hiring food columnists at around this time. One was Craig Claiborne, who wrote for *The New York Times*. "From the beginning, Earle MacAusland was interested in 'good living,' accessible through fashion, entertaining, dining, and leisure. It had nothing to do with money, class, or social status. It meant that the food you cooked and ate should be lovingly prepared and eaten with congenial company, and these could be enjoyed by everyone (*The Oxford Encyclopedia of Food and Drink*)." Decades before concerns were raised about junk food and fast food, *Gourmet*'s editorial policy stressed using fresh ingredients and cooking from scratch—no shortcuts or simplifications allowed. "Yet *Gourmet* was read by well-heeled people who wanted to enjoy a delicious, congenial meal with dazzling conversation in fashionable surroundings. It was also for those who could only imagine such occasions, whose trips to Paris, Rome, and London began and ended between the covers of a magazine." Today, because of the limitations of time, money, kitchen space, or energy, many Americans experience travel vicariously through reading the magazine. In turn, *Gourmet* created a market for upscale food; food magazines, food columns, in newspapers, specialty products, and upscale restaurants followed in the magazine's wake—as did other food magazines, which exploited the culinary fashion established by *Gourmet*.

How to Cook and Eat in Chinese

Buwei Yang Chao wrote this book, which was published in 1945. It is one of the first Chinese American cookbooks written. It had about 200 recipes and was written in a clear manner geared toward the Western audience while maintaining authenticity. It explained the process of stir-frying, step by step, and included information on Chinese ingredients, cooking tools, cooking terminology, and lore. Chao was a Chinese doctor who attended Tokyo Women's Medical College. She abhorred Japanese food, so she began to cook for herself. By the time she became a doctor, she was quite good at cooking. Her husband, a professor of comparative linguistics, basically wrote the book for her, since her English was poor. She cooked the dishes, her daughter Rulan translated them into English, and her husband translated back into Chinese, because he found the English dull. This book was the first to give dim sum recipes and explained the use of chopsticks. The professor developed a unique way of writing a type of English that he felt would be appealing. Terms such as "wraplings," meaning dumplings, were used. Future Chinese recipe books that were published elaborated on the basic recipes contained in that book.

Margarine

In the late nineteenth century, Emperor Louis Napoleon III of France wished to have a substitute for butter created. In response, Hippolyte

Mège-Mouriez invented margarine in 1870 using margaric acid—a fatty acid discovered in 1813 by Michael Chevreul, who noticed that the drops had a pearly appearance. He decided to name it after margarites—the Greek word for pearl. Soon after 1870, margarine began to be mass-produced in France. It became available in the United States by the end of the nineteenth century. However, the dairy industry felt threatened and began to lobby. As a result, the production of margarine was restricted and heavily taxed. There were fierce debates regarding the coloring of margarine. In some states, individuals had to knead yellow dye capsules into the margarine after they bought it because selling it in a form that looked too much like butter was not allowed. However, this all began to change during of World War II. At the National Nutrition Conference in 1941, the health benefits of this product were addressed, and individuals began to realize how the current legislation was keeping this product from them.

Since there were shortages of butter during the war, the government made margarine a lower ration point. During this period, margarine was less than half as expensive as butter. For the many people who thought butter tasted better than margarine, few products and recipes were available. For example, there was a recipe for butter spread that combined gelatin, evaporated milk, water, and salt with the butter to stretch it out. There was also a synthetic butter and vanilla-flavored liquid used for baking called Butta-Van. After World War II, many continued to use margarine, even though butter was no longer rationed. Prewar taxes and restrictions on the use of margarine resumed but were slowly repealed beginning in the 1950s. In the 1960s, margarine in tubs and vegetable oil spreads made their debut. Brands of margarine still available today include Mazola, Parkay, Blue Bonnet, and Imperial.

McDonald's

In 1930, Richard and Maurice McDonald moved to California from New Hampshire to make their fortune not in gold, but from the Golden Arches that were later to become ubiquitous throughout the world. In 1948, they opened up a hamburger shop in San Bernardino, California. To set themselves apart from other hamburger restaurants, they developed a "Speedee Service System," that is, a system that operated on principles used to run assembly lines, as applied to the restaurant business. Instead of having wait-staff and tables inside the restaurant as other hamburger places did, windows were placed on the outside of restaurants, where customers could place their orders. The customers then took the food and ate it in their cars.

Their menu was smaller than competitors', consisting of 15-cent hamburgers, 19-cent cheeseburgers, French fries, milkshakes, and sodas. Their food was served with a few condiments: ketchup, mustard, chopped onions, and two pickles. Disposable wrapping was used. The McDonald brothers franchised their operation. In 1954, salesman Ray Kroc met the two McDonald brothers. Soon, they changed the design of their restaurant to distinguish it from other restaurants with walls painted with red and white stripes. Richard McDonald thought up the famous golden arches. Kroc wished to make the restaurant into a nationwide and worldwide franchise business and opened up his first McDonald's in 1955 in Des Plaines, Illinois. The franchise grew rapidly, from 37 in 1957 to more than 100 in

McDonald's owner Ray Kroc eats a hamburger outside a McDonald's restaurant in 1961. (Art Shay/Time & Life Pictures/Getty Images)

1959. In 1961, Ray Kroc purchased the franchise from the McDonald brothers. He made sure that McDonald's was operated in a uniform manner in terms of menus, recipes, prices, trademarks, restaurant designs, and procedures. He even established Hamburger University to train his managers; it offered a degree in Hamburgerology. Kroc's slogan was "Quality, Service, Cleanliness, and Value." McDonald's served as a model for future fast-food restaurants. Kroc advocated heavy automation of processes, development of new products, and aggressive advertising—particularly toward children. In 1966, the clown character Ronald McDonald was invented. Playgrounds within McDonald's soon opened. The Happy Meal came out in 1979.

In 1967, McDonald's began growing into a worldwide operation beginning in Canada and has been expanding rapidly ever since. It has become a symbol of the United States and has inspired distrust and resentment, and has been accused of being environmentally irresponsible and helping to homogenize world food culture and erode local culinary traditions.

The phenomenon of McDonald's has been studied in academic has even become a hot academic topic. Books written about McDonald's and its effects include *The McDonaldization of Society* (1993) by George Ritzer, *Jihad vs. McWorld* (1995) by Benjamin Barber, and *Fast Food Nation: The Dark Side of the All-American Meal* (2001) by Eric Schlosser.

M.F.K. Fisher

Born on July 3, 1908, Mary Frances Kennedy Fisher was a prolific writer of culinary stories, articles, and essays for more than 55 years that changed the character of culinary writing across America. She attended private boarding schools, Illinois College, Whittier College, and Occidental College before continuing her education in 1929 at the University of Dijon, France, as the newly married Mrs. Alfred Fisher. The Fishers returned to California in 1932 and lived in Laguna Beach, doing odd jobs and writing. M. F. K. Fisher's first published article, "Pacific Village," appeared in *Westways* in 1934. Her first book was *Serve It Forth* (1937)—it was about the joy of eating and ancient culinary history books, such as *Apicius de re Coquinaria* and *Mrs. Beeton's Book of Household Management*. She wrote about the oyster's bivalve in *Consider the Oyster* (1941) to distract her second husband from his Buerger's disease. In *How to Cook a Wolf* (1942), she focused on the culinary conundrums posed by living on rations during World War II. In *The Gastronomical Me* (1943), she wrote about her best food experiences and how she used food to emotionally comfort herself. Later she moved to Hollywood and married her third husband. Soon after, she published a series of articles for *Gourmet magazine* about her current life in "The Alphabet for Gourmets" (1948). In 1954, all of the preceding books were compiled into one volume, *The Art of Eating*. She differed from other food writers at the time because her work was centered on the pleasures of gastronomy and not simply nutritionally balanced meals and cooking for company. Examples of other writers who wrote about gastronomy include George Wechsberg, Alexis Lichine Lucius Beebe, and A. J. Liebling. Besides writing her books and articles for *Gourmet magazine* Fisher wrote for *Vogue, Westways, Ladies Home Journal, The Atlantic Monthly, Esquire, Coronet,* and *Holiday*. Her work was extensively published in *House Beautiful* and *Gourmet* in the 1940s and in *The New Yorker* in the 1960s and 1970s. She also wrote an anthology titled *Here Let Us Feast: A Book of Banquets* (1946), the novel *Not Now But Now* (1947), and a translation of Brillat-Savarin's *Physiology of Taste* (1949). She lived in different parts of France and other places during her life. She also wrote about food she ate during childhood and her favorite recipes in her cookbook *With Bold Knife and Fork* (1969). She contributed to the Time-Life Books' publication *The Cooking of Provincial France* (1968). Fisher died on June 22, 1992, from Parkinson's disease.

M&M'S

These candies were inspired by the chocolate candies the soldiers ate during the Spanish Civil War from 1936 to 1937 as seen by the son of the Mars company founder, Forrest Mars. M&M'S were covered by a hard shell, which was significant because they did not melt in one's hands. Melting chocolate was not a trivial issue for a soldier who might have to put down his candy and pick up a gun. The invention of M&M'S was inspired by the British candy called Smarties developed by the Rowntree Company in 1937. In 1941, M&M'S were developed by company executives Forrest Mars and Bruce Murries, who used their initials in naming the candy. In 1940, M&M'S candies officially went into mass production and were added to American G.I. rations during the war as a high-energy field snack that melted in your mouth, not in your hand. These candies were then sold in brown plastic bags. The original colors were red, yellow, green, orange, brown, and violet. They became popular in the 1940s. Eventually, the company merged with Mars, Inc. Later on, in 1954, peanut M&M'S made their debut. M&M'S are still part of the daily food kit of soldiers—the MRE (meals-ready-to-eat). M&M'S colors and their combinations changed over the years. M&M'S are a part of our culture, our lore, and our history. M&M'S are included in recipes for baked goods and Chex snack mixes. The first change in the mix of M&M'S colors came in 1995 when blue replaced tan. An average batch of plain M&M'S is 30 percent brown, 20 percent each of yellow and red, and 10 percent each of green, orange, and blue. Different color combinations are offered during different holidays and for causes such as breast cancer awareness.

Rationing

After Pearl Harbor was bombed on December 7, 1941, the United States entered World War II. Since the soldiers fighting in Europe and Asia needed to be fed—as well as the Allies and the formerly Axis-occupied territories—the government implemented rationing. Besides food, other materials such as rubber, steel, tin, wool, cotton, soap, and nylon were also needed. Since domestic consumption was rising, there was fear of black

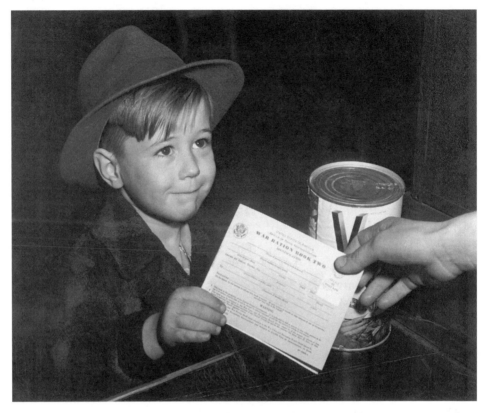

A young child turns in his family's ration book to purchase canned goods in February 1943. (National Archives)

markets, hyperinflation, and inequitable distribution of food across the country, which could lead to internal political instability. During this time, farmers were urged by the government and by monetary incentives to grow more food than during World War I. By May 1942, sugar was rationed, with meat and other foods soon to follow.

However, margarine and salad oils were cheaper and easier to get, because they were made with American grown seeds and grains like corn and sunflower seeds. The following foods were not rationed: poultry, fish, "innards," offals (feet, heads, and tails), honey, corn syrup, molasses, and flour. Each food was assigned a point value as determined by the Office of Price Administration (OPA) according to that food's availability and its consumer demand. Periodically, point values changed. The OPA published a booklet of coupons that was distributed by neighborhood schools, and teachers were asked to volunteer their time to give them out. Every month, each person was issued five blue stamps and six red stamps, with each stamp worth 10 points. The blue stamps were for processed foods and the red stamps for meats, fats, and some dairy products. Although Americans cut down on their consumption, the sacrifices brought about by rations did not change the basic structure of meals and eating habits long term. Many felt more deprived than they actually were. Ironically, food shortages were created as many hoarded food because they were under the impression that there wasn't enough. Although the government advocated that consumers create one-pot meals and stews with low-pointed ingredients, it also portrayed the ideal American meal as a large serving of red meat with two small vegetables on the side with the standard of three meals a day. This ideal was associated with the American image of abundance, stability, and familiarity. Food writers and dieticians worked to create recipes that conjured feelings of love and security. They also urged women to cook these dishes from scratch even though they were busy working. Despite the cozy portrayals of soybeans, casseroles, meat substitutes, and variety meats, these meals were viewed as inferior to the meat- and-potatoes meal. Most people felt that their rations were adequate and that the size of their meals remained the same. Americans with low incomes actually ate better than before the war.

Reynolds Foil

The first aluminum foil rolling plant, J.G. Neher & Sons, was opened in Schaffhausen, Switzerland, in 1886. The use of metal foil was nothing new; it had been around for hundreds of years. Foil is solid metal that has been reduced to a paper-like thinness by rolling or beating. Tin foil was used before it was replaced by aluminum. In the late 1800s, it was expensive to produce materials such as tinplate, glass, and paper for food packaging. The packaging often cost more than the food itself. Technical innovations made it more possible to produce packaging at less expense. Aluminum foil began being used as a protective barrier for items such as tobacco products and chocolate bars. In the United States, the first company to produce aluminum foil was the Reynolds Metals Company (RMC). The product was named Reynolds Wrap Aluminum Foil, and it came out in 1947. Reynolds Foil was sold in supermarkets and soon became popular with consumers. Many different uses of the foil have evolved including oven protection, lining for baking pans, and wrapping food for toaster and oven cooking. The Reynolds Metals Company helped to develop different uses for aluminum foil beyond the protection of food.

Examples of this include using it in the production of aluminum siding for buildings and in the construction of submarines. In 1982, the Reynolds Metals Company came out with Reynolds Plastic Wrap.

Seedless Watermelon

In 1949, Warren Barham, a student completing his Ph.D. in plant breeding, vegetable crops, and plant physiology, became interested in trying to modify the size of seeds in watermelons. He felt that average-sized watermelons took up too much space in the garden and that they consumed too much plant energy. He wanted to develop a better-quality, smaller fruit. He used small seeds that he obtained from a student from North Carolina State University, who had graduated in 1897 and said that his family grew this smaller variety. Although this seed produced a smaller-sized fruit, Braham wanted to grow a fruit that tasted sweeter. Over many years, he developed approximately 20 varieties of seedless and seeded watermelon hybrids by combining traditional farming with modern technology to select specific traits for seeds and plants. Barham developed Barham Seeds, Inc.—a family business that provides licenses for his watermelon hybrids to seed growers and brokers.

Shelia Hibben

Sheila Hibben advocated American regional cooking over the trend of cooking fancy foreign food. She was born Cecile Crack in Montgomery, Alabama, and lived from 1888 to 1964. She wrote restaurant columns for both *The New Yorker* magazine and *House Beautiful*. She wrote about American regional cooking and produced cookbooks such as *The National Cookbook* in 1932 and *American Regional Cookery* in 1946. Eleanor Roosevelt used Hibben as an unofficial menu consultant while FDR was in the White House. She also worked as an advisor to Rex Stout, a mystery writer, to help develop dishes for Nero Wolfe, one of his characters. In the early twentieth century, foreign dishes were slowly coming into vogue, but because of Shelia Hibben's influence, American regional cooking was making a comeback. Dishes such as corned beef and cabbage and dumplings were becoming popular in Manhattan. Hibben believed that Americans had lost their patriotism, and this was reflected in their food choices. As Hibben stated, to prevent "old-fashioned American cooking from going on the rocks . . . [there] has got to be a movement . . . How people could actually get themselves all worked up about saving the grizzly bear of the Rockies, and sit calmly by while such a magnificent dish as South Caroline Hoppin' John faces extinction, was more than I could ever understand!" She emphasized the link between food originally brought over by the settlers and the development of early American history and did not want it to be forgotten after World War II. She was also against the trend toward fast food and synthetic foods. Hibben urged Americans to relish the flavors of simple, well-made food and to abandon the "graceless routine of eating out of packages and cans."

Soy Products

The cultivation and consumption of soybeans is nothing new. They were first grown in China in 1000 BCE, and then spread to Korea, Russia, Japan, and other Asian countries. At first, when soybeans arrived in the United States, they were grown for hay and then for making oil for cooking and industrial uses. Other common soy products include soymilk, tempeh (a meat substitute), tofu (bean curd), miso (fermented soybean paste), natto (fermented soybeans), and soy sauce (fermented soybean sauce). Lesser known soy products include flour, grits, and materials used in the industrial production of bakery and meat products. During World War II, the use of soybeans in the form of grits was encouraged as a meat substitute, because they were not only full of protein but were also unrationed. There were many recipes for soy burgers. Soy grits were also used as meat extenders, that is, adding soy grits to meat in a recipe stretched the meat farther. Meatloaf with soy grits is an example. There were soy cereal and soy crackers. There was even soy butter that was said to have a slight honey and coconut taste and toasted soy butter that tasted like popcorn. These types of butters were used as sandwich spreads, as was peanut butter. Commercial bakers were baking cakes, breads, and cookies using soy flour in place of about 25 percent of the regular flour. The use of soy for human ingestion in the United States began during World War I with soybean oil in salad dressing and shortenings. People also grew soybeans in their victory gardens, because they took less space and are were less labor intensive than other crops. The government and the media promoted the use of soybeans for their nutritional value and abundance of calcium, protein, thiamine, and niacin. Despite the government and media accolades, many people resisted using soybeans because of the questionable quality of some soy products in the past and their unfamiliar taste when raw and unadulterated. After World War II, they fell out of favor until the 1960s, when the health food movement began.

Teflon

A host of new plastics were brought out at the National Plastics Exposition—a plastics industry tradeshow in New York City in 1946. Many of the plastics that are common today were first developed for use during World War II, when they were used as sealants in guns and machinery to prevent damage caused by rust and the elements. Peacetime uses for plastics included materials for home construction, furniture, paints, glues, textiles, kitchen appliances, and even contact lenses. Another important use of plastics was in cookware and bakeware in the form of Teflon. Teflon fluorocarbon resin was invented by accident in 1938 in the laboratories of the DuPont chemical company when Dr. Roy J. Plunkett, a chemist, found that this residue of refrigeration gases had unusual properties. First used only in defense projects, Teflon coating became a commercial product in 1948. The Happy Pan, an electric frying pan coated with Teflon material, made its appearance in 1961. Since then, Teflon has been commonly used to coat a variety of cookware found in supermarkets, department stores, and specialty cookware shops alike.

Uncle Ben's Parboiled Rice

In the 1940s Uncle Ben's rice was named after a poor African-American farmer from Texas, who was known for growing exceptionally good rice. Other than that, not much was known about Uncle Ben—not even his last name. He died not knowing that his name was famous or that there would be many food products named after him. During World War II, produce broker Gordon Harwell and English food chemist Eric Huzenlaub developed a special rice that was nutritious, cooked faster, and had a longer shelf life than standard rice. It was good for feeding the troops overseas. This rice retained 80 percent of its nutrients as compared to original rice, which only retained 5 percent of its nutrients. Long-grain rice underwent a process of pressure boiling before it was milled. This was the first change in the 5,000-year history of rice. This rice was sold only to the armed forces as converted rice. Ordinary citizens did not have access to it until after the war, when it was introduced by Harwell and Forrest E. Mars, his business partner. Uncle Ben's name was used along with the image of Frank C. Brown, who worked as a maître d'hôtel in Chicago. The image disappeared after customer complaints in the 1980s about how it depicts slave cultural stereotypes. The image returned after a couple years' decrease in sales. Uncle Ben's converted rice was one of the first convenience foods introduced in the

United States, and it illustrated acceptance of rice as an alternative to potatoes. The slogans "perfect every time" and "each grain salutes you" were used to advertise it. Over time, various grain products, including wild rice, brown rice, and a quick-cook product known as instant rice, were added to consumers' tables. Basmati, arborio, and jasmine rice have been joined by a no-cook brand of converted rice for commercial kitchens. Consumers are targeted with more than 60 products associated with rice and pasta in addition to a line of stir-fry and skillet sauces. Uncle Ben's products are sold in more than 29 countries in North America, Europe, and Asia and have developed many different flavors and varieties.

Victory Gardens

Due to the demands of the war, there was a shortage of fresh vegetables for civilians. The government urged people to grow their own food and stressed the patriotic significance of helping the war effort. Personal responsibility was stressed, and the government made this effort happen in concrete ways. In 1942, the Office of Civilian Defense began a program to be administered by the Local Defense Councils to start a Victory Garden Program in each community. The food grown in victory gardens was intended for use by the family growing it and for other members of the community. The government urged that the surplus be used for school lunch projects and emergency food needs. The extra food was also intended for use by the troops overseas as well as for other nations involved in the war, even after the war ended. There was a shortage of transportation available to transport food across the country. Railroad cars

Poster urges consumers to plant "victory gardens." During World War II, the government urged Americans to plant gardens for self-sufficiency, citing not only the shortage of food during war time but also the shortage of transportation. (National Archives)

were used to transport weapons, munitions, and other material for the armed forces. Fuel used for transportation also had to be conserved. In view of rising food prices and inevitable taxes, home-grown vegetables lightened the family budget. It was estimated that of every dollar's worth of vegetables and fruit bought at that time, 60 cents was paid out for transportation and handling. Home canning using glass jars was promoted so that steel could be saved. The importance of eating vegetables was emphasized, because it was thought that the lack of vitamins and minerals in the diet of potential soldiers was preventing them from being enlisted under the Selective Services Act. The Department of Agriculture published the following methods of preserving surplus fruits and vegetables: canning, storing root vegetables in the basement or underground, drying, and making pickles and sauerkraut. Families were urged to make plans about what and how much to grow, and people were urged not to waste. Seeds were available to be ordered. There was plenty of assistance and advice available to those who wanted it. Free or inexpensive classes and lectures were available at public schools, colleges, community centers, and places such as the Brooklyn Botanical Garden and the New York Botanical Garden. Books were published on different aspects of gardening, from growing fruits and vegetables to flowers and herbs.

Further Reading

Diner, Hasia R. *Hungering for America: Italian, Irish and Jewish Foodways in the Age of Migration.* Cambridge, Massachusetts: Harvard Univeristy Press, 2001.

"Du Pont to Erect Plant in West Virginia to Make Teflon, a Plastic." *The Wall Street Journal,* March 22, 1949.

Ellyn, Martha. "Dehydrated Foods Fill Vital Emergency Needs." *The Washington Post,* January 30, 1942.

Fisher, M. F. K. *The Art of Eating: 50th Anniversary Edition.* Hoboken, NJ: Wiley Publishing, Inc., 2004.

Gabaccia, Donna R. *We Are What We Eat: Ethnic Food and the Making of America.* Cambridge, Massachusetts: Harvard University Press, 1998.

Hoffman, David. *The Breakfast Cereal Gourmet.* Riverside, NJ: Andrews McMeel Publishing, Kansas City, Missouri, 2005.

Lewis, Rae. "Here's the Victory Garden Formula: Plant, Tend Well, Harvest, Then Can." *The Washington Post*, February 28, 1943.

Producing "Seedless" Watermelons: A Biotechnology Virtual Tour." http://www.accessexcellence.org/. June 7, 2010.

Smith, Andrew F. *Eating History: 30 Turning Points in the Making of American Cuisine*. New York: Columbia University Press, 2009.

6

1950s

Margaret Haerens

When people think of American food in the 1950s, they usually imagine the traditional image of the family meal: a happy, freshly scrubbed family sitting around the table enjoying a meal made by mom, who may have cooked for hours to create that dish. Of course, the reality of the situation is much more complicated. As the American economy boomed and many American families moved from urban centers to brand-new suburban housing developments, new food trends began to emerge. These trends reflected the larger societal changes going on in the country. More and more women were going out to work. Television became a profound influence on American eating habits, as cooking shows and advertising introduced new products, styles, and techniques. The era also signaled a transition in America's relationship to food and the food industry. As packaged foods became more available, advertisers began to push the idea that convenience was as important as quality. As a result of effective advertising in magazines, newspapers, radio, and television, homemakers and home cooks became more open to trying dried, packaged, and frozen foods. Although homemakers did not fully embrace the idea of packaged foods all at once, they judiciously began to use them when they did not hurt the quality of their cooking and offered significant time savings. The 1950s marked the decade when packaged foods and fast foods made major inroads in American markets and began to profoundly affect the buying and eating habits of the American consumer.

The 1950s were an era of abundance as well as transition. As the United States recovered from the tremendous economic, political, and cultural

Many people picture the ideal family of the 1950s, freshly scrubbed and seated around a dinner table set with a perfect home-cooked meal. (Lambert/Getty Images)

changes brought on by its participation in World War II, the attention of the American food industry shifted from supporting the war effort back to the American consumer. Products and ingredients that were scarce during the war years were available in abundance by the end of the 1940s. Rationing was long over, and new products were being developed at a breakneck pace. Many of these new products reflect a burgeoning interest in the exotic flavors returning G.I.s had enjoyed overseas, particularly Chinese, Italian, and Hawaiian foods. As a result, American home cooks had more opportunities than ever to create new dishes and experiment with new cooking styles.

Building on technology developed during wartime, the food industry began to introduce a wide range of packaged foods to the U.S. market. Products like dried soup mixes, frozen dinners, frozen juice concentrates, and cake mixes were developed to save women time and offer a convenient way to provide a nutritious and filling meal to their families. Advertising of the era pushed the idea that cooking was laborious and tedious and that every homemaker wanted shortcuts in putting together robust meals. Experts of the era note that to some extent this was true, but most homemakers wanted high-quality meals that they could be proud of cooking and serving. Homemakers were not excited about foods that required only adding water or opening up a can and then serving. With the quality of many packaged products inferior or inconsistent at best, it is fair to say that 1950s homemakers did not fully embrace packaged foods—or did so warily and with reservations.

There were some unqualified successes, though. After years of inconsistent quality, cake mixes became a staple in many American homes. The popularity of California Dip as an appetizer for cocktail parties or backyard barbeques led Lipton's Onion Soup Mix to become the most frequently used dried soup mix of all time. The proliferation of creamed soup in a can led to the rise of casseroles, which are still a favorite for many families today. Cheez Whiz, frozen fish sticks, Rice-A-Roni, and Eggo Frozen Waffles are also examples of products developed in that era that proved to have enduring popularity in the American marketplace.

Another theme in 1950s was the proliferation of television and its influence on American cooking habits. As the decade started, television was a relatively new medium, but its popularity quickly skyrocketed. In 1950, it was estimated that there were only one million televisions in the country. By 1960, 87 percent of American households owned at least one television. Many families gathered around to watch their favorite programs, such as *The Ed Sullivan Show, Gunsmoke, I Love Lucy,* and *The Jack Benny Show.* With growing numbers of families watching TV on a regular basis during the decade, television advertising became more influential with consumers. TV ads for packaged foods or new products affected the buying and cooking habits of the American homemaker, as many home cooks wanted to try the products they saw advertised on television.

TV cooking demonstrations also became a staple on daytime TV, either as cooking shows or as segments on other shows. Women watching during the day between household chores could see TV cooks make exotic and complicated dishes and explain new techniques they may have only read about in cookbooks or magazines. With this new knowledge, some home cooks became confident enough to try new methods at home. Some of these TV cooks also incorporated packaged foods into their cooking exhibitions, further encouraging home cooks to try unfamiliar packaged products.

Television also influenced the way people gathered to eat. As TV became more popular around the country, families began to eat in front of the television—whether it was a full meal or snacks. The food industry responded by coming out with meals convenient to the nation's burgeoning TV habits. TV dinners emerged during this era. Although frozen foods had been around for years—and entire frozen meals had been introduced in different forms—the quality of frozen dinners improved in the 1950s, and effective advertising led many families to try the new product. The TV dinner was a full frozen meal in a metal tray that could be popped into the oven, then put on a special TV tray to be consumed right in front of the screen. Snacks also were conceived with TV viewing in mind: they could be eaten with your hands, offered a variety of flavors and textures, and were easy to put together. One of the most enduringly popular treats that came from the 1950s is snack mixes, which are a combination of cereal, breadsticks, nuts, pretzels, and seasoning. Chex Mix is the best-known snack mix to emerge from the era.

For homemakers and home cooks, television wasn't the only source of information about recipes and new cooking trends. As in earlier eras, newspapers, magazines, and cookbooks also profoundly influenced American cooking habits. Newspapers and magazines printed trendy recipes, useful cooking and entertaining tips, and offered food columns and articles that explored new trends in depth. Cookbooks exploded during the decade, including the well-loved *Betty Crocker's Picture Cookbook* and new editions of the *Joy of Cooking*. The range of cookbooks was impressive: from barbequing and outdoor grilling to classic French cooking; from appetizers to desserts; and from using fresh ingredients to using packaged foods. Home cooks had a wide variety of cookbook subjects, styles, and trends to provide material for their own cooking.

Some of the trends that came to the forefront in the 1950s are still popular today. For example, barbequing and outdoor grilling became established as a great American tradition during that time. As more Americans were migrating from cities to suburbia, American families utilized backyards with picnic tables and grills, and outdoor parties became a regular feature of suburban life. With the invention of the Weber Kettle Grill, which allowed grilling all year long in different climates, outdoor cooks had a chance to develop their skills and techniques and perfect their recipes. The great American chef James Beard was also an avid outdoor cook and published his prominent cookbook, *The Complete Book of Barbeque and Rotisserie Cooking*, in 1954. Cocktail parties were all the rage as well. Cocktails became more daring, with interesting colors and fruity flavors, but the classics still were paramount: Manhattans, dry martinis, Sidecars, and Old-Fashioneds were staples at most cocktail parties. Plates of hors d'oeuvres, also called appetizers, were served as adults relaxed and socialized over cocktails. Theme parties were also a trend at that time. The hosts of the party picked a theme—such as the Old West, Mardi Gras, or

Hawaiian Luau—and guests dressed appropriately. The food at the party would also complement the theme of the evening.

Ethnic cuisines began to enter mainstream American cooking. Mexican cooking, already found in Mexican American enclaves in the American Southwest, proliferated with the development of Tex-Mex—a hybrid Mexican food influenced by Texan cooks, flavorings, ingredients, and cooking techniques. Tex-Mex can be traced back many years, but with the influx of growing numbers of Mexican immigrants into Texas and neighboring states in the 1950s, Tex-Mex established itself as an authentic American cuisine. For returning G.I.s, who had been exposed to Hawaiian and Asian flavors, Hawaiian buffets were a strong trend for a short time in American entertaining. Pizza also strengthened its foothold in American food culture, as more and more pizzerias opened across the country, especially in suburban areas.

The rise of fast-food franchises can be traced to the 1950s. Although the first McDonald's was opened in 1940, it wasn't until Ray Kroc bought into the company in 1955 that the modern era of McDonald's began. Today McDonald's serves 47 million customers a day. The first Burger King was opened in 1953 in Jacksonville, Florida. Based primarily on the West Coast, Jack in the Box opened its original restaurant in San Diego, California, in 1951. The first Kentucky Fried Chicken outlet was opened in 1952. Clearly, enterprising restaurateurs saw the need for convenient, quickly prepared food in the market during that time. They were right—fast food was a type of cuisine that appealed to a society dominated by cars and driving and would explode in popularity in the years to come.

Drive-in restaurants, another style of fast food, were also popular in the 1950s. Drive-ins enabled drivers to order food from their cars, as "carhops" came out to take orders and deliver meals on metal trays while diners sat in their cars. Some drive-ins had speakers through which you could order and then have your food brought out to you. Some carhops wore uniforms, and some even served food on roller skates. Many drive-ins featured music, hoping to attract a young, trendy crowd. Although the drive-in restaurant largely disappeared by the 1960s, a small number still survive as novelty restaurants, cashing in on 1950s nostalgia.

As some trends disappeared by the end of the decade, others endured and even grew in later decades. During the 1950s, American food culture continued to evolve, producing new trends, adapting to various influences, and incorporating new flavors and techniques. Home cooks were inundated with food advertising on the relatively new medium of television, as well as through magazines, radio, and newspapers. A wide range of cookbooks, TV food shows, and food columns helped home cooks navigate these changing waters to discover what worked best for their cooking and for their families. The bottom line was that as a wide range of packaged products became available and fast food promised convenient meals for a busy family, homemakers began to forge a new relationship with the American food industry, one that would continue to evolve in the next few decades of the American experience.

Entries

James Beard

Regarded by many experts to be one of the most significant influences on American cooking in the 1950s, James Beard wrote a number of cookbooks, opened a prominent cooking school in New York City, and brought to the forefront several culinary trends still in evidence today. Beard was born on May 5, 1903, in Portland, Oregon, and became interested in cooking at an early age. Under the tutelage of his mother, who was an expert cook, Beard learned particularly to love outdoor grilling, which his family did frequently at its summer beach home. A frustrated actor and singer, Beard opened a catering business with a partner in Manhattan in the late 1930s that also offered French, Italian, and Russian specialties for takeout. The success of the catering business attracted the attention of publishers, who commissioned him to compile his recipes and publish them in a cookbook, which in 1940 became *Hors d'Oeuvres and Canapés, with a Key to the Cocktail Party.* The book introduced several dishes that would become standard party fare, like deviled eggs and open-faced sandwiches. It also championed cocktail parties, which would become popular in the 1950s. After a stint in the U.S. Army during World War II as a cook, he returned to New York City and began advocating for an authentic American cuisine. In the preface to his *The Fireside Cookbook: A Complete Guide to Fine Cooking for Beginner and Expert* (1949), he expressed his wish for Americans to create a "truly national cuisine that will incorporate all that is best from our new, still-young nation." During the 1950s, Beard hit his stride, publishing four popular cookbooks and opening a well-received cooking school. Commentators cite his influence on the art of outdoor grilling, entertaining, fowl and game cookery, and the cocktail party. He often encouraged his readers and the viewers of his many TV appearances to use fresh, regional ingredients, acknowledging that even if home cooks had limited time, they could still create delicious and lovely dishes. He died in 1985. A foundation in his name was established a year later. The James Beard Foundation sponsors culinary exhibitions, educational programs, and scholarships for aspiring chefs and hands out the prestigious James Beard Foundation awards for culinary excellence every year.

Betty Crocker's Picture Cookbook

Published in 1950, *Betty Crocker's Picture Cookbook* is considered a classic and ground-breaking American cookbook, celebrated for the profound influence it had on American cuisine in the 1950s. Packaged in a bright red three-ring binder with loose-leaf sheets, the volume contained not only hundreds of recipes but also animated drawings, photographs of prepared dishes, and basic information for beginner cooks on measuring ingredients, choosing good yet economical cuts of meat, cooking and baking tips, and even setting the table or arranging your kitchen more efficiently. In the "Shortcut" section, the cookbook imparts useful tips on cleaning cooking equipment and finding inventive ways to rest—one suggestion was to lie down on the floor on your back for 3 to 5 minutes to recuperate from overwork. Recipes range from easy-to-prepare soups and casseroles to more adventurous dishes for the advanced cook, like Welsh rarebit and Chicken Tomato Aspic. Homemakers raved that the book made cooking easy and fun. It offered practical ideas and make cooking and homemaking less intimidating by introducing different ways to organize and innovate kitchens and menus. *Betty Crocker's Picture Cookbook* became a staple in American homes, going through a number of new editions throughout the ensuing decades. By 1991, 26 million copies of the cookbook had been sold, and in 2006, John Wiley and Sons released the 10th edition, *The Betty Crocker Cookbook*.

Cake Mixes

Cake mixes are dry baking mixes sold in supermarkets that make a moist cake batter when mixed with liquid ingredients such as eggs, milk, or oil at home. Mixes have been around for many years. Dry baking mixes originated in England with the introduction of a custard powder in the 1840s. In subsequent years, dry mixes for gelatin, pancakes, and biscuits appeared. In the late 1920s, the Duff Company of Pittsburgh, a molasses manufacturer, came up with a gingerbread mix and then regionally introduced white, spice, and devil's food cake mixes in the 1930s. During that same decade, a number of other food companies—including Pillsbury—produced versions of cake mixes, all of which had limited popularity because of their inferior quality. These early mixes tended to use dry milk

Improved cake mixes made homemade desserts more accessible during the 1950s. (Quentin Bargate/Dreamstime.com)

and powdered eggs, which led to poor flavor in the finished product. After World War II, food companies began to pour money into fine-tuning the flavor and quality, and in November 1947, General Mills introduced its Betty Crocker Ginger Cake Mix, which required only adding water. General Mills soon introduced mixes for yellow and white cake. A year later, Pillsbury introduced a chocolate cake mix. It was Duncan Hines, however, that really established cake mixes as a popular product for most 1950s homemakers. In 1951, it released the Three Star Surprise Mix, which proved to be popular because you could make a white, yellow, or chocolate cake from the same mix. In three weeks, it captured 48 percent of the market. In ensuing years, companies would reformulate cake mixes to make them more moist or require less mixing time. They have also developed mixes for specialty cakes, such as red velvet, tiramisu, or upside-down cake. During the 1950s, cake mixes became more popular as mixes improved and became even more convenient. It did not take long for them to become a staple in many American homes.

Carnation Instant Nonfat Dry Milk

Carnation Instant Nonfat Dry Milk (or Carnation Instant Dry Milk) is a powder product sold in packets that transforms from powder to milk when mixed with ice-cold water. Introduced by Carnation Company in 1954 as "magic crystals," the product became popular with cooks who appreciated the convenience when traveling long distances or camping. The product was a handy source of milk for coffee and cooking outside or in locations where fresh milk wasn't available, as well as for emergencies. It is especially useful in baking cakes and breads, as well as in keeping ground meat dishes moist. Dry milk can also enrich smoothies, egg dishes, dips, puddings, mashed potatoes, soups, and sauces. As nutritionists realized the value of a calcium-rich diet for healthy teeth and bones, families also found Carnation Instant Nonfat Dry Milk to be a great source for calcium, vitamin D, and protein. With more than 44 million American men and women aged 50 and older fighting symptoms of osteoporosis or low bone mass and many children not getting enough calcium in their diets, many Americans recognized the value of a product like Carnation Instant Nonfat Dry Milk. Founded on September 6, 1899, by grocer E.A. Stuart, the Carnation Company was originally the Pacific Coast Condensed Milk Company in Kent, Washington. The new company's first product was Carnation's Evaporated Milk, which became a staple in American kitchens, and cans of evaporated milk were carried by soldiers during World War I and World War II. Carnation Company later developed Fat Free Evaporated Milk and Sweetened Condensed Milk. In 1985, Nestlé, the largest foods company in the world, acquired the Carnation Company. The Carnation products are being produced under the banner of the Nestlé Carnation Company.

Cheez Whiz

Considered a "processed cheese sauce," Cheez Whiz was originally developed by a team led by food scientist Edwin Traisman and was first put on the market in 1953 by Kraft Foods. The intention was to capitalize on the success of Velveeta, a thicker processed cheese that had been available to customers since the 1930s. Whereas Velveeta was fairly solid, Kraft was looking to develop a spreadable product that would be soft at room temperature. When it finally reached the market in 1953, Cheez Whiz quickly became a popular product all around the country. Packaged as a spread and sold in a jar, Cheez Whiz is classified as a processed cheese food because it is made up of regular cheese reprocessed with additional ingredients such as emulsifiers and stabilizing agents. Products such as citric acid and flavoring ingredients may also be added to obtain the unique flavor of the product. It is used as a cheesy topping on corn chips, hot dogs, celery, crackers, nachos, and other foods—including the infamous cheesesteaks originating from the city of Philadelphia. In fact, customers at Philly cheesesteak stands often order their sandwich "Whiz wit," meaning the sandwich has a topping of heated Cheez Whiz and grilled onions. Cheez Whiz is also often used as a dip, which appealed to the 1950s homemaker who entertained frequently. One surprising use for Cheez Whiz is as a stain remover for grease-based stains; because it contains certain natural enzymes that can break up organic greases and oils, it has become a widely used prewash cleaning agent. Since its introduction in 1953, Cheez Whiz has remained a popular product in American households. In recent years, Kraft has changed the formula, redesigned the packaging—including a new, wider jar that allows dipping straight from the container—and has marketed several twists on the original recipe, offering products such as Cheez Whiz Tex Mex, Salsa Con Queso, and Cheez Whiz Italia. Today, Cheez Whiz can also be found in Handi-Snacks, which are packaged snack food collections.

Chex Mix

Generally made up of an assortment of Chex cereals, breadsticks, pretzels, nuts, or crackers, Chex Mix is a snack mix usually served at parties or in front of the television. Snack mixes, also called TV mixes, were popular in the 1950s, as families looked for interesting and convenient snacks they could eat with their hands comfortably while watching TV. In fact, even *Betty Crocker's Picture Cookbook* had a snack mix recipe. The story of Chex Mix originates with the introduction of Chex cereal in 1937 by Ralston Purina, an animal feed company that began to produce cereal in the early 1900s. In the 1950s, cereal companies printed recipes for mixing their cereals into snack mixes on the back of cereal boxes to sell more of their products. The recipe for Chex Mix first appeared in 1952 and became a staple throughout the years for casual parties and get-togethers across America, especially during the holiday season. People enjoyed the flavor and the checkerboard shape of Chex cereal, which is based on Ralston's Purina logo. Although Chex Mix was consistently popular for decades, Ralston Purina did not patent the recipe until 1990. Moreover, it wasn't available commercially in stores until 1985. Keep in mind that the recipe available on the box differs from the product you buy in stores—the recipe

Chex cereal mix is a classic staple for parties with the original recipe developed in the 1950s. (Danelle Mccollum/Dreamstime.com)

includes wheat, corn, and rice Chex, butter, bagel chips, pretzels, and nuts and is generously seasoned with garlic powder, onion powder, seasoned salt, and Worcestershire sauce, then baked in an oven. Today, there are at least 15 commercially available varieties of Chex Mix. Recipes for home-made Chex Mix are still available and found on Chex cereal boxes. In 1996, General Mills acquired the Chex brand and products and is now the sole manufacturer of Chex Mix.

Denny's

This national chain of restaurants is known for its round-the-clock breakfast and casual family dining. Harold Butler opened the first Denny's in Lakewood, California, in 1953 under the name Danny's Donuts. A year later, he opened several more Danny's Donut shops and introduced sandwiches and other entrees on the menu. Butler continued to open new restaurants and expand the menu, finally changing the name to Denny's in 1959 to avoid confusion with another chain, Doughnut Dan's. One of the restaurant's most successful menu items, the Grand Slam Breakfast, was introduced in Atlanta as a tribute to Hank Aaron in 1977. By 1981, there were more than 1,000 Denny's across America. Today, there are more than 1,500 restaurants nationwide and internationally in Canada, Costa Rica, El Salvador, Jamaica, Japan, Mexico, and New Zealand. One of the hallmarks of Denny's is its convenience: not only are they open 24 hours and on most holidays, but they also serve breakfast, lunch, dinner, and dessert around the clock, and many of their restaurants are located off free-way exists and in service areas for truckers and long-distance drivers. In the mid-1990s, the chain was affected by a wave of controversy when a series of discrimination lawsuits were filed alleging that several African American customers were denied service or given inferior service. A class action suit was settled in 1994, and Denny's made a commitment to pro-vide sensitivity training to its employees to avoid any such problems in the future. In 2006, Denny's was ranked at the top of *Black Enterprise*'s list of Top 40 Companies for Diversity. Denny's is recognized as the largest family-service restaurant in the United States and continues to attract fam-ilies and late-night eaters who enjoy their diverse and reasonably priced menu, particularly their Grand Slam Breakfast special.

Diners Club Card

Widely accepted as being the first independent charge card, the Diners Club card was thought up by Francis McNamara in 1950. The operator of a small loan company in New York City, McNamara came up with the idea when one of his clients began a business of lending out his department-store credit cards to friends and charging for their use. Inspired, McNamara created the Diners Club card, which allows members to charge expenses on the card and pay them off in full by the end of each month. Up to this point, there had only been department store credit cards—not fully independent cards that enabled their members to charge at a variety of merchants. The Diners Club card was designed with restaurants in mind, creating what would be later classified as the "travel and entertainment" (T & E) card market, which was meant for high-end travelers with a taste for expensive travel and food. It was first used in February 1950, when McNamara charged a dinner at Major's Cabin Grill in New York City for his partner Ralph Schneider on the Diners Club card—a legendary dinner known in the credit-card industry as the First Supper. In one year, 20,000 people become card members, allowing Diners Club to expand to other major U.S. cities. By 1952, more than 400 restaurants accepted the card. By 1955, the Diners Club card went global with more than 200,000 members. However, Diners Club's monopoly in the T & E market was quickly challenged by the American Express card, which would eventually surpass it and become America's most popular charge card. In 1981, Diners Club International was acquired by Citibank and in 2004 announced an agreement with Mastercard, which enabled Diners Club to be used wherever Mastercard can be used.

Drive-In Restaurants

A drive-in restaurant allows customers to drive in, park their cars, have full meals brought out, and then eat them in their cars. Although drive-in restaurants reached the height of their popularity in the 1950s, the concept had been around since before World War II. The growing number of cars in the United States enabled the drive-in trend to reach its zenith during the decade. Most drive-in restaurants served diner food: burgers, hot dogs, French fries, cole slaw, shakes, and ice cream sundaes. To be served at a drive-in, you would drive your car into a designated space and park it.

Cars park in the lot surrounding Stan's Drive-in Coffee Shop at night in Hollywood, California, on March 26, 1958. (AP/Wide World Photos)

You would then place your order through a speaker system, or a waitress—servers at drive-ins were primarily women called "carhops" or "curb girls"—would come out to give you a menu and take your order. You would then be brought your food on a special tray, which would be attached to your half-open car window. When you were finished, the carhop would come out and collect the tray and resolve the bill. Consumers were drawn to the speedy and efficient service and liked the concept of eating in their cars. Some restaurants attracted customers with music or with themes or with dressing their staff in roller skates and uniforms. Drive-in restaurants often became a magnet for young people, who would take a date there or end up there after a night of cruising around in their parents' cars. The novelty began to wear off, however, with the introduction of fast-food restaurants. In the 1960s and 1970s, many drive-in restaurants closed, except major chains like A & W Restaurants. Some interest has revived in recent years, however, as older generations look to revisit their youth or introduce a touchstone from their past to a new generation. This nostalgia boom has led to a growing number of novelty drive-ins across America. These restaurants tend to depend heavily on 1950s music and ambiance, even providing live bands, dance contests, and sock hops.

Dunkin' Donuts

A U.S. chain of coffee and baked goods stores, Dunkin' Donuts has for many years been a popular place for people to pop in to buy coffee and doughnuts. In 1950, Bill Rosenberg opened the first Dunkin' Donuts shop in Quincy, Massachusetts. Rosenberg had a simple philosophy: "Make and serve the freshest, most delicious coffee and donuts quickly and courteously in modern, well-merchandised stores." The company began franchising five years later, licensing the first of many new Dunkin' Donuts stores. The menu quickly expanded and now offers 52 varieties of donuts and more than a dozen types of coffee as well as bagels, breakfast sandwiches, flatbread sandwiches, and other baked goods. The company grew rapidly; by 1963, there were more than 100 Dunkin' Donuts shops, and by 1979, there were more than 1,000. Today, there are almost 9,000 Dunkin' Donuts stores in the United States and 31 other countries. Dunkin' Donuts serves more than 3 million customers per day. These stores are owned by Dunkin' Brands Inc., which also owns the nationally known ice cream chain Baskin Robbins. The two chains are often integrated into one, offering convenience for customers looking for delicious treats. In recent years, Dunkin' Donuts introduced a plan to significantly reduce trans fats in its products by switching to a combination of palm, soybean, and cottonseed oils. These low-trans-fat products became available nationwide since October 2007. That same year, they also launched Dunkin' Donuts coffee in retail locations, such as supermarkets and club stores. In 2008, Dunkin' Donuts introduced DDSMART, a healthy new menu with low-calorie, low-fat, and low-sugar items and launched their all-day oven-toasted menu, including personal pizzas, flatbread sandwiches, and hash browns.

Eggo Frozen Waffles

A brand of frozen waffles that is stored in the freezer and cooked in a toaster or conventional oven, Eggo Frozen Waffles were created in 1953 in San Jose, California, by three brothers, Tony, Bill, and Frank Dorsa. In the mid-1930s, the Dorsa brothers came up with a dry waffle batter that required only adding milk to make fresh waffles with a waffle iron. The mix proved to be incredibly popular, so Frank began experimenting and invented a machine that could make thousands of waffles in an hour. The brothers then froze and shipped them to supermarkets all over the United States. They initially called these waffles "froffles," a combination of "frozen" and "waffles." However, when their customers started calling them "eggos" because they had an "eggy" taste, the Dorsa brother named them Eggo Frozen Waffles in 1955. Homemakers love them; they don't require a waffle iron, are stored easily in the freezer, and cook quickly in a toaster, toaster oven, or conventional oven. The ease of cooking Eggo waffles enables children to make their own breakfasts. Eggo waffles have long been a staple in American homes and college dorms. In 1970, the Kellogg Company purchased Eggo and, in 1972, introduced the catchy advertising slogan "Leggo My Eggo." Variations of the classic waffles were introduced, such as cinnamon, blueberry, chocolate chip, and banana. Kellogg also expanded the brand by introducing pancakes, mini waffles, French toast, and muffin tops. Eggo is by far the market leader in frozen waffles; as of 2009, it was reported that it represented 73 percent of the frozen waffle market.

Frozen Fish Sticks

One of the biggest success stories of the 1950s was the popularity of frozen fish sticks. A processed food usually made of cod, which is then battered, deep-fried, and frozen, fish sticks are a convenient dish for home cooks, who take them out of the freezer and pop them in the oven. They are especially popular with children, who eat them with ketchup, tartar sauce, or other flavorful dips. In the United States, Birds Eye introduced a line of fish sticks in 1952, and within a few years, they had proven to be a surprising hit: by 1954, more than 30 million packages of frozen fish sticks were produced and shipped to supermarkets all over the country. Mothers loved the product not only for the time saved and ease in preparation, but also because their children loved them—in fact, children, who do not like to eat fish usually like fish sticks. The explosive popularity of frozen fish sticks led to a number of other food manufacturers coming out with their own versions of the product. It also inspired manufacturers to experiment and formulate a range of other breaded, fried, and frozen products: veal sticks, ham sticks, eggplant sticks, and dried lima bean sticks are examples of these failed attempts. Although none of those products were successful, frozen fish sticks were. They became a reliable and familiar product for American families looking to introduce fish to picky young children who wouldn't eat it in any other form. They remain a favorite dish in American homes today.

Jif Peanut Butter

Jif is the most popular peanut butter on the U.S. market. It is the base ingredient in the ubiquitous peanut butter and jelly sandwich, which has been such a staple in American homes for decades. It would not be a stretch to say that a majority of American kids have had peanut butter and jelly sandwiches. The history of peanut butter goes back hundreds of years to a time when Aztecs used to grind and mash peanuts into a paste. In more modern times, it can be traced to Montreal, Canada, where Marcellus Gilmore Edson patented a peanut product similar to peanut butter in 1884. In 1903, the first peanut butter-making machine was invented. The Jif brand is owned by the J. M. Smucker Company, which is one of the top food manufacturers and marketers in the United States. In 1958, the original Creamy Jif peanut butter was introduced and quickly became one of the top-selling peanut spreads in the country. Part of the brand's success can be attributed to its effective advertising campaign, which featured the slogan "Choosy mothers choose Jif." It did not take long for discerning mothers to try it—and stick with it. To capitalize on the enduring brand, Smucker developed several new varieties throughout the years. Extra Crunchy Jif was introduced in 1974 and became another popular product. In 1991, Smucker's debuted Simply Jif, which featured less sodium and sugar than the original recipe. They continued to develop healthy variations of the product with the introduction of Reduced Fat Jif in 1995. Jif also updated its advertising slogan to "Choosy moms and dads choose Jif."

Lipton's Onion Soup Mix

Introduced to the U.S. market in 1952, Lipton's Onion Soup Mix is a dry onion soup mix that, when combined with water, transforms into soup. It became incredibly popular in the mid-1950s as the base ingredient of California Dip, which is regarded as one of America's most beloved dips. Made from a combination of sour cream and Lipton's Onion Soup Mix, California Dip is easy to make, convenient to store, and can be served with a number of snacks, including potato chips, corn chips, crackers, bread-sticks, tortilla chips, or melba toast. The recipe is thought to have been invented in early 1954 by an anonymous cook in Los Angeles. It did not take long for the recipe to spread around the city as women realized that they could make an easy and delicious dip for home entertaining. The rec-ipe was printed in the local paper, and sales of the soup mix soared. In 1958, when Lipton executives learned that the California Dip was driving sales of their mix through the roof, they perfected the recipe and began to print it on every box. For Lipton, the timing was perfect: with the explosion of cocktail parties, backyard barbeques, and theme parties that raged during the 1950s, California Dip was a convenient, tasty dish that everyone enjoyed. Today it is still a popular dip. Lipton's Onion Soup Mix is also used as flavoring in meatloaf, meatballs, and other dishes.

PAM Cooking Spray

The most popular nonstick cooking spray, PAM is considered to be a perfect substitute for sautéing with high-fat butter, margarine, or oils. It is sold in cans and sprayed on cooking or baking equipment to prevent stickiness, allowing food to cook evenly and then be removed easily from the pan. Chefs and home cooks find PAM to be a convenient and useful product that saves valuable time in the cooking process and is a healthier option than heavy butters, oils, or margarines. The first patent for nonstick cooking spray was issued to Arthur Meyerhoff and Leon Rubin in 1957, who then introduced PAM Cooking Spray in 1959. Two years later, Rubin and Meyerhoff formed Gibralter Industries to market PAM All Natural Cooking Spray—PAM stands for "Product of Arthur Meyerhoff." In the early 1960s, the host of a local Chicago TV cooking show introduced PAM and used it during cooking demonstrations. Carmelita Pope, a well-known Chicago personality, demonstrated its many uses and as a result, PAM gained a loyal group of customers. As word of its usefulness spread, PAM quickly became a product used in growing numbers of American households. In 1971, Gilbralter Industries merged with American Home Products, then International Home Foods, and finally ConAgra Foods. Along the way, PAM developed variations on the original nonstick spray, such as PAM Butter Flavor in 1985 and PAM Olive Oil in 1986. Recognizing that it could improve on the nutritional value, PAM switched to canola oil in the 1990s, eliminating many of the saturated fats in its products. In 2003, PAM introduced PAM Baking, which includes real flour. A year later, it released PAM Grilling, which is created to work at high grilling temperatures.

Pillsbury Bake-Off Contest

The premier cooking competition in the United States, the Pillsbury Bake-Off, enables amateur cooks to submit recipes and then compete in a bake-off for a cash prize—as well as the prestige of being the Grand Prize winner. The contest started in 1949, when executives at Pillsbury decided

Pillsbury Bake-Off winners Mrs. Bernard Derousseau of Rice Lake, Wisconsin, and Mrs. Peter Wuebel of Redwood City, California, pose with the Duchess of Windsor, Pillsbury Mills President Philip W. Pillsbury, and the prize-winning Kiss Me Cake on December 12, 1950. (AP/Wide World Photos)

to celebrate Pillsbury's 80th birthday and promote its Pillsbury flour by sponsoring a contest. The company invited homemakers to send in their best recipes containing Pillsbury flour, and the finalists competed at the Waldorf-Astoria hotel in New York City. The first winner was Theodora Smafield with her No-Knead Water-Rising Twists recipe. She received a $50,000 prize. Response to the contest was so overwhelming that Pillsbury decided to make it an annual event. During the 1950s, the Pillsbury Bake-Off Contest established itself as the most popular food competition in the United States. Home cooks looked forward to trying the most successful recipes, which were reprinted in magazines and cookbooks. Many also aspired to enter the contest with their own creations. During the decade, most entries in the contest were from-scratch cakes, followed by quick breads, pies, and cookies. In later decades, packaged ingredients, such as refrigerated dough, became more prevalent in the recipes submitted to the contest, as did the use of microwaves and other time-saving kitchen appliances. The contest remained so popular throughout the years that the reward for the winner eventually climbed to $1 million in the 1990s. It continues to be an institution in amateur cooking competitions.

Rice-A-Roni

A mixture of rice and macaroni, Rice-A-Roni is one of America's favorite side dishes. Based on an Armenian-style rice pilaf recipe, Rice-A-Roni was developed by Vince DeDomenico, a member of the family that owned the Golden Grain Macaroni Company in San Francisco. One day in the plant, Vince mixed a dry chicken soup mix with rice and vermicelli to create a product he called Rice-A-Roni. They key was to sauté the rice and pasta in butter before the liquid was added, a process that provided a distinctive flavor. The convenience of its preparation was also an advantage: it required little effort to make a heaping pan of flavored rice and macaroni. When the product was introduced in 1958 in stores in the U.S. Northwest, home cooks were delighted. What really catapulted Rice-A-Roni into America's consciousness was its catchy advertising. With its distinctive jingle and its slogan as "The San Francisco Treat," Rice-A-Roni became a product familiar to every American who watched TV or listened to the radio. The company quickly began developing new flavors and variations, such as beef, chicken, rice pilaf, and Spanish rice. Today, Golden Grain boasts dozens of flavors and whole-grain and lower-sodium versions. Many of these flavors are taken from international influences, like Chicken Teriyaki, Fried Rice, Mexican Style, and Red Beans & Rice. Golden Grain also produces Pasta Roni, a line of pasta dishes such as Fettuccini Alfredo, Stroganoff, and Angel Hair.

Saran Wrap

Designed for commercial use in 1949, Saran Wrap was introduced for household use in 1953. It is a cling wrap used for food packaging and storage, enabling cooks to wrap or cover food to protect it from oxygen, moisture, chemicals, and heat. Saran Wrap is made of polyvinylidene chloride (also known as PVDC), a compound discovered by Ralph Wiley, a Dow Chemical lab worker, in 1933. When Ralph, who cleaned glassware in the Dow Chemical lab, discovered a stubborn substance on a vial that he couldn't scrub clean, Dow researchers developed the substance into a greasy, dark film. Called Saran—which became its commercial name—the substance was then sprayed on military planes to protect them from the elements, particularly salty sea spray. The automobile industry sprayed the substance on upholstery to protect fabric. It was also used to make ventilating insoles for boots and to make high-quality doll hair. Realizing that Saran could be adapted for commercial markets, Dow Chemical got PVDC approved for use in food packaging. Dow Chemical also refined the formulation of Saran, eliminating its green hue and ridding it of its offensive odor. They then used it to create a thin, clingy plastic wrap sold in boxed rolls with a serrated edge for cutting. For homemakers in the 1950s, it quickly became a popular alternative to tin foil. When environmental concerns were raised about the use of PVDC, scientists began making plastic wrap from other substances. In 2004, the name Saran Original was changed to Saran Premium, and it was announced that Saran Wrap would be made of low-density polyethylene (LDPE). Although Saran Wrap is still a registered trademark of the Dow Chemical Company, it is recognized as a brand of S. C. Johnson & Son.

Sweet'N Low

Immediately recognizable in its bright pink packets, Sweet'N Low is a brand of artificial sweetener made up of granulated saccharin, dextrose, and cream of tartar. Since its introduction in 1957, it has been a familiar product in diners, restaurants, and homes and is frequently used in coffee and tea in lieu of sugar. Its origins can be traced back to 1945, when Ben Eisenstadt purchased a tea-bag machine, which packaged single servings of tea in paper packets, for his diner in Brooklyn, New York. Looking to find a more sanitary way to provide sugar than in a bowl, which often attracted insects and bacteria, he decided to use his tea-bag machine to create individual sugar packets. These first packets of granulated sugar caught on, and Eisenstadt even provided packets of sugar to the U.S. government for shipment to European countries recovering from the devastation of World War II. However, he had failed to patent his product, and he began to look around for other ideas for packaging opportunities. In 1956, the company began developing machines to package a range of products, including ketchup, soy sauce, and flour. In 1957, Ben and his son, Marvin, came up with a powdered sugar substitute, calling it Sweet'N Low, which is a name borrowed from Ben's favorite song, which was written by Sir Joseph Barnby in 1863. Sugar substitutes are preferable for individuals with diabetes and for dieters looking to limit their caloric intake. Interestingly, the name Sweet'N Low and the musical staff used as its symbol were given the Federal Trademark Registration No. 1,000,000. Throughout the decades after its introduction, Sweet'N Low has remained one of the top sugar substitutes in the United States and is still manufactured in Brooklyn.

Tang

An orange-flavored, noncarbonated soft drink, Tang is legendary for being the drink of the NASA space program. It is available as a powder—which is simply mixed with water—and as a liquid and provides the essential vitamins A, C, E, and B6 as well as calcium, riboflavin, and niacin. William A. Mitchell invented Tang for the General Foods Corporation in 1957, which first marketed it in 1959 in powdered form as a breakfast drink mix. It did not sell well until NASA began using it on Gemini space flights in 1965 to flavor the water to mask the flavor of certain byproducts. General Foods advertised its association with the manned spaceflight program, and sales of Tang increased dramatically. Consumers were enamored with a product used by astronauts in outer space—especially children, who became loyal customers of the orange drink that the astronauts drank. Tang can be used as a flavoring in smoothies and also in cocktails. In addition to the original orange version, General Foods has developed a range of new flavors over the years, including grape, strawberry, fruit punch, watermelon, and Jamaica Hibiscus. Some flavors are sold only in certain regions, according to regional tastes. All in all, there are 38 flavors of Tang. General Foods has also come up with a sugar-free version and has reformulated the original orange flavor to improve the taste. Today, Tang is manufactured by Kraft Foods, one of the top food manufacturing companies in the United States.

Tuna Noodle Casserole

Although there have been many variations on the traditional recipe, the traditional tuna noodle casserole contains tuna, egg noodles, cream of mushroom soup, onion, shredded cheese, and either bread crumbs or crushed potato chips sprinkled on top. Casseroles became popular in the 1950s as cooks discovered the convenience of combining meat, vegetables, noodles, and sometimes cheese into a casserole dish with little time-consuming preparation. The result was a delicious, hearty meal with little effort or time spent. The popularity of casseroles was also facilitated by the discovery that creamed soups could be effective and delicious binders in casseroles or used as sauces with meat. In the 1950s, a variety of creamed soups came on the market, and cooks began to experiment in making variations of basic casseroles with different meats, vegetables, and cheeses. In particular, Campbell's Cream of Mushroom soup turned up as a binding ingredient in a variety of different casserole dishes during the decade, including the king of casserole dishes in the 1950s: the tuna noodle casserole.

TV Cooking Shows

With the proliferation of television in the 1950s, TV cooking shows quickly became a staple of American television programming. Many American homemakers watched local and national cooking shows, which provided useful information on new recipes, cooking techniques, and trends that home cooks could use and adapt in their cooking. Shows also offered in-depth demonstrations on how to cook featured dishes, explaining complicated or confusing techniques to aspiring cooks who had never seen them done. Reading about how to make a dish in a cookbook was one thing; seeing it prepared in front of your eyes provided another perspective and level of understanding for many home cooks. Cooking shows can be traced back to the early years of television. In 1946, James Beard had a short-run show on NBC called *I Love to Eat!* which ran right before *Friday Night Boxing* from Madison Square Garden. Although the Beard's show did not last long, it spurred a number of other aspiring TV cooks and local networks to try their own versions on daytime television—when homemakers would be at home, planning their evening meals. By the early 1950s, there were cooking shows in some form in almost every television market. One of the most well-known TV cooks of the time was Josie McCarthy, who hosted a show on the NBC network. McCarthy was known for her clear explanation of complicated recipes and cooking techniques, which provided home cooks an easy-to-follow model for their own culinary experiments. Most of the recipes on TV cooking shows were fairly simple, familiar dishes—not too exotic or sophisticated for the audience. These shows were educational, but they also injected a level of confidence and inspiration for homemakers at all levels of experience. Cooking shows have proven to be an enduring genre of entertainment, eventually spawning an entire TV network, the Food Network, and motivating ensuing generations of aspiring cooks and homemakers.

TV Dinner

Called the golden age of American television, the 1950s introduced a number of classic TV programs that entertained millions of Americans. For families that once depended on the radio and reading for entertainment, the explosion of TV's popularity during the decade allowed families to sit together in front of the TV in the evening and watch much-loved programs

An aluminum tray holds a reheated frozen TV dinner, ca. 1955. TV dinners offer a quickly prepared dinner in packaging to serve conveniently in front of the television. (Stringer/Hulton Archive/Getty Images)

TV Dinners: What's on the menu?

The first TV dinner to gain popularity in the United States was the Swanson TV Dinner. In 1954, these frozen meals sold for 98 cents each. The meal consisted of turkey, cornbread stuffing, buttered peas, and sweet potatoes.

Within 10 months, Swanson had sold 10 million TV dinners. By the end of 1954, it had sold 25 million. TV dinners were a smash hit. Different varieties quickly began developing featuring fried chicken, meatloaf, and Salisbury steak.

---

such as *I Love Lucy, The Ed Sullivan Show, Dragnet,* and *Gunsmoke.* One food company, Swanson, soon realized that frozen meals served in trays and easily reheated in the oven would be a perfect alternative for harried mothers too busy to make a home-cooked meal or for families more interested in sitting in front of the TV than sitting at the dining room table. In 1954, Swanson introduced the first nationally available TV dinner: a Thanksgiving meal of turkey, cornbread dressing, frozen peas, and sweet potatoes, each placed in its own compartment in an aluminum tray. It sold for 98 cents. It proved to be a tremendous success; more than 10 million turkey TV dinners sold in the first year of production. The Swanson frozen dinner became known as a TV dinner not only because it was meant to be eaten conveniently in front of a TV, but also because the tray was shaped like a television set. The term quickly became synonymous with any prepackaged frozen meal purchased in the supermarket that came in an aluminum or plastic tray that could be heated in the oven or the microwave.

Weber Kettle Grill

A grill with a rounded bottom and lid and fit with a dome-shaped grill, the Weber Kettle Grill is one of the most popular American barbeques ever sold. The barbeque grill was invented by George Stephen Sr., who became so frustrated with the uneven flame of his old brazier grill in his backyard in Mount Prospect, Illinois, that he resolved to come up with a better one. Stephen had a background in metalworking—he was the part owner of the Weber Brothers Metal Works in Chicago—and he began experimenting with some water buoys his company produced. Determined to design a grill with a lid that would enable grillers an opportunity to grill year round, he cut one of the buoys in half: the dome-shaped bottom was the grill, and the rounded top was made into a lid that easily shut and opened.

Once he got it home and began using it, the new-fangled grill began to garner admiration from his neighbors, who called the grill Sputnik. They began to ask if they could order one of his specially designed kettle grills, and soon producing them became a full-time job. Stephen began selling them commercially in 1952, and the grill's popularity led the Weber Brothers to establish a special barbeque division. Stephen eventually bought out the business and changed the name to Weber-Stephen Products Company. As the Weber Kettle Grills became popular all over the country in the late 1950s and 1960s, the product became known simply as the Weber, which became a generic term for a barbeque grill. Weber-Stephen manufactures a range of grills today, and in 2004, it acquired some assets of the Ducane Company, including the rights to distribute Ducane grills in the United States and Canada.

Poppy Cannon White

An influential food writer and cookbook author, Poppy Cannon White was a prominent figure in American cooking in the 1950s. Born in South Africa in 1906 as Lillian Gruskin, she moved with her family to the United States in 1909. She ended up in advertising, working with a number of food companies. She also worked as a food writer, which she felt was her true calling. In 1940, she got her first full-time journalism job as a food columnist for *Mademoiselle*. She was a food editor for a number of popular magazines for women, including *Mademoiselle, Ladies Home Journal, House Beautiful*, and *Town & Country*. She was also a frequent commentator on food and cooking on TV and radio shows. In her food columns, she often advocated the use of packaged and canned foods, assuring her readers that they were just as good as homemade. If anything, she believed, a little seasoning could liven up any mixed, canned, or bottled product. Yet she made it clear that her ambition was not to create inferior food but to imitate great food. She also promoted shortcuts, proposing that finding ways to save time in the kitchen was a benefit to all cooks. She published her first cookbook, *The Can-Opener Cookbook*, in 1952. She proved to be a prolific cookbook author and had a high-profile collaboration with the writer and personality Alice B. Toklas. Her later work shifted to emphasize fresh ingredients, but she never disavowed her belief in the benefits of shortcuts and packaged products in cooking. She committed suicide in 1975.

Further Reading

Jakle, John A. and Keith A. Sculle. *Fast Food: Roadside Restaurants in the Automobile Age.* Baltimore: Johns Hopkins University Press, 1999.

Lembert, Phil. "6 Things You Need to Know about Frozen Dinners." *Today.com,* April 4, 2007. http://today.msnbc.msn.com/id/17937719/ns/today_food_and_wine-before_you_bite_with_phil_lempert/.

Shapiro, Laura. *Something from the Oven: Reinventing Dinner in 1950s America.* New York: Viking, 2004.

7

1960s

Margaret Siggillino

For the United States as a nation, the 1950s were a prosperous, stable period. The economy was doing well, and many Americans bought new houses, appliances, and cars. Families moved to the suburbs, and the nuclear family became the norm with most cooking done at home. The trend of gourmet cooking, barbequing, and the fascination for exotic foods that began in the 1950s was still going strong. However, the 1960s brought a great deal of societal and technological change. At this time, most people were happy and optimistic about the state of the world and felt things would keep getting better and better. People enjoyed things that were modern and futuristic, and this was one reason for their enjoyment of instant food. Changes that began taking place in the early 1960s included the space race, modern feminism, the environmental movement, and the civil rights movement.

During this time, the Cold War was in full effect, and the space race between the United States and the Soviet Union began in the early 1960s. Yuri A. Gagarin was the first person to go up into space and orbit the earth. The United States soon followed with astronaut Alan B. Shepard, Jr. making the first U.S. debut in space. The two countries continued to compete in space. Inventors and manufacturers of space food began to develop products such as freeze-dried food and semi liquefied food in tubes.

At the same time, the modern feminist movement began to take off with the help of Betty Friedan's book *The Feminine Mystique*, published in 1963. Her book was geared toward middle-class women who lived in the suburbs and addressed the deep-seated frustration, boredom, and depression that resulted after marrying and raising children. Many felt they had lost all identity except that of a caretaker. Friedan's book gave voice to their previously unspoken woes, and it became popular. In terms of cooking, two categories of cooks developed: those who executed complicated gourmet recipes from scratch and those who used instant, processed ingredients to make food fast. Because more and more women started working outside the home, they began to buy premade food or cook with ready-made canned or boxed ingredients to save time. Those who enjoyed cooking bought books like Julia Child's *Mastering the Art of French Cooking*. Those who did not like to cook or were afraid to cook gravitated toward less intimidating cookbooks such as the *I Hate to Cook Book* by Peg Bracken published in 1960. Bracken's cookbook was one of the first of its kind, because it provided relief for women who were tired of trying to live up to the standard of being perfect housewives. Unlike many of Julia Child's recipes, Peg Bracken's recipes were designed to be inexpensive and created with ready-made ingredients quickly and with minimum preparation.

The trend of gourmet cooking with instant foods began in the 1950s and continued into the 1960s. People wanted to learn to become gourmet cooks but not spend a lot of time and effort doing it.

People began to want to cook gourmet food for many reasons. After World War II, the American economy was booming. This new wealth brought the means to travel, and international flights were becoming more and more affordable. When people came home, many wished to re-create the dishes they tasted overseas. Food writers and cookbook authors such as M.F.K. Fisher and James Beard along with *Gourmet Magazine* helped this trend along. At first, French cuisine and Italian cooking were the most popular. These were followed by Asian cuisine, especially Chinese, Japanese and Hawaiian. Later on, Scandinavian cuisine with its smorgasbord parties and Swedish meatballs came onto the gourmet scene. Time–Life Books came out with a *Foods of the World* encyclopedia in the late 1960s. Famous writers such as M.F.K. Fisher, Julia Child, and James Beard contributed to this project. With the increased travel and exposure to other cultures, people began to take an interest in other types of cuisines including Italian, French, Spanish, Scandinavian, Asian, Indian, Middle Eastern, and South American. Whatever was deemed the most sophisticated was the most popular. Gourmet clubs developed in tandem.

In the 1960s, a new attitude developed that deemed frozen and canned convenience food better than fresh, homemade food made from scratch, because modernity and all things futuristic were prized. The image of foods being produced under sterile, scientific conditions by technician-like chefs became appealing. Thus, artificial foods and nonfoods were being produced and enjoyed by many. In 1964, General Foods created a powdered orange juice drink called Awake that was similar to the more popular Tang drink that came out a year later, which was touted as the drink astronauts consumed in space. Toppings made from artificial whipped cream came out, which were first made by mixing a boxed whipped topping mix with water and beating it until frothy. This was the predecessor to Cool Whip that was made in the 1970s. Advertisements attested that these toppings were healthier than whipped cream that had been made from real cream and that they spoiled less quickly than whipped cream.

Esther Riva Solomon legitimized and glamorized cooking gourmet dishes with ready-made ingredients in her 1963 cookbook *Instant Haute Cuisine*. She learned to make veloute, a type of gravy, while a student at Le Cordon Bleu Paris. After spending considerable time and effort making it, she realized that it tasted much like a good canned gravy she bought in the United States. After this, the quick cooking trend began, and new cookbooks came out that reflected this. They fell into three categories: gourmet, instant gourmet, and "hate to cook" cookbooks.

At about the same time, another movement took place: cooking from scratch, without using ready-made ingredients. The popularity of Julia Child's cookbook *Mastering the Art of French Cooking* and her television program helped this along, and people began to pursue cooking as a hobby. There were some naysayers to the trend of cooking gourmet with instant ingredients. In the October 1961 issue of *Esquire* magazine, Joseph Wechsberg equated instant gourmet cooks to piano students who attempt to play a Chopin piece after five lessons, whereas, with gourmet cooking, one was encouraged to take one's time to become familiar with raw ingredients and various cooking techniques. A new edition of the *Joy of Cooking* came out in 1964. It had been written originally in 1931 and had a friendly, chatty, user-friendly style that was good for the novice cook. For the more advanced cooks, anything by Julia Child, Elizabeth David, and Robert C. and Richard Olney was popular.

The average American cooked a mixture of simple dishes and multi stepped dishes prepared from scratch and did not cook French food all the time. Even though condensed soup became popular in the 1950s, it was still used as an ingredient in dishes. Dried soup mixes were used in the same manner, for example in California Dip, a sour cream dip, and in Sweepsteak, a popular recipe for foil-wrapped roasts that was included in Peggy Bracken's *I Hate to Cook* cookbook. Cocktail parties continued to be popular, but there were new snacks and hors d'oeuvres that included stuffed Edam cheese, porkers, and franks 'n' sauce.

Dips were bought premade in the supermarkets. The Ruffles potato chips and Bugles corn chips that came on the market were sturdy enough not to break when dipped. As for desserts, "gooey" desserts that brought one back to childhood were the rage. Examples of these include Jell-O cake and cheesecake with pineapple glaze. Desserts made with liquor were popular, too. These included Irish coffee pie, grasshopper pie, and Kahlua pie. Other dishes that were popular in the 1960s included beef Wellington (beef baked in a puff pastry) and green beans amandine (green beans topped with toasted almonds). Many restaurants served beef Wellington— it symbolized elegance. Gazpacho and paella were also featured menu items. Instant versions of these dishes came out. One example includes a recipe for beef Wellington as ground beef baked in a store-bought pie dough. The practice of flaming food became a fad, because it made dishes seem more sophisticated. *The Pyromaniac's Cookbook* featured recipes for flaming food, including one with baked beans and rum called Baked Beans au Glow-Glow. Upscale restaurants embraced this trend and often featured carts of flaming food pushed by costumed personnel. Cooking with liquor and drinking during and after meals gained popularity. Fondue, originally a Swiss peasant dish made with stale bread chunks dipped into a warm sauce of melted cheese and wine, was popularized by Konrad Egli, a chef at the Chalet Suisse restaurant. It was an easy-to-make dish that people ate by dipping their bread chunks into a common pot. Fondue encouraged interaction between hosts and their guests. The fad took off, and many began having fondue parties. Different variations on fondue appeared, including fondue made with beef dipped into a wine sauce and fruit dipped into chocolate sauce made at first with Toblerone chocolate.

While these three types of cooking were popular in the early 1960s— quick recipes from ready-made ingredients (Bracken), gourmet dishes with instant, ready-made ingredients (Riva Solomon), and gourmet dishes from scratch (Julia Child)—environmental consciousness was developing. During the twentieth century, there were a great many technological advances in agriculture in the form of pesticides, herbicides, hormones, and fertilizers. This enabled more crops to be grown that were less susceptible to diseases. It enabled livestock to grow bigger, which led to more meat. Small farms with varied crops began disappearing, and big factory farms that specialized in one crop took their place. Food was being processed with chemicals, and crop strains were being homogenized. With these advances came environmental and social concerns. As the population of the United States grew, so did industrial activities. With this growth came air and water pollution. People became nervous about the effects of pesticides, fertilizers, and nuclear fallout.

This new environmental consciousness was inspired by the publication of Rachel Carson's *Silent Spring* in 1962, a book that expounded upon the dangers of DDT and its long-term effects on the food supply, humans, other animals, and potentially the whole ecosystem. Although Carson wrote many other books about the environment during her career as a marine biologist, this particular book inspired many attacks and lawsuits from chemical companies. The government called her an alarmist and tried to silence her. Two other books have also had a significant influence on the public consciousness. *The Poisons in Your Food* by William F. Longgood (1960) described the perils of chemicals added to American food. In the book *Appetite for Change: How the Counterculture Took on the Food Industry, 1966–1988,* Walter Belasco describes how many different groups and individuals began to protest big food corporations and the government

Scientist and author of *Silent Spring* Rachel Carson speaks to a Senate Government Operations subcommittee to discuss pesticides in 1963. (Library of Congress)

subsidies they were receiving. During this time, the practice of organic farming grew popular. Jerome I. Rodale created a system in 1940 in which he stressed the importance of the biological control of pests without chemicals and encouraged the practices of composting and soil building. He advocated a return to small-scale farming, growing food to be consumed locally to cut down on the pollution created by trucking and shipping foodstuffs long distances.

Many individuals who were environmentally conscious and in the counterculture movement chose not to consume food that was grown or processed with chemicals. Although it was cheaper for Americans to buy food during the postwar years, the quality of that food was not as good because cheaper artificial flavorings and preservatives were being used. Many foods commonly available were now marketed as frozen, canned, or boxed products. The health food movement began—an anti establishment movement against society, parents, and those who cook instant gourmet dishes with artificial foods and preservative-laden ingredients. Growing and eating organic produce were in vogue. People also consumed raw milk products, brown rice, yogurt, brewer's yeast, wheat germ, sunflower seeds, blackstrap molasses, honey, different types of sprouts, and anything made with wheat flour. Hippies opened food co-ops and tried to recreate what they thought food tasted like before food production and farming became industrialized. They also baked their own bread. Hippies were not interested in eating the same foods their parents did. They stopped consuming bread and other products made from white flour, white sugar, margarine, canned vegetables, processed cheese, condensed soups, and instant white rice as well as other instant products. After a while, major corporations in the food establishment began to take notice and made pronouncements that organic farming would cause famines; these establishments were openly skeptical of the true nutritional benefits of organic food. For supporters of health food, the nutritious and "natural" aspect of foods trumped the factor of good taste. Many in the movement did not know how to cook.

Another sort of anti establishment movement arose in 1961: the Civil Rights Movement. The speeches of Martin Luther King, Jr. inspired many. John F. Kennedy became president and passed legislation to ban discrimination based on race. The Civil Rights March occurred in Washington in 1963, and Blacks, joined by many Whites, demonstrated for improvements in rights and equality. About 250,000 people in all staged demonstrations to dramatize their demands for rights and equality. After John F. Kennedy was assassinated in 1963, Lyndon B. Johnson became president and passed many more civil rights laws, including the Civil Rights Act of 1964, which outlawed discrimination in employment and public areas. The Civil Rights Act of 1968 was passed to end discrimination in housing sales and property rentals. Johnson's war on poverty helped to provide financial aid to the needy. Despite the government aid, poverty was still an issue. In the mid-1960s, there were riots in poor African American neighborhoods in New York City, Newark, Los Angles, Chicago, Detroit, Cleveland, and other cities. When Martin Luther King, Jr. was assassinated in 1968, there was more rioting. Around this time, other minority groups such as the Mexican Americans, American Indians, and women began to demand equal rights.

African Americans aimed to get in touch with their roots in the late 1960s when the Black Power Movement began. Chemically straightened hair was out, and Afros were in. Western clothing was replaced by African clothing. Soul food and southern food were basically the same thing. Examples of soul food dishes include cornbread, ham hocks, collard greens, chitterlings, black-eyed peas, BBQ ribs, and fried chicken. Hippies and gourmet cooks took an interest in this kind of food and began to go to soul food restaurants and try to cook soul food dishes for themselves. By the end of the 1960s, the country was divided politically and culinarily. Cooks no longer prepared their moms' and grandparents' food. Most regional dishes were lost. Sometimes, they were made for special occasions.

Entries

Alice's Restaurant Cookbook

Alice May Brock, originally from Brooklyn, moved to Great Barrington, Massachusetts, because she did not enjoy living in the city. During her youth, she was a rebellious teenager who kept getting in trouble and ended up going to a reform school in Hawthorne, New York. While there, she became a sous chef in the school's kitchen. Soon after she moved to Massachusetts, she found a job as a librarian at the Stockbridge School. She met a student there, Ray Brock, in 1961, got married, and moved to a church that they bought a few years later using the $2,000 given to Alice by her mother. She opened a small restaurant six miles away from the church in April 1966. Alice's Restaurant became famous because of the song of that name written by Arlo Guthrie, which detailed the saga of his trying to do a good deed for Alice, being arrested, and managing to avoid being drafted into the Vietnam War. The song and the restaurant became famous because they reflected the clashes of the counter-cultural hippies and the establishment. From the popular song came a movie called

Alice's Restaurant. The *Alice's Restaurant Cookbook* was published by Random House in 1969 and contained recipes and pictures with humorous, free-spirited advice that encouraged her readers to relax and enjoy cooking and not be intimidated by foreign cooking or get bogged down by rules. Alice wrote that "recipes aren't as important as the philosophy behind them.... Good food is food you eat with your friends, ... everybody ... having a good time is the key to a successful meal." She also wrote: "Other books say, 'Do not, do not! Do not try to make a soufflé unless you have a soufflé dish.' They make cooking sound like a fantastic science, and that makes a lot of people afraid to cook." She encouraged people to improvise and advised her readers to use car hubcaps lined with tin foil if they ran out of plates. She also advised: "You have to have one really big pot, something you can boil macaroni and rice in, wash your dog in. Get one that's big enough so that a mop will fit." She also said that "wine and liquor are great for cooking, and also for the cook. In fact, more important for the cook than for cooking." She tells her readers to advertise and tell others how great their cooking is: "If you tell people that what you're cooking is absolutely fantastic—if you squeeze their arm and whisper in their ear that this meal is the greatest yet—they're going to love it. They'll never suspect that that strange taste in the potatoes is just that you've burned them." Brock encouraged her readers to use fresh, natural foods instead of the canned vegetables and processed food many were raised on. She also urged her readers to bake bread and to learn to garden.

Examples of her dishes include basics such as beef Stroganoff, chicken Kiev, mussels steamed in white wine, olive oil and garlic, and English trifle. Her Mexican Heartburnger is a bit more unusual: it is made with two pounds of meat and a half a box of bay leaves. She also tells her readers that if they happen to enjoy eating shrimp with chocolate sauce, then "it's good." The décor of her restaurant included an old sneaker on the table filled with flowers. People tended to dress down when they went to her restaurant; they could come as they were. This was a relatively new concept back then. Her restaurant had stops and starts, but it has inspired the opening of similar Alice's Restaurants in other parts of the country.

Arby's

The idea for this restaurant chain began in 1949 when two brothers, Forrest and Leroy Raffel, bought their uncle's restaurant equipment business in Youngstown, Ohio. This business exposed them to the restaurant trade and its many trends. They sought a more upscale niche in the fast-food industry selling something other than hamburgers. The idea for Arby's came to them while waiting in line to buy roast beef sandwiches at a popular sandwich shop, and they decided to base their menu on selling that one item. They created the name Arby's by combining the initials of Raffel Brothers, the name of their restaurant equipment business, into Arby's. The first Arby's restaurant opened in 1964 in Boardman, Ohio. They wanted to evoke an old Western feel, so the restaurant was decorated with wood and stone décor. The Arby's sign was neon and shaped like a 10-gallon hat. Their menu contained 69-cent roast beef sandwiches, iced tea, and potato chips. During this time, hamburgers were around 19 cents each. Later on, Arby's added curley fries, fresh wraps, chicken sandwiches and Reuben turkey sandwiches to the menu. Soon after opening, they franchised the restaurant. The Royal Crown Cola Company in Atlanta, Georgia, bought the restaurant chain in 1976, and it became international in 1981, when they opened the franchise in Tokyo. There were about 2,000 Arby's restaurants throughout the world by 1988. Arby's decided to lighten up its menu in 1991 and began offering low-calorie meals to their consumers. In 1996, Arby's bought the TJ Cinnamon Classic Bakery chain, which offered desserts, snacks, and breakfast foods. The Arby's restaurant chain became the Arby's/TJ Cinnamon in 1997.

Buffalo Wings

Buffalo wings were invented by Teressa Bellisimo in Buffalo, New York, at the Anchor Bar on October 30, 1964. There are three different views of what may have inspired Bellisimo to invent this dish: the wings may have been a snack for Teressa's son and his friends; they may have been created for Catholic bar customers, who wished to break their meatless Friday night at midnight Saturday morning; or Teressa may have been trying to use up wings delivered to her by accident. At first, these wings were broiled. Later they were deep fried. The buffalo wing cooking continued to evolve, and John Young, an African-American cook, became famous in Buffalo for breading the wings first, deep frying them, and then serving them with a spicy "mambo" sauce. Buffalo wings are made by dividing the wings into two pieces, deep frying, and coating them with a mildly hot oily sauce. They are served with celery sticks and blue cheese dressing on the side. The dish first came to national attention in 1980 with an article written by Calvin Trillin for *The New Yorker* magazine. The Hooter's national restaurant chain began serving the wings in 1983. Pizza Hut and Domino's pizza followed suit in the 1990s. Television commercials created by these companies aired during sporting events. This is how buffalo wings came to be associated with watching sports on television. Buffalo wings are still served at two bars in Buffalo, the original Anchor Bar and another bar named Duff's.

Counterculture Food

In 1968, the term "counterculture" came into existence. This antiestablishment movement championed the struggle for women's rights, civil rights, consumer rights, and workers' rights; the movement also opposed the Vietnam War, the government, and the capitalist system as a whole. The hippie and new age movements grew out of this. Communes, food co-ops, urban gardens, health food stores, and green markets also began to blossom at this time. Counterculture foods included organic fruits and vegetables, brown rice, nuts, seeds, herbal teas, beans, soy products, dried fruit, granola, honey, whole-grain bread, natural cheese, yogurt, juices, and vitamin and mineral dietary supplements. The counterculture discouraged meat consumption because of the ecological damage it caused and the waste involved in its growth and production. The teachings of Buddhism and Hinduism, popular during the time, were also used to discouraged meat consumption. Submovements and diets sprang out of this movement, including a purifying macrobiotic diet based on Taoist principles. Many believed that this primarily vegetarian diet could help the world as a whole. Euell Gibbons' book *Stalking the Wild Asparagus* (1962) helped the idea of foraging for food catch on; this idea was incorporated into subsequent natural food and vegetarian movements. The counterculture movement continued into the 1970s. Popular commune-based, natural-foods cookbooks published during that time include *The Commune Cookbook* (1972) by Crescent Dragonwagon and *Eat It: A Cookbook* (1974) by Dana Crumb and Sherry Cohen. In the 1970s, the counterculture food movement caught the attention of the mainstream. Feeling threatened, the big corporations either put down the food countercultural followers or tried to mimic countercultural food products by manufacturing their own natural-food products to blur the distinction between the countercultural and the establishment. Despite this, the countercultural food continued to evolve and move on. Some companies begun back then are still in business. One example is the Celestial Seasonings tea company started in 1969.

Issues raised by the counterculture food movement persist in concerns about the globalization of food and the resistance to genetically modified foods. In 1986, Carlo Petrini launched the slow food movement, which embodies many of the original concerns, as a response to the opening of a McDonald's restaurant in Rome. It is dedicated to saving America's food heritage and to supporting and celebrating the food traditions of North America. Slow Food USA encourages the organic movement and supports the raising of old livestock breeds and heirloom fruit and vegetable varieties, as well as the production of handcrafted wine and beer, farmhouse cheeses, and other artisanal foods that are at risk of succumbing to the effects of culinary industrialization and degradation of farmland.

Flaming Foods

The practice of flaming foods—officially called flambé—came into vogue in the 1960s. Different types of foods and dishes were set alight to make them seem sophisticated and spectacular. Liquor is poured onto food and set alight soon after it is added to a hot pan; it is then brought to the table. It is done for show and to impress guests. The Moors originated this practice in the fourteenth century. Flaming, as it was done in the 1960s, had its origins in Monte Carlo in 1895 when a waiter, Henri Carpentier, set fire

Foods served flambé became the rage during the 1960s, though its origins date back to 1895. (Shutterstock)

to crepes he had prepared for Edward VII of England. Although it was an accident, igniting the sauce on the crepes created a pleasing and unique taste. Alcohols such as rum, cognac, brandy, sherry, and whiskey are used in flaming because they contain about 20 to 40 percent alcohol. Different liquors were chosen to enhance the food they were flaming. Whiskeys were often used for poultry and fish dishes, and sweet liqueurs for desserts. To enchance the color and the size of the flames, salt was added to savory dishes and sugar to desserts. This was a trend in the gourmet cooking era in the 1960s. In restaurants and in homes, various dishes, desserts, and beverages were flamed. These included meats, crepes, omelets, and side dishes such as beans and even cocktails. People experimented and tried to flame other types of food from soup to salad and even ice. These attempts did not typically succeed. Upscale restaurants such as The Pump Room in Chicago jumped on the flaming trend. They had various carts used for flaming. Ernest Byfield, the restaurant owner stated, "We serve almost anything flambé in that room. It doesn't hurt the food much." *The Pyromaniac's Cookbook,* published in 1968, taught home cooks the art of flaming and provided many recipes for flaming food from entrees to desserts. Examples of popular flambé desserts include Bananas Foster, Bombe Alaska, and Crepes Suzette. A few accidents occurred during flaming. Housewives have accidently set their hair or their clothes on fire. Sometimes diners were burned by the flaming items on their tables. Eventually, the flambé trend fizzled out.

Fondue

Fondue is a Swiss cheese melted in white wine and other ingredients in a chafing dish, fondue pot, or electric saucepan. The Swiss invented fondue during the 18th century. The Swiss winters were long and cold, and the Swiss sustained themselves eating bread and cheese that were made during the warmer months. They found that stale bread and cheese tasted better when heated. Cheese was melted in a pot over fire, and the bread was dipped into it, making the bread softer. As this dish evolved, white wine and other flavorings were eventually added to the melted cheese to improve the taste. Fondue was probably eaten out of one pot around a table because poorer Swiss villagers did not have enough plates and cutlery for each person. They also huddled around the fire to stay warm. Depending on the type of fondue that was served, "dunkables" included French bread, fruit, meat, or pieces of cake. The dish was introduced in the United States at the Chalet Suisse restaurant in New York by Konrad

Egli. Although fondue made its debut in the 1950s, it became popular in the 1960s. Different types of fondue evolved beyond the original recipe made with Swiss cheese. Variations include the following types of fondue: beef bourguignon, chocolate and other sweet sauces, and different types of broth. Fondue parties were a trend in the late 1960s. Guests would do their own cooking. The host would set up the fondue pot on a coffee table or a regular table. Guests would sit around the table and dip their bread, fruit, cake, or meat into the fondue pot with a fork or a skewer. A green salad and wine or other beverages were served on the side. This type of party was popular for single or married women to throw because it was quick and easy to put together. It did not require much time in the kitchen, and it encouraged hosts and guests to interact. This fit in with the communal culture of that period. Around 37 varieties of fondue pots were available in the United States during that time. Cheese used for fondues included emmentaler, gruyere, beaufort, comte, and fribourg. These cheeses can be mixed. Garlic, nutmeg, salt, and pepper were common seasonings to add to the mix. Egli and employees of Toblerone Chocolate invented chocolate fondue for dipping pieces of bread and fruit. Other cooks invented different varieties of dessert dipping sauces, which included strawberry, lemon, and butterscotch.

Gatorade

The inspiration for the invention of Gatorade began in the form of a question. In the summer of 1965, Dwayne Douglas, the assistant football coach for the Gators at the University of Florida, noticed that his players lost a great deal of weight during practice but did not feel the need to urinate. He then met with a team of university physicians to inquire about how his players were affected by heat and why they were afflicted with heat-related illnesses. Robert Cade, a kidney disease specialist, decided to investigate the problem and invited research fellows Dana Shires, Jim Free, and A.M. DeQuesada to join his quest in researching the effects of heat on the human body. They determined that sweat contained potassium and sodium in the form of electrolytes. They theorized that when the players sweat during games and practice, they were being robbed of their energy, endurance, and strength by the loss of these electrolytes, which are responsible for keeping the body in balance. Oddly enough, during this time, sports team players were encouraged to abstain from drinking water or other liquids because it was thought to cause stomach cramps and nausea. To determine the validity of this theory, Cade obtained football coach Ray Graves's permission to collect samples from a freshman football team. It was found that the players' blood sugar was low, their blood volume was low, and their electrolytes were completely out of balance. Heat exhaustion caused many players to collapse. Cade decided to put salt and little bit of sugar in the water for the players to drink. Cade's wife added lemon juice to improve the taste of the drink. They called the drink Gatorade. Over time, the fluid evolved into a formula of glucose, fructose, sucrose, potassium, and sodium. During one game, freshmen were given the drink, and their performance improved noticeably against the opposing team, who were not given the solution. Graves observed and then asked Cade for some of the drink for the varsity team to use for a game the next day against the Louisiana State University team. By 1966, this drink was given to all of the players at the University of Florida. Over the next five years, only one player had to go to the hospital for heat exhaustion treatment—a big improvement over the 17 who were admitted during the first month of that first year. In 1967, Stokely-Van Camp Co. began producing Gatorade. Production began after a conversation between one of Cade's research fellows, who accepted a position at Indiana University, and the vice president of the company. Soon after, sales of Gatorade skyrocketed. After dealing with a series of legal disputes, the University of Florida and Cade's research team—The Gatorade Trust— began to receive royalties in 1973. The Quaker Oats company bought Stokely-Van Camp in 1983, and then Gatorade became famous with endorsements from athlete Michael Jordan. From then on, Gatorade became the standard sports beverage. Quaker Oats created the Gatorade Sports Science Institute, funded for scientists to research the effects of exercise, nutrition, and the environment on the human body.

Gourmet Food

Gourmet food and gourmet cooking gained popularity in the early 1960s. Before then, many dishes were made using instant or ready-made ingredients. The movement really began to take off in 1962 when Julia Child's television show *The French Chef* began airing on a Cambridge, Massachusetts, television station. The show was based on the recipes in *Mastering the Art of French Cooking*, a book which was written by Julia Child, Simone Beck, and Lousiest Berthold and published in 1961. Child's unpolished, informal, and enthusiastic approach inspired many Americans to attempt to cook French dishes themselves. People began cooking dishes such as beef bourguignon, beef Wellington, green beans amandine, and chocolate mousse on a more regular basis. People began to also experiment with eating and preparing foods from other countries. During this time, more people were affluent and tended to travel abroad. This helped foster a desire to recreate at home the dishes they experienced abroad. Magazines and newspapers began to include more exotic recipes. Gourmet food and international food were synonymous. Dishes that were considered peasant food in some countries, such as homemade pasta, fondue, and soufflé, were seen as gourmet dishes in the United States. Exotic ingredients became more widely available throughout the country. There were always some small specialty stores that carried ingredients from particular countries. However, gourmet stores were opening up at a rapid rate. International Safeway, a supermarket that carried ingredients from around the world, opened in Washington, DC, in 1964. When it first opened, foreigners and party planners shopped there, soon followed by first- or second-generation Americans who wanted to be able to cook like their ancestors. Then, average Americans began making forays. Exotic meats such as tiger and kangaroo were stocked there along with fruits, breads, cheeses, honey, and spices. Cooking schools were growing in popularity during the 1960s. People could attend classes to learn how to create French, Italian, Japanese, Chinese, and Indian dishes and more. Baking classes were also available.

I Hate to Cook Book

Peg Bracken, a copywriter at an advertising agency, published the *I Hate to Cook Book* in 1960. This was different from other cookbooks that came out during that time and was inspired by a conversation she had while lunching with friends, "all of whom hated to cook but have to. . . . We decided to pool our ignorance, tell each other our shabby little secrets, and toss into the pot the recipes we swear by instead of swear at." Bracken's book was written in a wry, humorous style that directly addressed those women, particularly in the suburbs, who secretly hated to engage in daily monotonous domestic duties. There was societal pressure on women to be good at domestic duties. Not being good at such duties was equated with not being womanly. This was reflected in the media, especially in magazine articles and cookbooks. Bracken's message to women was radical during that time, telling women that cooking did not define them or determine their status in the household. Her recipes were designed to be fast and easy. She pointed out that her recipes were not " . . . tested by experts. That is why they are valuable . . . Even we can make these taste good." The recipe titles were humorous and so were the instructions. She instructed women in her recipe for Skid Row Stroganoff to "add the flour, salt, paprika, and mushrooms, stir, and let it cook five minutes while you light a cigarette and stare sullenly at the sink." Other recipes included were Stayabed Stew, Sole Survivor, and Sweep Steak. Most of her dishes were made with canned and processed food. The book was immediately popular and rapidly became a bestseller, because during the 1960s, about two-thirds of women were working outside the home. Women were tired and frazzled when they came home from work and "didn't want to spend endless hours in the kitchen." They prepared dinners from "convenience products." Women "who found themselves trapped in an endless whirlwind of domestic chaos" felt tremendous relief when this cookbook was published, because there was still a societal pressure for women to remain in the traditional familial role.

Instant Mashed Potatoes

Instant mashed potatoes came into vogue during this time when instant food was seen as chic. Like other instant foods, they were mass produced in factories. First, the potatoes were washed several times in water and then steamed to soften the skins. The skins were then removed by churning the potatoes in a rotating drum with steel bars on the inside. Then, the potatoes went to an assembly line, where workers removed the potato eyes by hand. After that, the potatoes were sliced in one-half-inch pieces and put into a pre-cooker and then a steam-cooker. Soon after, they were mashed and then dried into flakes. These flakes were used to make instant mashed potatoes; they were also used in other recipes, from savory items to desserts. One popular recipe was frosted meatloaf. Instant mashed potatoes were spread onto baked meatloaf as icing frosted a cake. Other recipes followed similar trends, including one for Snow-Capped Casserole, a mashed potato-covered casserole. Instant potatoes were used in fancier dishes such as Potato Clouds. This was a soufflé made with potatoes and cottage cheese served with sour cream and onions on top. These were typical side dishes. Instant mashed potatoes were even used in desserts. A couple of examples include Potato Doughnuts and a recipe for Pecan Crescents, a cookie made with instant mashed potatoes, pecans, and vanilla.

Julia Child

Julia Child was born as Julia McWilliams in an upper-class family in Pasadena, California. She met her husband Paul Child while posted in Asia working for the Office of Strategic Services during World War II.

Julia Child displays the Salade Niçoise she prepared in the kitchen of her vacation home in Grasse, southern France, on August 21, 1978. Julia Child made French cuisine accessible to American cooks through her cookbook, *Mastering the Art of French Cooking*. (AP/Wide World Photos)

Her culinary career began at the age of 37, when the Childs moved to Paris, and she enrolled in the Cordon Bleu cooking school. Julia Child became famous in 1961 for writing her first cookbook, *Mastering the Art of French Cooking*, with two Frenchwomen, Simone Beck and Louisette Bertholle. Although the book took more than 10 years to publish and was first rejected by a publisher, this best-selling cookbook was the first to popularize the principles of French cooking to an American audience. It contained detailed step-by-step instructions and took into account ingredients available to the average American. This detailed style set a precedent for future cookbooks of different ethnic cuisines. Beginning in 1963 and lasting until 1973, Child had her own television show on a Boston public television station. Her clumsy, down-to-earth style combined with her solid knowledge of classical French cooking techniques attracted an audience of cooks and non cooks alike; many watched it for the entertainment value alone. She introduced average Americans to simple classical French dishes and to the concept of foreign ingredients and specialty equipment.

Because of her show, cooking went from being seen as drudgery to something fun. This inspired many to enroll in cooking schools and buy special cooking utensils and other cookbooks. She helped to elevate the status of the culinary profession in the United States and contributed to its development. She was primarily an educator, and she was crucial to the formation of the American Institute of Wine and Food and the International Association of Culinary Professionals. Although she was devoted primarily to the home cook, she helped to mentor professional chefs and women in the field. When her second book, *The French Chef Cookbook*, was published in 1968, many Americans were enjoying cooking French.

Pop-Tarts

Kellogg's Pop-Tarts made their debut in 1964. Pop-Tarts are actually based on Country Squares, a similar product that Post created in 1963. This was part of a long-term goal set by Post, which was to develop non cereal products after World War II that did not require refrigeration. These products included the orange-flavored beverage called Tang and Gaines-Burgers dog food. Based on the same principles, Post then developed an enclosed, flat, fruit-filled pastry that did not require refrigeration. The pastries were designed to accompany Post's cold cereals and were enclosed in foil packaging to keep from spoiling. Post mistakenly informed the press about the product six months before it was ready to go public. Kellogg's—Post's biggest competitor—took advantage of this blunder and quickly created its own version. The name Pop-Tarts was inspired by the pop art movement occurring during that time. Pop-Tarts were first sold in the grocery stores in Cleveland, Ohio. Kellogg's instructed store managers to stock the Pop-Tarts in the baked goods or baking supplies aisle and not in the cereal aisle, because they did not want Pop-Tarts to be substituted for cereal. Pop-Tarts rapidly grew popular because of a television commercial for them that featured a talking cartoon toaster named Milton. Pop-Tarts are in size thin enough to fit into a toaster. Originally, they were unfrosted and came in four varieties: strawberry, blueberry, brown sugar cinnamon, and apple currant. Since then, their flavor offerings have expanded to chocolate chip, French toast, s'mores, and many more. Some varieties were frosted on the outside, and sprinkles were added to others. Although Pop-Tarts were designed to pop out of the toaster when toasting finished, some did not. This led to unfortunate accidents causing trapped Pop-Tarts to ignite their toasters. In 1992, Thomas Nangle sued Kellogg's for damages because of this. This highly publicized case led to experiments by the humorist Dave Barry and Texas A&M University Professor Joseph Delgado. Many subsequent lawsuits followed before this warning was placed on the box: "Due to possible risk of fire, never leave your toasting appliance or microwave unattended."

Slurpee

The Slurpee was created from an accident by the owner of a Dairy Queen in Kansas, Omar Knedlik, in the late 1950s. He began storing bottles of soda in the freezer because his soda machine was not working. He left the soda in the freezer a little too long, and it became partially frozen. When he served it to his customers, they raved about it. He then became inspired to invent a machine to create the carbonated concoction. He began working with a Dallas industrial manufacturer that was trying to develop a way to get air conditioning in cars to see if they could assist in developing his machine. Knedlik used this technology to develop the ICEE machine during a five-year period. The convenience store bought three machines in 1965. Bob Stanford, a 7-Eleven company employee, came up with the name Slurpee in 1967 at an advertising meeting because of the sound the drink made when sipped through a straw. At first, the Slurpee machines were kept behind a counter; they became self-serve units later. Now, there are more than 200 flavors of Slurpees ranging from cherry to mochaccino. Most Slurpees are sold during the summer months. A straw-spoon was created to help patrons consume the Slurpee. Many young people throughout the decades grew to love Slurpees and drank them so quickly they developed a BrainFreeze—that term is now a 7-Eleven trademark. Smoothies and Starbuck's Frappucino have developed from the same idea.

Soul Food

During the racial strife of the Civil Rights Movement in the 1960s, African Americans demonstrated renewed pride and interest in the documentation of their recipes and foodways. Soul food had been considered Southern food—the African influence was so tightly interwoven into the fabric of American cuisine, it had not been noticed. The use of the word "soul" to describe the state of "Blackness" arose in the 1930s. The word "soul" was applied to anything African American, from "soul music" to "soul food." The use of the term "soul food" dates from 1964. Soul food—the food from the days of slavery and poverty—became all the rage and there was great interest in the study of African culture and cooking, not only among African Americans, but also with society at large—especially White liberal cooks. In the late 1960s, the Black Power movement emerged. African Americans wanted to get in touch with their African roots and stop attempting to imitate the ways of White American society. African slaves brought their culinary know-how and managed to bring seeds for some of their produce to the United States during their perilous journey from West Africa. Those who worked in the kitchens of their owners in the 13 colonies introduced their methods of cooking and some of the ingredients. Those who worked in the fields cooked greens, fried chicken, salted pork, barbequed food, corn dishes (for example, cornmeal mush, hoecakes, and cornbread), sweet potatoes, and other types of meat or fish that they happened to catch. African Americans have written cookbooks since the 1800s. In 1962, *Ebony* magazine columnist Freda DeKnight's cookbook was republished as *The Ebony Cookbook: A Date with a Dish: A Cookbook of American Negro Recipes*. The first commercial use of "soul food" in a book title was *Soul Food Cookery* (1968) by Inez Yeargan Kaiser. A revised edition, also published in 1968, carried the title *The Original Soul Food Cookery*, perhaps to distinguish Kaiser's work from other similarly named volumes. Gourmet home chefs who tired of cooking other types of exotic food wanted to try something new. European Americans began venturing into places like Harlem and Watts to try soul food restaurants. Slvia's was and still is a popular soul food restaurant in Harlem. Hippies involved in the anti-establishment flower power movement also embraced soul food. Though many thought it was unhealthy, many associated it with those that were poor and oppressed, and this made it seem more authentic. White middle- and upper-middle-class people had trouble embracing all of it, especially chitterlings, pigs' feet, pigs' tails, and possum.

Space Food

The development and evolution of space food came about when John Glenn took a five-hour flight into space on February 20, 1962, during Project Mercury. He was the first American who orbited the earth and ate in space. Since space lacks gravity, this posed unprecedented challenges. For example, crumbs from food can float in the air and have the potential to damage equipment, which is what happened at first. Astronauts ate bite-sized cubes, freeze-dried powders, and tubes of semi liquefied food. The astronauts found it unappetizing, experienced difficulties in rehydrating the freeze-dried foods, and did not like having to squeeze tubes or collect crumbs,

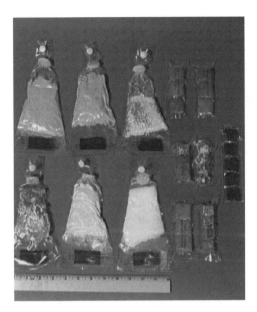

NASA displays samples of food used by Mercury astronauts, ca. 1952. Packages contain dehydrated soups and juices, fruits, vegetables, and meats in specific proportions for maintaining nutritional balance while in space. (NASA Johnson Space Center)

and the food did not taste good. A Paradoxically, weight was also a problem in space. During subsequent journeys, the food quality was improved. During the Gemini program in 1965, food cubes coated with gelatin to prevent crumb dissipation replaced aluminum tubes. Freeze-dried food was rehydrated, and food choices were expanded to include desserts. Astronauts were allowed to choose their meals, as long as the calories added up to 2,800 calories per day with a precise ratio of protein, fat, and carbohydrate per meal. In the late 1960s with the Apollo and Skylab moon programs, the food got better. Astronauts began to carry "spoon bowls," pressurized plastic containers that could be opened with a plastic zipper and the contents eaten with a spoon. Because it had a high moisture content, the food clung to the spoon, making eating seem closer to the earthbound experience. During the Apollo program, freeze-dried ice cream was provided on one flight, but this product was abandoned because it was not at all like ice cream. Freeze-dried ice cream, however, is sold as space food in the gift shops and visitor centers of the U.S. National Aeronautics and Space Administration (NASA). The Skylab program in 1973 and 1974 had larger spacecraft and vast culinary improvements over menus used in the Apollo, Gemini, and Mercury flights. Unlike previous space vessels, Skylab had enough space for a dining table—essentially a pedestal on which food trays were mounted. Conventional knife, fork, and spoon were used, as were scissors for cutting open plastic seals. The spacecraft featured amenities such as a freezer for filet mignon and vanilla ice cream and a refrigerator for chilling fresh fruits and vegetables. Results of Skylab experiments showed a need for changing the nutritional content of space foods. After long periods in space, astronauts lose calcium and other vital minerals, so all future menus reflected these needs. Over time, space food specifications were refined. Less crumb-prone food is favored; for example, flour tortillas are used instead of bread for the most part. Salt, pepper, and other spices are liquefied to prevent particles from floating around.

Taco Bell

The idea for the Mexican-American fast-food chain got its start when Glenn Bell, owner of a hamburger and hot dog stand in San Bernardino, California, noticed that there were many taco stands in that area. He liked eating food from these taco stands but began to wonder if he could apply the principles of fast food to improve the speed and efficiency of the Mexican taco stand food and make it into fast food. Bell invented a hard taco shell. Before then, hard taco shells were made by frying soft tacos. He found that having a ready-made hard taco shell saved time. He soon began to find more ways to speed up service. In 1954, Bell opened the Taco Tia restaurant and began opening more branches in other nearby areas. Soon after, Bell sold this group of restaurants and then teamed up with some partners to create the El Taco restaurant chain. The first El Taco opened in 1958 in Long Beach, California. Finally, Bell sold his stake in El Taco to his partners and opened Taco Bell in Downey, California. His menu contained tacos, burritos, and drinks. Soon after, Bell opened eight stores in Los Angeles, Paramount, and Long Beach and turned his chain into a franchise. The restaurant exteriors were California-mission-style. These establishments generated $50,000 per year, and Bell decided to franchise the operation. The resulting Taco Bell chain used the symbol of a sleeping Mexican sitting under a sombrero. The chain expanded to 868 restaurants in 1978. Soon after, Bell sold his franchise to PepsiCo. The franchise was then managed by John Martin, who had worked for many fast-food companies. He began serving discounted value meals and kept introducing new products such as wraps, fajitas, gorditas, and chalupas. By 1980, the chain has 1,333 franchises. Currently, the franchise has around 6,400 branches in the United States. In 1997, the Taco Bell franchise became a part of Yum! Brands Inc. Yum! also owns KFC, A&W restaurants, Pizza Hut, and Long John Silver's. Before the 1950s, most Americans were not familiar with Mexican food until Glenn Bell established his restaurant chain.

Time–Life's Foods of the World Series

Time–Life Books published its Foods of the World series in 1968 in a 27-volume set. Each volume was written by famous food writers during that time. The history and culture of each cuisine were included in each volume along with authentic recipes. During this time, many Americans were interested in recreating international dishes at home after traveling to different parts of the country and the world. The set of books consisted of seven volumes dedicated to American regional cooking (Schact, 1969). These included *Creole and Acadian, The Eastern Heartland, The Great West, The Melting Pot, New England, The Northwest,* and *Southern Style*. Nine volumes were dedicated to Europe. Each title began with the words *The Cooking of . . . .,* and the set included *The British Isles, Scandinavia, Provincial France, Germany, Italy, Spain & Portugal, Vienna's Empire, Russian Cooking,* and *Classical French*. The rest were as follows: *African Cooking, The Foods of Latin America, Middle Eastern Cooking, Pacific and Southeast Cooking, A Quintet of Cuisines,* and *Wines and Spirits*. Notable volumes published in 1968 include *American Cooking* by Dale Brown, *The Cooking of Provincial France* by M. F. K. Fisher, *The Cooking of Italy* by Waverley Root, and *The Cooking of Vienna's Empire* by Joseph Wechsberg. This was the first series of books of its kind.

Vegetarianism

Vegetarianism became popular in the 1960s during a time when conventional American values were being examined and called into question. Some members of the counterculture saw a vegetarian diet as a way to improve one's health, help fight hunger in the United States and around the world, and practice compassion. Vegetarianism is nothing new in the United States or the history of the world at large; it existed in ancient Greek times and became popular throughout various periods of world history. In the western world, it began with the mathematician Pythagoras, who founded the first vegetarian society in the sixth century BCE. He believed in having compassion for animals and did not approve of the widely practiced rites of animal sacrifice—a part of Greek religious rites. Like the Buddhists, the Pythagoreans also believed that animals have souls and that those souls would transmigrate into the bodies of other living creatures. Other ancient vegetarians include Socrates, Empedocles, Plato, Epicurus, and Plotinus. Pythagoreanism arrived in the United States in 1817 when William Metcalfe came from England to start the first vegetarian church in the United States. In the early 1840s in England, the term "vegetarian" was coined. This church survived into the early 1900s. Famous vegetarians in early American history include Ben Franklin and Benjamin Lay. In 1960, H. Jay Dinshah started the American Vegan Society. One reason that vegetarianism became popular during that time is because of the influence of Asian religions that became popular in the United States. For example,

Taoism brought in the concept of macrobiotics; diet was based on principles of yin and yang. Other influences include the Hare Krishnas (a East Indian Hindu sect) and the practices of yoga and Zen. This is because in Buddhist religions, eating animals created a block from enlightenment because it harms living creatures. China and Japan temple cuisine introduced Americans to mock meats made of wheat gluten and soy. Influential vegetarian cookbooks began to surface. Examples include *The Vegan Kitchen* (1966), written by Freya Dinshah. Some members of the counterculture saw a vegetarian diet as a way to improve one's health and help fight hunger in the United States and around the world. The popularity of the vegetarian diet during the 1960s was not necessarily revolutionary. The lifestyle had been embraced as far back as the times of Greek mathematician Pythagoras. In fact, vegetarians had been called "Pythagoreans" until the 19th century. The 1960s' American counterculture philosophy of embracing peace can be seen as an analog to the ancient Buddhist practice of vegetarianism for the sake of not harming other living beings.

Weight Watchers

Weight Watchers started when Jean Nidetch, a 35-year-old housewife from Queens, New York, was trying to lose weight but couldn't. She was 5'7" and weighed 214 pounds. After trying many different diets, she enrolled in the New York City Department of Health's obesity clinic. She went on a diet advocated by Dr. Norman Joliffe and lost 21 pounds. She was happy with the results but felt she needed moral support and stamina from others. She decided to ask six of her heavy friends to join her in the diet program. The women met at Nidetch's home and talked about their weight and offered support to one another in an Alcoholics Anonymous meeting style. Over a period of one year, Nidetch lost 72 pounds, and her friend Felice Lippert lost 50 lbs. In 1963, Jean Nidetch, Felice Lippert, and her husband Albert Lippert founded the company Weight Watchers International. Nidetch trained leaders and led groups so other Weight Watchers groups could form. Weight Watchers became a franchise and went on to produce cookbooks, videotapes, a television program, and low-fat foods. Over the years, similar weight-loss groups were established. Before Weight Watchers, the practice of dieting in the United States had a long history, beginning in the 1800s with Sylvester Graham and John Harvey Kellogg; they both believed that obesity and gluttony were the cause of ill health and low energy. Kellogg instituted the practice of counting calories at his sanitarium in 1904. The science of counting calories became more precise when scientist Wilbur O. Atwater created the calorimeter and developed calorie tables for everyday foods. In 1910, Upton Sinclair began fasting and advocated the practice to cleanse the body. In the 1930s, there were many fad diets, and slimness came to be idealized and favored over the corpulence of yesteryear. TOPS (Take Pounds Off Sensibly), a program similar to Weight Watchers, was started in 1948 by Esther Manz. She was inspired by the Alcoholics Anonymous meeting style because it advocated support from one's peers. Unlike TOPS and Alcoholics Anonymous, Weight Watchers was a for-profit company.

Wendy's

R. Dave Thomas opened this fast-food hamburger chain in downtown Columbus, Ohio, in 1969. He had been in the restaurant business since he was 12 and had worked in the army as a cook. Since he was creative and resourceful, he quickly rose up the ranks and began to manage restaurants. He improved the menu options and helped to increase daily profits in the enlisted men's club, where he was stationed in Germany, from $40 to $700 a day. After he came home, he worked at a Hobby Horse restaurant in his hometown in Indiana and met Colonel Harlan Sanders. Sanders was elderly at the time, trying to sell his chicken recipe. He convinced Thomas that his chicken would be a popular menu item and that it should be sold in the Hobby Horse restaurant. It was, and it did well. Thomas helped Sanders establish the Kentucky Fried Chicken chain and helped it grow. So many hamburger restaurants existed during that time that many were failing. Thomas thought that this restaurant would be different, so he opened it despite the naysayers telling him not to. He thought that people would be willing to pay more for good food and good service. His restaurant managed to change the public's perception of fast food. It is now the third most popular food chain, following first McDonald's and then Burger King. Wendy's was named after his youngest daughter. His restaurant was different because his burgers were made to order. Each burger was twice the price of other places. The setting was different, too. He made it more appealing with Tiffany lamps, carpeting, and wooden chairs. The workers were dressed in aprons, bow ties, and chef's hats for the males. The menu was small for his Wendy's Old Fashioned Hamburger Restaurant. Special condiments were included. French fries came with the burgers. Chili was on the menu, as were frosty shakes. Wendy's did well and was quickly successful. More locations sprang up the same year it opened. They even included an automobile pick-up window in an attempt to increase sales volume. By 1976, there were more than 1,000 franchise locations spread throughout the country. Thomas added salad bars to his franchise, chicken sandwiches, baked potatoes, stuffed pitas, and Caesar salads. He targeted the middle class as his customer base. Following today's trends, Wendy's has embraced consumer environmental and health concerns by offering biodegradable napkins and packaging, and half-sized salad options.

Further Reading

Birtles, Bryan. "Provenance History of the Slurpee." *Vue Weekly: Hot Summer Guide 2010*: June 9, 2010: Issue 764.

Blake, Mary. "Carnation Cooking Hints." *Atlanta Daily World*, January 20, 1961: 2.

Cannon, Poppy. "Fast Through French." *Chicago Daily Defender*, February 26, 1968: 18.

Claiborne, Craig. "Cooking Classes This Fall Stress International Flavor." *The New York Times*, September 20, 1962.

"Flame Your Way to Flavor with Chateaubriand." *The Hartford Courant*, December 1968: 1E.

Hewitt, Jean. "For Dips or Dinners, Fondue is Popular by Jean Hewitt." *The New York Times*, November 17, 1969.

Kays, Joe, Phillips–Han, Arline. "Gatorade, The Idea That Launched an Industry." http://www.research.ufl.edu/publications/explore/v08n1/gatorade.html.

Meade, Mary. "Make Puffy 'Clouds' of Instant Potatoes." *Chicago Tribune*, February 13, 1967.

Schact, Doris. "Foreign Influence on Cooking Told in Series of Books." *Chicago Tribune*, June 13, 1969.

Witt, Doris. *Black Hunger: Soul Food and America*. Minneapolis: University of Minnesota Press, 1999.

8

1970s

Hilary Schenker

By all measures, the 1970s were tumultuous. After a two-decade military involvement in Vietnam, the United States finally pulled out, achieving neither victory nor closure. The war had cost the country not just 58,000 lives and billions of dollars, but Americans' faith in the efficacy and morality of its government. Watergate and Nixon's impeachment followed not long after, leaving most Americans cynical and apprehensive. In 1973, the energy crisis underlined the vulnerability of the United States as fuel shortages and price increases wracked the nation, with the government suddenly encouraging consumers to drive more slowly and lower their thermostats.

In the past, the United States had seen itself as "the bread basket of the world," generously showering poorer nations with bountiful surpluses of grain. Suddenly faced with an energy crisis and new environmental concerns, the once limitless future began to feel less certain. World hunger took center stage, with the United Nations convening a World Food Conference in Rome in 1973, attended by 1,000 government and private delegates from 130 countries. Reacting to the public concern over malnutrition even in the United States, the government greatly expanded the food stamp and free school lunch programs.

In his 1976 cover story for *New York* magazine, Tom Wolfe called the '70s the Me Decade, but it was a decade of contradictions. While agribusiness and fast food grew increasingly powerful, local, natural foods also gained a foothold. The truly revolutionary ideas of the 1960s—organic farming, vegetarianism, local food—which had been exclusive to hippy enclaves and communes hit the mainstream, where they threatened but were ultimately capitalized on by an expanding food industry hungry for profit.

There was no denying that in the 1970s, what you ate was a political choice. As Warren Belasco summarized in his book *Appetite for Change: How the Counterculture Took on the Food Industry*, "White versus brown was a central contrast. White meant Wonder Bread, White Power, Cool Whip, Minute Rice, instant mashed potatoes, peeled apples, white coats, white collar, whitewash, White House, white racism. Brown meant whole-wheat bread, unhulled rice, turbinado sugar, wildflower honey, unsulfured molasses, soy sauce, peasant yams, 'black is beautiful.'" While suburbanites bought up the newest processed wonder foods, young revolutionaries searching for new diets began to explore macrobiotics and even to buy books like *Stalking the Wild Asparagus*, the 1962 book by outdoorsman Euell Gibbons, which taught foragers how to nourish themselves with the lichen, grasses, and other fresh edibles growing wild around them. *Organic Gardening and Farming*, a publication which had begun in the 1940s, saw its readership increase by 40 percent in just one year, to 700,000 in 1971. Backyard vegetable gardens became more common, with some local papers labeling them "inflation gardens" or "energy gardens."

In gourmet circles, French food remained a staple, with Julia Child enjoying continuing popularity. Her show, *The French Chef*, which was produced by Boston's public television station WGBH, aired first from 1963 to 1966 in black and white, and then again from 1970 to 1972 in color. Viewers couldn't get enough of the loony tall woman, and her passion for French cooking inspired home cooks across the nation. Chuck Williams, the owner of Williams-Sonoma, the French-inspired cooking supply store, knew what had happened on *The French Chef* the night before because the next morning customers would "come into the store demanding a charlotte mold or whatever pan Julia had used, and it had to be the exact size. Because they had to make what she'd made *that night*." The same went for grocery stores. Shallots, which had been an uncommon food item in the past, were suddenly in high demand.

Hosted by the handsome and charismatic Graham Kerr and riding the coattails of Julia Child's success came another TV cooking show, *The Galloping Gourmet*, which first aired from 1968 to 1971. Though hated by the established food world for being high on antics and low on cooking expertise, Kerr's show was an instant success. TV executives realized that the success of *The French Chef* wasn't just an anomaly and that the United States was a ripe audience for TV cooking shows.

In 1970, Julia Child published volume two of her classic, *Mastering the Art of French Cooking.* By this time, Child had achieved nearly rock-star status and was happily crisscrossing the country with her husband Paul for book signings and cooking demonstrations.

After Julia Child made a quiche on her 87th television show in the mid-1960s, the popularity of that dish took off. Quiche was not a new invention, but its versatility suited the 1970s perfectly. Child had encouraged her viewers to be creative, to add anything from bacon to spinach, asparagus, mushrooms, chicken livers, or shellfish. Standard Quiche Lorraine became boring, as restaurants and cooks experimented with every type of quiche, from leek and anchovy to moussaka quiche with eggplant, tomatoes, onion, and lamb. One contributor to *Bon Appetit* recommended a cottage cheese quiche topped with canned french-fried onion rings as a "light supper dish that is an excellent source of protein." In October 1971, *Gourmet* published a recipe for a cranberry-carrot dessert quiche with whipped cream on top. By the early 1980s, quiche had become so ubiquitous—at every restaurant and corner deli, bad quiche abounded—that it finally outstayed its welcome. Chef Craig Claiborne, who had initially praised quiche, announced that he wouldn't be caught dead serving it.

Throughout the 1970s, food tended toward the gooey, heavy, and rich. If there was veal, or fish, or vegetables, there was sauce to pour on top. If there was spinach salad, there was rich cheddar dressing. Since 1954, a man named Steve Henson had been serving a special dressing at his dude ranch, Hidden Valley. His packet of seasonings, to be mixed with mayonnaise and buttermilk to make a thick dressing, became so popular that he gave up the dude ranch and devoted himself to making the dressing full time. In 1973, Clorox Corporation bought the rights to Hidden Valley Ranch and distributed it countrywide, where it became a popular topping for everything from salads to sandwiches to fish.

The increasing popularity of rich foods spurred a counter trend catering to an increasingly weight-conscious country. "Low-fat" foods became popular. Food manufacturers produced more "lite," low-cholesterol, and low-sodium products. In 1970, Morton introduced Salt Substitute, and in 1973, Lite Salt. McCormick introduced its first low-fat product, Lite Gravy, in 1978. Nutritionists began recommending a bowl of healthy cereal with nonfat milk and a small glass of orange juice as a more balanced breakfast. Breakfast in general was increasingly eaten quickly or grabbed on the run. In 1973, McDonald's introduced the nation's first fast-food breakfast item, the Egg McMuffin. Other chains followed suit with their own breakfast menus. In general, the Great American Breakfast of old was changing and even disappearing. Eggs, toast, and bacon were tainted by fears of high cholesterol. Meanwhile, sugary breakfast cereals proliferated, with Post Fruity Pebbles and Cocoa Pebbles making their debuts in 1971.

Despite the shrinking breakfast trend, brunch enjoyed huge popularity. Though the term "brunch" was coined back in 1895, it fit the laid-back, hedonistic 1970s lifestyle perfectly. Drinks were an important part of the brunch meal, and though Bloody Marys and mimosas remained popular, new drinks were also invented, such as the Elmer Fudpucker and Harvey Wallbanger. Supposedly the Wallbanger was named after a surfer named Harvey who, after drinking too many of the galliano and vodka concoctions, walked into a wall. Crepes, another popular '70s dish, could be served at brunch or any other meal. In 1977, Aunt Jemima even came out with a crepe mix and frozen crepe batter.

At the same time, a food revolution was brewing. While some Americans were busy gussying up quiche and crepes, others were searching for food purity. In France in the late '60s, young chefs Paul Bocuse, Pierre Troisgros, and Roger Vergé were throwing off the yoke of rigid, classical French cooking and embracing innovation with lighter, fresh ingredients. Dubbed "la nouvelle cuisine" by the *Gault Millau* magazine, the movement sparked new ideas in California as well. Influenced by the nouvelle as well as natural food movements, Alice Waters, a young Berkeley graduate, opened the famous Chez Panisse in 1971. The mantra of the restaurant was "fresh, local, seasonal ingredients." While at first the menu was entirely French, Waters began to realize that French recipes replicated in California could never be as good as the originals, which were made with fresh, local, French ingredients. Slowly, the new California cuisine was born. Embraced immediately by diners and critics, the restaurant was one of the most influential in American history.

The same year, in 1971, a surprise bestseller by a young woman named Frances Moore Lappé revolutionized Americans' attitudes toward food. Her book, *Diet for a Small Planet*, was a political tract and food guidebook, framing food choices as moral choices. Lappé's revelation was that the problem of world hunger was not one of overpopulation or insufficient resources, it was one of inefficiency and bad policy. She pointed to "The Great American Steak Religion" as the crux of the problem. Cattle consumed 16 pounds of grain to produce just one pound of meat, she said, and half of American grain went to feed livestock in feedlot operations, where cattle were force-fed cheap grain surpluses. "Although we lead the world in exports of grain and soy," she concluded, "this incredible volume 'lost' through livestock was twice the level of our current exports. It is enough to provide every single human being on earth with more than a cup of cooked grain each day of the year!" In other words, we could solve world hunger by changing our diets. The book included guidelines for how to mix complementary proteins as well as a collection of vegetarian recipes in the vein of Millet Cauliflower Soup and Soybean Pie. Selling nearly two million copies in the '70s, Lappé became known in the mainstream press as the "Julia Child of the soybean circuit." Moreover, her advocacy of vegetarianism brought meatless eating into the mainstream consciousness.

At the start of the '70s, vegetarianism was not fully understood. All the talk of protein grams and complementarity seemed complicated, and in an effort to compensate, many vegetarian recipes offered either tons of heavy cream and butter or long, unwieldy lists of ingredients. Vegetarianism was also tainted by nutty advocates who recommended chewing mouthfuls of brown rice in meditative silence for 10 minutes or by recipes for "nut-loaves" made from stomach-churning combinations of nuts, cream cheese, dried fruits, and shaved carrots. Still, ideas were spreading, and even a mainstream cookbook like Virginia Pasley's *In Celebration of Food* included a selection of menu ideas for "your vegetarian young people home from college."

In 1973, a young chef named Molly Katzen opened the Moosewood Restaurant, a vegetarian collective, in Ithaca, NY. Katzen had been inspired by the vegetarian food scene in the San Francisco Bay area while there studying at the San Francisco Art Institute. The restaurant was an instant success, and demand for Katzen's spiral-bound collection of recipes grew until Ten Speed Press finally published *The Moosewood Cookbook* in 1977. By 1981, the book had sold more than 250,000 copies, and its sequel, *The Enchanted Broccoli Forest*, was on the way. Another cookbook from 1972, *The Vegetarian Epicure*, by Anna Thomas, was also popular. Meanwhile Deborah Madison, a young Zen practitioner on a quest for pleasurable, natural food, began an apprenticeship at Chez Panisse in Berkeley, where she trained before opening her own celebrated vegetarian restaurant, Greens, in 1979.

As public awareness and apprehension of additives and artificial colorings in processed food intensified, the natural food movement gained traction. In 1974, a former FDA scientist, Jacqueline Verrett, wrote an exposé of government failure to protect consumers from dangerous chemicals and additives entitled *Eating May Be Hazardous to Your Health*, which became a best seller. Mainstream magazines including *Bon Appetit* began presenting "natural foods" columns. Home bread-making enjoyed huge popularity, with *Woman's Day* and *Gourmet* featuring articles on its joys. Edward Espe Brown's *Tassajara Bread Book* (1970) sold 400,000 copies. In response to the new natural food trend, manufacturers rushed to churn out more vitamin-enhanced and high-fiber products, advertising use of brown versus refined sugar. There were now "home-style" breads, yogurts with no additives, and truckloads of mass-market, "natural" granola. The term "natural" began to lose meaning.

Processed foods and convenience foods proliferated and were marketed increasingly to working women who no longer had time to prepare laborious dinners. Some of the newest processed foods included Carnation's hot chocolate mix (1972) and boxed meal mixes like Hamburger Helper, first sold in 1970, and Cup-O-Noodles and Stove Top Stuffing, both introduced in 1973. Unlike the younger crowd, older suburban Americans embraced processed foods wholeheartedly, especially in their desserts. They began a love affair with cake mixes, pudding mixes, and Cool Whip, often using soda pop as an ingredient. In 1975, American consumption of soft drinks surpassed that of coffee. For the older generation, using a processed food

---

Watergate Cake

Two popular recipes circulated in the 1970s were for Watergate Salad and Watergate Cake. Watergate Cake was a mixture of pistachio-flavored pudding, marshmallows, crushed pineapple, nuts, and whipped cream. The cake often featured a cake mix combined with green food coloring and nuts, with "cover-up" frosting. *The Watergate Cookbook (Or, Who's in the Soup)*, by The Committee to Write the Cookbook, and *The Watergate Cookbook* both appeared on bookshelves in 1973. The following list contains a selection of the former's 108 "unimpeachable" recipes:

Nixon's Perfectly Clear Consomme
Ellsberg's Leek Soup
Liddy's Clam-Up Chowder
Magurder's Dandy Ly'in Salad
Sauteed Slippery Eels a la Deanoise
Republican Peeking Duck
Mitchell's Cooked Goose with Stuffing
Cox's In-Peach Chicken
Martha's Sweet and Sour Tongue
Nixon's Hot Crossed Wired Buns with Tapping
GOP Cookie Crumbles
Pick Your Own Hero Sandwich

as a shortcut in an entree became not just acceptable but sometimes even fashionable. Popular dishes like broccoli-mayonnaise casserole and lobster-asparagus mousse—made with canned asparagus, canned lobster, and canned condensed cream of asparagus soup—typified the trend.

The way Americans shopped was also changing. According to the Cooperative League of the U.S.A., between 5,000 and 10,000 food co-ops were established during the 1970s, with sales of $500 million in 1975. Similarly, the number of health food stores increased from 500 in 1965 to 3,000 in 1972. Grocery stores were also making changes. Their interiors were becoming less austere and more brightly colored. Plastic grocery bags were introduced to supermarkets in 1977 and took hold despite some initial resistance from consumers. With the introduction of the Universal Product Code (UPC) in 1974, checkouts became automated. There was also a new hot food trend, with grocery stores offering more bakery and prepared hot food deli items, and there were new specialty departments. Discount food stores and warehouses were grocery stores' response to consumer price concerns, with chains like A&P having to offer bulk discount stores to stay in business.

American kitchens were also flooded with new appliances and technologies. In 1970, resealable plastic bags and Reynolds oven bags were introduced, and in 1972, Ziploc bags. Soda now came in recyclable plastic soda bottles, invented in 1973 by engineer Nathaniel Wyeth. Microwave cooking, though long used by restaurants and airlines, was becoming more common in the home. Some food manufacturers began to include microwave cooking instructions on their packaging. In 1978, General Electric offered the first over-the-range, space-saving microwave, the SpaceMaker. There were new Cuisinarts, Mr. Coffee coffeemakers, and Crock-Pots. Some other newfangled "time-saving" appliances, such as the combination freezer-oven, which could be set on a timer to convert from a freezer to an oven for frozen dinners to be ready right at dinner time, were never "the next big thing" as predicted.

Eating out in the '70s was often less about the food and more about the experience, as singles bars and zany, goofy restaurants, often with a theme, gained in popularity. By 1975, TGI Fridays had 10 locations and doubled as a singles hangout. Its decor of hanging junk and potted plants inspired copycats and helped give rise to the slang term "fern bar" (meaning a hangout decorated with potted plants and tiffany lamps for well-dressed singles). Among the more popular theme restaurants was Spats in New York, with a 1930s theme, La Biblioteque, which served such dishes as veal scaloppini Voltaire and filet mignon Camus, Tumbledown Dicks in Cos Cob,

Connecticut, and Frog & Nightgown in Raleigh, North Carolina. In New York, one theme restaurant, Maxwell's Plum, enjoyed particular success. Warner LeRoy, son of famous Hollywood producer-editor Mervyn LeRoy, opened the restaurant in 1966. Like many '70s restaurants, the name had no meaning but was meant to evoke an atmosphere of fun. Every surface glittered with mirrors and cut glass or was studded with art nouveau and Art Deco figures and objects and potted plants, while huge Tiffany chandeliers hung from the ceiling. Maxwell's Plum was so popular throughout the '70s that even a reservation did not guarantee seating. It finally closed in 1989.

Salad bars were another popular '70s invention. Though it's unclear who opened the first salad bar, one of the first and definitely the largest was at R.J. Grunts in Chicago. Opened in 1971, R. J. Grunts' cofounder, Rich Melman, followed a macrobiotic diet. His expansive salad bar offered a selection of 40 different items. As the salad bar trend grew, however, it was not always so healthful. Salad bars were most commonly found at surf and turf restaurants. Fixtures of the salad bars were large bowls of iceberg lettuce (possibly browning at the tips) and smaller bowls of spinach leaves, cherry tomatoes, pickled beets, sliced cucumbers, sliced onions, sliced radishes, shredded carrots, garbanzo beans, sprouts, sunflower seeds, artificial bacon bits, shredded cheese, and a choice of gloppy, mayonnaise-based dressings to spoon on top. Most restaurants that featured salad bars followed a formula. They strove for an old-time, quasi-Victorian feel, with dark wood paneling and brass fixtures. To go with the salad, there would be "fresh" baked bread, which was baked in the restaurant from frozen dough. The rolls would be served alongside little pots of swirled non-butter. For entrees, there was steak, lobster, or a shrimp kebab, often frozen mass-market, and the desserts were huge and gooey.

The tastes and palates of Americans were expanding in the 1970s, though, as ethnic foods spread away from the coasts to the rest of the country. Local papers began announcing the arrival of such foods as bagels, soul food, sushi, and gyros. Ethnic food festivals, where visitors could sample everything from Greek spanakopita to Japanese yakisoba, spread even to small towns. The word "fajita," derived from the Spanish word "faja," meaning "girdle," or "strip," and referring to the actual cut of meat, appeared for the first time in print in 1975, though it remains unclear who originally coined it. Taco Bell restaurants opened in the most secluded reaches of the Midwest. Even so, in 1976 on a campaign visit to San Antonio, President Ford still made the embarrassing gaffe of biting into a tamale he was offered without first removing the husk.

President Gerald Ford is given guidance by two daughters of the Republic of Texas after mistakenly biting into a tamale without removing the husk on August 9, 1976. (AP/Wide World Photos)

While French food was still the king of gourmet, it had begun to seem a bit classical, and the most fashionable cooks were looking to the Mediterranean for inspiration. Greek and Italian foods became the fashion, while German and Scandinavian foods popular in the 1950s and 1960s fell from favor. One Greek dish that enjoyed wide popularity in the 1970s was moussaka, a baked eggplant, lamb, and tomato dish topped with béchamel sauce and egg. Cioppino, the Italian American fish stew, Italian osso-bucco (braised veal shanks), and caponata, a Sicilian appetizer made from eggplant, all gained in popularity. At Italian restaurants, red sauce was out and rich, white, creamy sauces were in—fettucini alfredo, spaghetti carbonara, pasta primavera.

Food was changing in the '70s, and Americans' reactions varied. There were the natural food advocates, counting protein grams, experimenting with soy and searching for more organic options; there were the suburban housewives whipping up ketchup casseroles and Hamburger Helper; and then there was the birth of California cuisine and the fresh, local, seasonal food movement. Most importantly, perhaps, there was dialogue, as the different camps tussled over what makes food food, what mealtime should be, and the larger repercussions of our food choices.

Entries

Ben & Jerry's Ice Cream

Sweet, mushy foods were popular in the '70s, and ice cream was no exception. Locals first flocked to an ice cream shop in Somerville, Massachusetts, called Steve's Ice Cream, opened by Steve Harrell in 1973. At Steve's the concept of the "mix-in" or "smoosh-in" was created, and you could get such creative "smoosh-ins" as Oreos, Heath Bar, dried fruits, or nuts to fit your fancy. Stoned customers "attuned to strange blends of thick fresh cream, tropical fruits, and crushed candy bars" perhaps gave rise to the new trend, speculates Warren Belasco in *Appetite for Change*.

Among the imitators of the popular Steve's Ice Cream Shop were Ben Cohen and Jerry Greenfield, two Vermont Deadheads who had dreamed of opening their own ice cream company. They observed Steve's Ice Cream

Jerry Greenfield (left) and Bennett Cohen stand in front of a Ben & Jerry's RV nicknamed the Cowmobile in Burlington, Vermont, on June 15, 1987. (AP/Wide World Photos)

carefully, making pilgrimages there to take pictures and see the workings of the ice cream machine. They took a correspondence course in ice cream making from Penn State University and finally invested $12,000 to open up Ben & Jerry's Homemade Ice Cream and Crepes in a renovated gas station in Burlington, Vermont, in 1978.

Ben and Jerry began promoting their ice cream at supermarkets, and Pillsbury tried to freeze out the newcomers, hoping to restrict shoppers to just one gourmet ice cream, the Pillsbury-owned Häagen-Dazs brand. After Ben & Jerry's received an out-of-court settlement, their ice cream was distributed to supermarkets across the country and was an instant success. With its innovative flavors and funny names like Cherry Garcia (named for Jerry Garcia), Chubby Hubby, and Chocolate Chip Cookie Dough, the ice creams were a hit with Baby Boomers.

Initially, the ice cream was promoted for having all natural ingredients and supporting local farmers. All farmers who provided dairy had to agree to use no bovine growth hormone (BGH). Going even further in their marketing to socially and environmentally conscious consumers, Ben & Jerry's proudly advertised the use of recycled materials to make their cartons, that 7.5 percent of their pre-tax profits went to charity, and the fact that their highest-paid executives would never make more than seven times the salary of their lowest wage earners. This corporate pay policy was rescinded in 1994 to allow for greater growth. Cohen and Greenfield decided to take the company public to expand profits and distribution, and unfortunately lost control to investors. In August 2000, the company was bought by the Unilever conglomerate, which also owns the Dove and Breyer's ice cream brands. Finally, in 2002, Ben & Jerry's was forced to remove the "All Natural" tagline from its labels after the Center for Science in the Public Interest accused them of using artificial flavors, hydrogenated oils, and other "unnatural" ingredients. Ben & Jerry's continues to be extremely popular, especially in urban markets.

Celestial Seasonings Herbal Teas

Celestial Seasonings was founded on righteous principles: good for the environment and for your health, non caffeinated, organic, additive-free, and gathered by idealistic youth in the wild. The company was founded by Morris (Mo) Siegel, a long-haired young entrepreneur in his 20s who had been foraging for herbs in the Rocky Mountain foothills since 1969, bagging them together in a mix he labeled Mo's 24. In 1972, the business began to take off with the introduction of the popular Red Zinger tea, a mix of hibiscus flowers, rose hips, and lemongrass that produced a bright crimson tea.

From the beginning, the company marketed itself aggressively as natural and hip. Tea boxes were decorated with trippy drawings, crunchy health advice, a full ingredient label, spiritual quotes, and even drawings of medicinal plants. In a mutually beneficial pairing, Moosewood Restaurant, Molly Katzen's successful vegetarian cooperative in Ithaca, New York, began stocking boxes of Celestial Seasonings tea.

Workers for Celestial Seasonings were treated to free lunch, T-shirts, and a shareholding plan, though they were paid less than the going wage in Boulder, Colorado. In an interview, Siegel admitted that his aim was to "defeat the unions by providing more and better benefits for his workers than any union could." The benefits proved to be mostly spiritual. By 1978, Celestial Seasonings employed 200 people and was grossing more than $9 million a year. Many original supporters were put off by Siegel's bald corporate ambition, seeing him as selling out his organic, revolutionary roots. He invested in new overseas supply lines, production facilities, and distribution outlets, and in 1977, the company switched from its own in-house advertising to a mainstream San Francisco ad agency. Following the move, Celestial Seasonings stopped selling to local co-ops and health food stores and began dealing exclusively with larger supermarket chains. Finally, in 1984, Siegel sold the company to Dart & Kraft, Inc., for a reported $8 million to $10 million.

Chez Panisse

Alice Waters's Chez Panisse, one of the most influential restaurants in America, opened its doors on August 28, 1971. Packed every night, it was an immediate success. Celebrated in the press, in a 1975 *Gourmet* magazine feature, and later by James Beard and other critics, it rose to national prominence.

Chez Panisse is unassuming in appearance, occupying a nondescript stretch of Shattuck Avenue in Berkeley, California, two floors, the bottom dining room decorated in a dark wood mission style, and an upstairs cafe where you can see chefs in the open kitchen work the grill and bake pizzas in the wood-burning oven. A single bill of fare is printed each night, generally unfussy and always ingredient driven. But Alice Waters, the proprietor, along with an influential early chef at the restaurant, Jeremiah Tower, can take credit for popularizing the mantra now repeated by chefs across America: "fresh, local, seasonal ingredients."

Alice Waters graduated from UC Berkeley in 1967 with a degree in French cultural studies. What and how one should eat, in the late '60s and early '70s, was an issue of hot debate, and opposing camps argued over what foods suited a revolutionary spirit. "Just because you're a revolutionary doesn't mean your idea of a good meal should be Chef Boyardee ravioli reheated in a dog dish," Waters is said to have told a friend in the late 1960s. She was inspired by her first trip to France in 1965, which, she said, "awakened [her] in a sensual way to food." She did not go through the traditional routes for a chef but instead taught herself to cook.

At first, the menu at Chez Panisse was based on the cuisine of Provence, but realizing that lacking the same ingredients, it could never taste the same, Waters began to seek out a network of local California farmers, local seafood, and wine. The restaurant was a social, sensual experience, though it nearly foundered in its first year because of the owners' lack of business acumen. Organic foods were prominently advertised; some now well-known gourmet brands like Niman Ranch meat and Laura Chenel's chevre got their start there. It was the first restaurant to employ a full-time "forager," someone whose job was to seek out the best local ingredients—mussels from the bay and flowering mustard from Napa—and establish relationships with local farmers and suppliers. At Chez Panisse, Waters threw out the rule book, using French cuisine as a launch pad for a new California cuisine based on local ingredients. Many dishes that have now become identified as California cuisine, such as oven-baked pizza with unusual toppings, baby green salads with warm goat cheese, or grilled fish and vegetables, were served at Chez Panisse. As an institution, Chez Panisse was a training ground for many influential chefs who later went on to their own careers, including Jeremiah Tower, Judy Rodgers, Deborah Madison, Mark Miller, Paul Bertolli, Jonathan Waxman, Mark Peel, and Joyce Goldstein.

Crock-Pot

In the 1970s, new appliances were proliferating in kitchens across America, but perhaps the appliance that most typified the decade was the Crock-Pot. Crock-Pot is a name trademarked by the Rival Manufacturing Co., but it has become a generic term for any slow cooker. In the early 1970s, Rival acquired a smaller company, Naxon Utilities, which was manufacturing a small electric bean cooker called the Beanery. The Beanery was a simple, brown-glazed crock liner housed in an aluminum casing with a lid. Rival redesigned the slow cooker by modifying the look of the outer wrapper and adding a glass lid and handles. Rival also offered buyers a cookbook with a variety of recipes. In August 1971, Rival released the product, branding it the Crock-Pot Slow Cooker. Rival advertised it with the slogan "cooks all day while the cook's away."

Slow cooking, of course, was not a new concept. In the 1940s, some electric stoves came with a built-in well cooker that could be left on all day for slow cooking a stew or pot roast, and down-easterners have always buried bean pots. Part of what may account for the Crock-Pot's popularity in the 1970s was the economic downturn that forced households to find more economical ways of cooking, paired with a rising national interest in cooking in general. In the Crock-Pot, cheaper, fattier cuts of meat tasted better when cooked long hours. The Crock-Pot also appealed to suburban working women, who were embracing more processed foods. These women could come home to their slow-cooked chicken made with frozen lemonade concentrate, or good and easy stew made with onion soup mix and condensed cream of mushroom soup. By 1981, Rival was reporting more than $30 million in sales. Many other appliance brands followed suit with their own slow cookers.

Cuisinart Food Processor

When Carl Sondheimer first introduced the food processor at the 1973 National Housewares Exposition in Chicago, it received only lukewarm interest. Even with its solid, squarish base, wide, clear, plastic bowl, 6-inch, S-shaped blade, and slicing and shredding disk attachments, viewers dismissed it as an overpriced, glorified blender, balking at the $140 price tag.

Sondheimer was a retired MIT-educated electronics engineer from Greenwich, Connecticut, with a passion for cooking. In 1971, Sondheimer had travelled with his wife to the Paris housewares exhibition, where they had seen Le Magimix, a powerful, versatile machine that could chop, slice, shred, and puree, assisting cooks with everything from pastry dough to salmon mousse. Le Magimix was a home version of industrial Le Robot-Coupe, also invented by Pierre Verdun. Impressed by the Magimix, Carl Sondheimer took a few of the machines home to his own workshop, where he took them apart and created a whole new electrical underwiring so that they could work in the United States, aided by a powerful new motor. Finally, he added additional safety features, streamlined the design, and christened it Cuisinart. He acquired the distribution rights from the French company Robot-Coupe to sell his modified machines under the new name.

Disappointed but undaunted by the initial lukewarm response to Cuisinart, Sondheimer tried another tack. He approached famous food writers across the country and offered them demonstrations of the device. In 1975, in *The New York Times Magazine*, Craig Claiborne and Pierre Franey hailed the Cuisinart as an invention that "in the minds of serious cooks, ranks with that of the printing press, cotton gin, steamboat, paper clips, Kleenex, wastebaskets, contour sheets, and disposable diapers." They marveled at the machine's ability to chop 50 pounds of cabbage for sauerkraut in mere minutes, something that would have been highly tedious by hand. James Beard put Sondheim in touch with Chuck Williams at Williams-Sonoma and other buyers. With endorsements from top chefs including Julia Child, sales hit the roof. Cuisinarts were such a hot item that in the Christmas of 1976, some retailers ran out and were forced to resort to selling empty boxes as promises for future delivery.

Sondheimer continued to improve the Cuisinart throughout the '70s and '80s, adding pulse buttons, larger bowls and feed tubes (to slice larger foods like apples and tomatoes), and a plethora of new accessories including thick and thin slicing disks, coarse and fine shredding disks, french-fry cutters, citrus reamers, egg whips, and pasta makers. In 1988, Sondheimer sold the company to a group of investors who then sold it to the Conair Corporation.

Dean & DeLuca

Giorgio DeLuca was the son of a specialty Italian foods importer who sold in New York's old Washington Square Market on the Lower West Side. His father sold his imports—olive oil, dried figs, chocolates, parmigiano-reggiano cheese, panettone, soppresatta—to wholesalers who, in turn, sold them to specialty shops in Italian American enclaves.

Giorgio DeLuca, born in 1944, grew up in the Italian American community in Queens. After graduating from City College, DeLuca moved into an apartment in Greenwich Village, where he became friendly with the gay couple downstairs, Joel Dean and Jack Ceglic. Dean was a composer and pianist with a master's in literature from Columbia, and the two became friends. Through Dean, DeLuca received an education in art, opera, and good eating. With this new perspective, he realized the purity and value of the supposedly low-end Italian foods his father imported. Dean and Ceglic soon moved to SoHo, and DeLuca became infatuated with their new bustling, bohemian community. Seeing the potential, in 1973, DeLuca opened a specialty cheese shop in SoHo, which he called the Cheese Store.

In this aesthetically beautiful store, he served up samples of emmentaler cheese and fresh chevre from France with olive oil and fresh thyme to the bustling neighborhood.

Meanwhile, Dean had been interested in opening a pots and pans store, and when a large space across the street from the Cheese Store became available, Dean and DeLuca decided to combine forces. Imported pots and pans hung from the ceiling. Cheeses were free of refrigerators and available for whiffing, and open bags of fresh coffee overflowed near the door. DeLuca ordered the food and did marketing, Dean took care of kitchenware and the business end, and Ceglic designed the store, giving it its industrial-chic feel. (Though Ceglic was also part owner, he graciously declined naming rights, agreeing that Dean & DeLuca had a certain ring.) While SoHo was becoming the "in" neighborhood, with curious tourists from out of town as well as the Upper East Side making pilgrimages to the area, business boomed. In-store chef Felipe Rojas-Lombardi rolled out chickens tandoori-style, grilled salmon on cedar planks, and created pasta salads with sun-dried tomatoes. With more working mothers, the market for prepared gourmet foods was taking off, and with it Dean & DeLuca.

Egg McMuffin

Breakfast was changing in the 1970s. More women were working and had less time to cook breakfast. More often, people were turning to convenient breakfast items. In addition, concern was increasing over rising rates of obesity and high blood pressure, and the great American breakfasts of old—eggs, toast, bacon, orange juice—had became an object of suspicion as more consumers turned to cereal.

Observing the new fast breakfast trend, McDonald's, which had previously served only lunch and dinner, introduced the new Egg McMuffin in 1973. The McMuffin consists of an English muffin, an egg formed in a Teflon circle with the yolk broken, topped by a slab of pasteurized processed American cheese, Canadian-style bacon, and liquid mayonnaise.

McDonald's gives credit for the invention of the Egg McMuffin to Herb Peterson, a California McDonald's franchisee who saw the demand for a fast-food breakfast. Peterson began his career at McDonald's as vice president of the company's advertising firm, D'Arcy Advertising, in Chicago. Along with the invention of the Egg McMuffin, he is credited with creating the company's first national advertising slogan, "Where quality starts fresh every day." Another McDonald's franchise owner, Harold G. Fulmer, claims he began serving breakfast at his McDonald's franchises in

Pennsylvania as early as 1970. He calculated that local roadside diners were making half their sales in the morning, and so he started offering coffee, orange juice, and pastry at his McDonald's, a move he claims originally angered McDonald's.

As the nation's first fast-food breakfast item, the Egg McMuffin was enough of a new phenomenon that newspapers across the country covered it. One local newspaper headline proclaimed, "Idea good, but reality of Egg McMuffin weak," though the author conceded, "it was certainly better than no breakfast at all," and that it was economical. Even *The New York Times* carried an article on whether correct plural usage would be Egg McMuffins or Eggs McMuffin.

Frozen Yogurt

Though Europeans had been enjoying it for 2,000 years, yogurt actually originated in central Asia. The word is Turkish (in Turkish the "g" is silent). In the 1970s, yogurt expanded from the exclusive domain of specialty Greek and Middle Eastern stores to the mainstream. *New York Times* readers learned that Jimmy Carter's septuagenarian mother, Miss Lillian, ate yogurt as an appetizer before every meal and that author Ken Kesey raised his own cows in Oregon so he could make yogurt just to his liking. Gourmet chef Craig Claiborne hailed it as "a sensational ingredient for cooking."

In 1975, Americans ate 200,000 tons of yogurt, nearly $300 million worth according to *The New York Times*, which was up from $25 million in 1967. In 1974, Yoplait Yogurt was introduced. Enthusiasts credited yogurt as prolonging life and improving digestion. Some women even promoted it as a face mask. Capitalizing on the healthy associations of yogurt, Dannon released a commercial in the '70s featuring 125-year-old yogurt-eating Soviet Georgians. But it was perhaps frozen yogurt that really hit America's soft spot.

To make frozen yogurt, yogurt and stabilizers plus flavors are mixed in soft ice cream machines. After 10 minutes, the thick, creamy swirl can be eased into a cone. Frozen yogurt contained about 57 percent fewer calories than ice cream; one eager purveyor of yogurt at a store in Alexandria, Virginia, exclaimed, "It's ice cream without guilt. It's magic."

The first frozen yogurt was sold in Cambridge's Harvard Square from a hole-in-the-wall store called Spa, starting in 1972. The frozen treat was first conceived of by Bostonian Walter Simonson, an employee of H.P. Hood Dairy Co. Harvard students lined up at the door, but they were alone. Alan

J. Philips, the owner of the company, found another opportunity to market frozen yogurt in New York City. Bloomingdale's department store was opening a new boutique and was looking for a small health food bar "just for atmosphere." Philips convinced them to try his frozen yogurt idea. When Bloomingdale's customers devoured 2,400 gallons of mix in the first two hours, he knew he'd hit on the next big thing. Simultaneously, in southern California, Knudson's began to freeze yogurt like a popsicle and impale it on a stick within a paper cylinder. These yogurt pops did not see the sudden roaring success of soft-serve frozen yogurt, though they did enjoy steady but modest increases in sales.

Miller Lite

Meeting consumer demand for a beer that was low in calories and carbohydrates, Miller Lite was a huge success, helped also by an aggressive marketing campaign. Whereas a regular beer has about 138 calories per 12-ounce bottle, light beer has between 95 and 102. Light lagers have been described as "a watery interpretation of the Pilsener style." The Association of Brewers' 2004 guidelines describe light lager as "extremely light straw colored, light in body, and high in carbonation. Flavor is very light/mild and very dry. Hop flavor, aroma and bitterness is negligible to very low. Alcohol by volume is between 3.5 to 4.4 percent."

Miller beer was born in 1855 when Frederick Miller, a German immigrant, purchased the Menomonee Valley Brewery in Milwaukee. In the late 1960s, the head of the Miller family was tragically killed in an airplane crash, and in 1970, Philip Morris and Company purchased the brand. In 1972, Miller bought the Meister Brau line of products, which included Meister Brau Lite beer. Lite beer was much cheaper to produce than other beers, but Miller chose to market it as a premium beer. By making this low-calorie, low-carbohydrate brew into a national best-seller, Miller broke new ground in the beer industry. By 1975, sales reached four million barrels a year. The successful marketing campaign featured the well-known, well-liked former football player Matt Snell with the slogan, "New Lite Beer from Miller is all you ever wanted in a beer . . . and less." The success of Miller Lite started a revolution in light beers. In 1978, Miller surpassed even Pabst and Schlitz to become the number-two top-selling beer after Anheuser-Busch. Before long, these top two were producing more than 50 percent of the beer sold in America, as smaller, independent brewers were pushed out of the market.

The birth of the light beer market reflected America's growing concern over obesity and high blood pressure. In the '70s, many manufacturers introduced "lite" versions of their products. In 1973, Morton released its Lite Salt, and in 1978, McCormick rolled out its first low-fat item, Lite Gravy.

Mrs. Fields Cookies

The sweet, warm smell from the Mrs. Fields cookies now wafts through malls across the country. By 2005, the franchise had more than 450 locations in 11 countries. The first Mrs. Fields cookie store was opened in August 1977 by Debra ("Debbi") Fields and her husband, Randall K. Fields. Mrs. Fields was a 22-year-old mother with no previous business experience and her husband was a Stanford graduate. The store, which they opened near Stanford University in Palo Alto, California, was named the Mrs. Fields Chocolate Chippery. They specialized in extremely rich chocolate chip cookies, which they baked throughout the day and sold warm.

They later renamed the store simply Mrs. Fields Cookies to allow for a greater variety of cookie types. In 1983, the first store opened in New York, and in 1990, Mrs. Fields began franchising. In 1993, tough economic times forced Mrs. Fields to sell her company to private investors in Utah. Debbi Fields was featured on television cooking shows. Her first cookbook, released in 1992, *Mrs. Fields Cookie Book: 100 Recipes from the Kitchen of Mrs. Fields,* sold more than 1.8 million copies and was the first cookbook ever to reach the top of the *New York Times* best seller list.

Orville Redenbacher's Gourmet Popping Corn

Orville Redenbacher was born in 1917 in Brazil, Indiana. He grew up on a large farm, going on to study agronomy and genetics at Purdue University, where he conducted experiments on the first popcorn hybrids. In 1940, Redenbacher became the manager of a 1,200-acre farm in Princeton, Indiana, where he built a hybrid seed corn plant and continued his hybrid popcorn experimentation.

In 1951, Redenbacher went into partnership with Charles Bowman, who was the manager of the Purdue Ag Alumni Seed Implement Association of Lafayette, Indiana, and together they purchased the George F. Chester Seed Company at Boone Grove, Indiana. In 1965, all of their popcorn experimentation paid off when they developed a new popcorn hybrid, one that would expand to nearly twice the size of the current commercial brands and left almost no unpopped kernels. They christened this new variety Red Bow, which they derived from the first three letters of each of their names, and began trying to market it to the major processors.

For five years they had no luck. Processors rejected Red Bow because yields were smaller, and it cost more to harvest. In 1970, Redenbacher decided to stop producing popcorn seed and focus all his energy on Red Bow. He travelled first to local stores, distributing samples and talking to customers. A Chicago public relations firm convinced the team to change the name from Red Bow to Orville Redenbacher's Gourmet Popping Corn. Next, they began using the slogan, "The World's Most Expensive Popcorn" in an effort to convince buyers of their products' superior quality. They'd become a success locally, but in order to expand nationally, they joined Blue Plate Foods, a subsidiary of Hunt-Wesson Foods. By the time Hunt-Wesson sold Blue Plate in 1974, Orville's popcorn was so popular that Hunt-Wesson decided to retain the rights to it. By 1975, it was the most popular brand in America. In 1976, Hunt-Wesson launched a new campaign featuring Redenbacher himself. His bow tie, dark-framed glasses, and midwestern accent seemed to suggest he was a down-home kind of guy. Consumers remembered his folksy image and bought his popcorn again and again. In 1996, while lounging in his hot tub, Redenbacher suffered a heart attack and drowned.

Pasta Primavera

One of the most enduring legacies of the '70s, pasta primavera with its cream sauce and hodgepodge of vegetables created a stir when it was first served at Le Cirque, one of New York's luxury French restaurants. Originally meant as a seasonal springtime dish, though almost immediately served year-round, it reflected the '70s conflict between French cuisine, which had reigned as the gourmet standard for decades, and Italian, part of the newer trend toward Mediterranean cuisines. At least three chefs lay claim to having created the dish. Ed Giobbi, artist and cook, claims to have served a non cream version of the dish to Le Cirque owner Sirio Maccioni and Le Cirque's original chef Jean Vergnes at his home. Maccioni claims that the dish arose on a trip to Canada when his wife Egidiana threw together a pasta dish using what was in the cupboard, including frozen peas, mushrooms, garlic, tomato, cream, and parmesan, and no olive oil. Whatever its origins, Pasta Primavera was called "by far the most talked-about dish in Manhattan today," by Craig Claiborne and Pierre Franey in their feature on the dish in *The New York Times Magazine* in October 1977.

Pop Rocks

Pop Rocks were invented in 1956 by William A. Mitchell, a chemist for General Foods (GF). He invented the candy while searching for a way to

William Mitchell, inventor of Pop Rocks candy, samples the candy with a group of New York schoolchildren in 1986. (AP/Wide World Photos)

make instant carbonated soda from a tablet. The formula wasn't a success as instant soda, and General Foods, unsure how to market it, shelved the idea for 20 years. Later, another GF chemist came across the idea and turned it into the Pop Rocks we know today: tiny, brightly colored, gravel-size candy that bursts on the tongue when eaten. Pop Rocks are made from sugar, lactose, corn syrup, artificial flavor, and artificial color, all gassified with carbon dioxide. Upon contact with the moisture in the mouth, they release the pockets of carbon dioxide gas, causing a snapping and crackling. Pop Rocks came initially in three flavors: grape, cherry, and orange. When they were released in 1975, Pop Rocks caused an immediate buzz. By 1976, they were the most popular candy in the United States with everyone from elementary to college kids.

At first, General Foods marketed the candy mostly in California, with other test sales around the country. The one-fifth-of-an-ounce package was sold for 20 cents, though there was such high demand for the candy that eager entrepreneurs bought their own supplies to sell at a profit elsewhere, at prices of up to 50 cents a package. One Brooklyn distributor said,

"The kids are like junkies—hungry for the stuff. It's the fastest-moving new candy I've ever seen."

Shortly after the release of the product, the trouble started. Worried customers began flooding their local Food and Drug Administration offices with reports that Pop Rocks had caused injuries in children. Though the reports were unsubstantiated, Pop Rocks samples were sent to the FDA's Washington laboratories, where volunteers conducted experiments to ensure that the product could cause no injury. The FDA even set up a telephone hotline to reassure worried parents. But in spite of these assurances, fears spread. A widespread urban legend held that drinking carbonated soda and eating Pop Rocks at the same time could cause a person's stomach to explode, and that in fact little Mikey of Life cereal commercial fame had died this way (he did not).

Sales of Pop Rocks boomed to 500 million a year until 1978, when sales began to drop significantly. General Foods launched a large-scale campaign to combat the rumors, spending an estimated $500,000 on a full-page letter directed at parents printed in 45 major newspapers, and the inventor, Williams, was sent on a speaking tour in the East to discuss the product's safety. Still, General Foods discontinued Pop Rocks in the 1980s amid swirling rumors, though they were re-introduced shortly afterward and have remained on shelves ever since.

Quaker Oats Granola

Introduced to supermarkets in 1972, Quaker Oats 100 Percent Natural was the first, but certainly not the last, mass market granola. In the 1970s health food, which had been the domain of hippie enclaves in the 1960s, hit the mainstream. Food magazines including *Bon Appetit* started up health food columns, and even *Gourmet* offered recipes such as soybeans with feta and peppers. The food manufacturing giants realized that natural foods could sell and began to meet the demand.

Among the new mass-marketed "natural" foods, perhaps none was so instantly popular as granola. Almost every big cereal manufacturer scrambled to put out its own: General Mills had Nature Valley, Kellogg's made Country Valley, Pet put out Heartland, and Colgate-Palmolive had Alpen (unfortunately for Colgate-Palmolive, consumers found the name too similar to that of the dog food Alpo). In 1974, Quaker Natural Granola was one of the top five selling brands of cereal. No other new cereal had made the top five in almost 30 years. In 1975, General Mills introduced the portable granola bar as a "healthy" alternative to sweets.

It's no mystery why people loved granola—it's loaded with honey, oil, and calories. But it was all okay because they were natural, good calories, or at least they were when made at home or bought in bulk at health food stores. Of course, with mass market granola, the calories weren't all of the

---

Test your knowledge of 1970s American eating habits with this quiz, adapted from *The Changing American Diet.*

1. How many eight-ounce servings of soft drinks did the average American drink in 1976?

   a) 86

   b) 367

   c) 493

2. Of all the fresh fruit that we bought in 1976, what proportion was bananas?

   a) 18 percent

   b) 36 percent

   c) 52 percent

3. How much cheese (including cottage cheese) did Americans eat (on the average) in 1976?

   a) 20.7 pounds

   b) 35.3 pounds

   c) 55.5 pounds

4. How much red meat (beef, lamb, pork, and veal) did Americans consume on average in 1976?

   a) 85.2 pounds

   b) 165.2 pounds

   c) 242.5 pounds

5. How much of the ice cream and ice milk we ate in 1976 was vanilla?

   a) 72 percent

   b) 42 percent

   c) 24 percent

6. Did Americans in 1976 get more or fewer of their calories from fat than Americans in 1910?

   a) less than 5 percent more or less

   b) 17 percent more

   c) 31 percent more

Answers 1-c, 2-b, 3-a, 4-b, 5-b, 6-c

"good" variety. Supermarket brands were often packed with sugar, brown sugar, corn syrup, and highly saturated palm and coconut oils. It wasn't until the 1990s that some granola manufacturers would produce low-fat granola using fruit juice for sweetener. Meanwhile, in 1973, a new cookbook called *The Granola Cookbook* showed home cooks how to incorporate granola into almost everything. There were recipes not just for granola, but for granola eggs Benedict, granola quiche Lorraine, granola eggplant Parmesan, and even granola fondue.

Starbucks Coffee

Starbucks is everywhere now, its green and white mermaid logo ubiquitous in small towns and along highways across America. In New York, you can sometimes find multiple Starbucks on a single block. But this chain was yet another product of the specialty and gourmet food awakening that began in the 1960s.

Since World War II, instant coffee had ruled the scene, with different coffee manufacturers engaging in price-cutting wars in which the real loser was coffee taste, which came from reconstituted inferior robusta beans. Soda was increasing in popularity, with most baby boomers choosing Pepsi or Coke over Nescafé. In the 1960s, however, an increased awareness of the social issues involved with coffee production, advocacy for a fair trade policy, which guarantees fair pricing for coffee cooperatives, and a rediscovery of the joy of coffee brewed from freshly roasted, high-quality arabica beans all contributed to the popularity of local, specialty coffees.

In 1966, a Dutchman by the name of Alfred Peet opened a shop in Berkeley called Peet's Coffee & Tea. Locals and students quickly grew addicted to his rich, heady roasts. One of Peet's early devotees was a University of San Francisco graduate named Jerry Baldwin. Baldwin subsequently moved to Seattle, where he ordered bags of Peet's coffee to roast for himself at home. Then, in 1971, with Peet's as the supplier and roaster, Baldwin and two friends, Zev Siegel and Gordon Bowker, opened their own coffee company at Pike Place Market: Starbucks Coffee Company.

By the time Siegel sold out in 1980, Starbucks had six retail outlets and was selling wholesale beans to restaurants and supermarkets. In 1983, the company came full circle by purchasing Peet's Coffee. In 1987, Baldwin sold Starbucks to his former head of marketing, Howard Schultz, deciding he would rather focus on Peet's coffee. Schultz expanded the Starbucks Company throughout the Northwest and to Chicago and Los Angeles. On a trip to Italy in 1983, he was inspired by the communal feel of the coffee bars and decided to focus on espresso-based milk drinks like lattes and cappuccinos. With little advertising, Starbucks spread across the country and is now opening outlets in Europe, Asia, and Latin America. Its unique lingo is now spoken by millions (that is, "I'll have an Iced Quad Venti with Whip Skinny Caramel Macchiato"). The company went public in 1992.

Further Reading

Belasco, Warren J. *Appetite for Change: How the Counterculture Took on the Food Industry.* Ithaca and London: Cornell University Press, 1989.

Brewster, Letitia and Michael F. Jacobson. Ph.D. *The Changing American Diet.* Washington, DC: Center for Science in the Public Interest, 1978.

Bundy, Beverly. *The Century in Food: Americas Fads and Favorites.* Portland: Collectors Press, 2002.

Kamp, David. *The United States of Arugula.* New York: Broadway Books, 2007.

Lappe, Frances Moore. *Diet for a Small Planet.* New York: Ballantine Books, 1971.

Sacks, Daniel. *Whitebread Protestants: Food and Religion in American Culture.* New York: St. Martin's Press, 2000.

9

1980s

Judith Yablonski

The shift from the Carter administration to the Reagan era of the 1980s encompassed a dramatic change in the attitude toward wealth in America. The Baby Boomers, those born during the post-World War II era, were in the prime of their careers. They were experiencing the wealth of a booming stock market, which began as a steady and steep rise in the early 1980s and did not decline until the latter part of the decade. These Baby Boomers became known as yuppies, short for "young urban professional" or "young upwardly-mobile professional." Jerry Rubin, who went from being a notorious radical antiwar organizer to working on Wall Street at the end of the 1970s, serves as a symbol for the cultural shift that was occurring for most in his generation. The Baby Boomer generation was fed up with blasting corporate America and was ready to embrace the security, status, and wealth offered by joining corporate America. The yuppies were interested in spending, luxury housing, fancy clothes, fancy cars (BMWs), condos, and country vacation homes. *If you got it, flaunt it* was a watchword, as was *shop till you drop*. Naturally, the yuppies could not get enough of the fanciest, most ostentatiously luxurious food.

Statistics show that the 1980s were a period of the strongest growth and prosperity in this country's history. Reagan's tax cuts led to a long period of continuous economic growth and expansion. In accordance with the higher stock market, yuppies, unlike their parents, were generally two-income family households. Psychologically, American confidence returned. The failure in Vietnam was in the past, the American hostages had returned from Iran, and the Carter era, with its emphasis on anti-elitism and simplicity, was over. Carter installed solar panels on the roof of the White House, and Reagan pulled them off. Further, there was a general feeling that the 1970s energy crisis was over and that inflation was on the decline. When Ronald Reagan ran for reelection in 1984, his television advertisement touted, "It's morning again in America" and suggested that improvements in America's economy were due to Reagan-era policies. The concept spread like wildfire.

Yuppies dressed for success, wearing power ties to their power lunches. Their food choices were all about image and status. The popularity of Lee Bailey's books on how to entertain glamorously and luxuriously, intended for readers with a country house big enough to accommodate several different entertainment locations, exemplifies the mood of the era. His recipes specified the location suitable for serving each dish, such as by the pool, on the boat dock, or under the arbor. Similarly, people looked to Martha Stewart for advice on how to make the presentation of the dining room table extraordinary—using the right types of ornate platters and expensive flowers.

Generally, there was a decrease in home cooking. High-priced restaurants, which boasted status and bragging rights, were in. If not eating out, people would buy high-priced take-out from restaurants or eat frozen gourmet meals from the supermarket heated up in the microwave. When the yuppies did cook, it was for parties, and the recipes would be complicated dishes with outrageous, exotic ingredients, as was dictated by their glossy coffee table cook book written by a favorite celebrity chef. The ingredients were difficult to procure, and the preparation required skilled labor. Often, hosts chose to rely on paying the high price directly to the source itself. Nothing ordinary would do.

Health concerns played a nearly fanatical role in determining food choice during the 1980s. Despite the fashion of chocolate decadence and ice cream mix-ins, for the most part, the yuppies and the general population of the 1980s became increasingly aware of how their food choices affected their health and body weight, and all sorts of health food products appeared on the market as a result. Health food and health food stores began to reach more mainstream customers in the 1980s. A 1985 report from the Federal Food and Drug Administration, for example, stated that oat bran could lower cholesterol. The report created a health food frenzy, as it was the first time that the government suggested that you could improve your health with food. Yogurt and wheat germ were still "in," as were whole grain bread and cereal. Americans were eating more fruits and veggies. Star chefs often chose to incorporate fruit into every dish and to use organic food and free-range poultry, and people were choosing chicken over red meat and cooking dried beans and fish. People were eating light, even if taste was sacrificed. The Baby Boomers, interested in status and image, did not want to look overweight.

In 1985, *The New Doubleday Cookbook* appeared, providing for the first time per-serving calorie, sodium, and cholesterol counts for each recipe. That same year, Jane Brody published the *Good Food Book: Living the High-Carbohydrate Way*, which offered nutritional information and low-fat, high-carbohydrate recipes that tasted good geared toward lower-income people who wanted to eat healthfully. More and more Americans were becoming aware of the health benefits that certain food choices have to offer. For example, it was becoming part of the collective knowledge that high-fiber foods can help or prevent constipation, lower one's risk of developing heart disease, and prevent certain cancers. The demand for bread and cereals high in fiber increased as a result. Other health benefits that were beginning to shape American knowledge came from a study of the Greenland Inuit people, who consumed large amounts of fat from seafood. The omega 3 fatty acids contained in the seafood were found to be the source of the low incidence of cardiovascular disease among the tribe.

Sushi became a popular food in the United States during the 1980s because it contained fish and vegetables with specific health benefits. (Shutterstock)

Similarly, Mediterranean cooking was believed to allow for a longer life. Fruits and vegetables became well known to have anticancer compounds called antioxidants. And the list of the health benefits of various foods seemed almost infinite. Sushi became popular because of its healthy ingredients and because it allowed people to experience a taste of an ancient culture in modern times.

Along with the promotion of the benefits of certain foods, there were also warnings in the media, although they served as more of a conversation piece than advice that the majority of Americans heeded. These warnings related to the dangers of hydrogenated and polysaturated vegetable oil, artificial dyes, nitrates, and pickled foods. Furthermore, Americans were beginning to learn that the advances in agricultural technology that allowed them to buy produce from around the world and their local supermarkets for low prices were produced with methods that could have adverse health effects. Thus, more people were beginning to demand organically grown foods to ensure that their produce was grown without the use of cancer-causing pesticides and that their meat and milk be free of antibiotic residues from the agricultural fields. Corporate food giants were quick to churn out products that catered to all of the hype in the media about food choices. The 1980s saw a deregulation of advertising restrictions, and advertisers could legally make stronger health claims. Advertising focused on foods that lower cholesterol and provide other health benefits, such as decreasing incidences of cancer. For example, Kellogg's All-Bran and Lipton Tea were pitched as cancer fighters, butter was promoted as containing "zero carbs," and in 1986, Hormel Foods Corporation came out with Spam Less Sodium, a healthy alternative to the canned luncheon meat manufactured of pork shoulder and ham. In 1988, lower-fat dairy products gained widespread acceptance. Low-fat and skim milk sales combined exceeded whole milk sales for first time. During the 1980s, margarine, developed in 1869 as a product of animal fat and milk, outsold butter based on its promotion as the healthier, cheaper butter. A notable influx on the market of soft drinks and sodas geared toward people on a diet appeared, such as diet Coke.

Despite the popularity of health food, the 1980s saw an increase in the incidences of obesity. According to the Centers for Disease Control and Prevention, obesity began to grow in the United States during the later part of the 1980s. The reasoning for this could be that alongside the interest in health food, there was an interest in chocolate decadence, Ben & Jerry's, and desserts. There was a divergence of desires and a belief that one healthy meal bought you the right to a decadent dessert. Furthermore, when people were not at fine restaurants, they were eating more and more processed foods and munching on the multitude of processed junk food popular in the 1980s. Between products such as Slim Fast or Richard Simmons aerobics videos, people were eating Doritos and drinking Diet Coke.

Food and politics were constant companions during the final decades of the twentieth century. In 1981, Reagan tried to cut federal funding for school lunches for the poor by announcing that ketchup could be counted as a vegetable. There was huge public protest, and Senator Heinz gave a speech arguing that ketchup was clearly a condiment, not a vegetable, and exposed the politics behind this reclassification.

In 1985, Americans were frightened by the news that a hole in Earth's ozone shield had been discovered over Antarctica. People's concern for the planet was growing. The 1980s saw heightened organized activity to address these issues ranging from animal rights and world hunger awareness to creative new approaches to agriculture. Furthermore, many companies attempted to address these issues through their corporate policies. For example, Paul Newman founded Newman's Own Food in 1982, devoting the profits to charity. Applying concepts of sustainable business practices, Ben & Jerry's adopted a policy of donating 7.5 percent of its pretax profits to charity and that its highest paid executives would never make more than seven times the salary of its bottom wage earners. This policy ended in 1995 when co-founder Ben Cohen resigned as CEO and was replaced by Chuck Lacey, who earned six figures annually.

Gregory McNamee describes in his book, *Moveable Feasts,* that in the late 1980s, London Greenpeace accused McDonald's of destroying rainforests, producing meat using hormones, using pesticides and antibiotics in cattle feed, and torturing and murdering animals. They argued that the rainforests of Central America and the Amazon were being turned into cattle pastures mainly because of the fast-food industry. McDonald's was also criticized as being junk food. In response, McDonald's began selling salads, reducing the fat content of its hamburgers, and changing the way it made french fries.

The People for the Ethical Treatment of Animals (PETA) was formed in 1981 with a focus on all animal rights issues, including factory farming. That same year, Farm Animal Reform Movement (FARM) was formed with the intention of promoting vegan, plant-based diets to save animals, protect the environment, and improve health. In 1985, FARM organized its annual event the Great American Meatout—modeled after the Great American Smoke out—in which programs were scheduled to promote a vegetarian diet that includes fruits, vegetables, and whole grains in lieu of eating meat. One year later, Farm Sanctuary, a refuge for abused farm animals, opened. All of these organizations published vegetarian cookbooks to promote their causes. Animal rights groups also became vocal in their denouncement of the wearing of fur. As a result, fur wearing went permanently out of fashion, and hunting began to decline. According to the *Oxford Companion to American Food and Drink,* hunters numbered 21 million in 1981 and are now estimated to be closer to 13 million. Trappers declined from 800,000 in 1981 to the current 100,000.

The 1984 to 1985 famine in Ethiopia was widespread and affected the inhabitants of today's Eritrea and Ethiopia due in part to record low rainfalls. In response, pop musicians organized themselves to make "We Are the World," a rock fund-raising music video. The song was a charity single, originally recorded by the group USA for Africa in 1985. It was written by Michael Jackson and Lionel Richie and coproduced by Quincy Jones and Michael Omartian for the album *We Are the World.* "We Are the World" was a worldwide commercial success and became the fastest-selling American pop single in history. It was the first single to be certified multi-platinum. However, commentators in the rock press were disappointed that the song did not challenge listeners as to why famines occur in the first place. According to Voice of America News, as of 2009, *We Are the World* had sold more than 20 million copies and raised more than $63 million for humanitarian aid in Africa and the United States. Other efforts to address hunger issues included 6 million Americans participating in Hands Across America in 1986 by holding hands and singing across 4,150 miles of road in support of the hungry and homeless.

The latter part of the twentieth century experienced a rapid increase in the amount of pesticides and insecticides used in agriculture and the introduction of many lab-oriented solutions to global hunger. In 1982, the first genetically engineered crop plant was developed—the tomato. In 1984, the first transgenic farm animal was born. The average commercial fertilizer use on U.S. farms during the 1980s was about 47.4 million tons per year, grown from 27 million tons in 1960.

The first collective farming operation started in western Massachusetts in 1985, which the owner, Robyn Van En, named "community-supported agriculture" or CSA. A CSA aims to preserve farmland jeopardized by farmers unable to compete with imported produce and corporate agriculture. The business model is based on local buyers of the collective paying in advance for their seasonal produce and agreeing to accept a portion of the risks and benefits of the growing season. The buyers receive fresh local produce on a regular basis in return and a connection to the land on which their food is grown. Some buyers even volunteer to work the fields in lieu of a portion of their annual dues. According to data collected by the U.S. Department of Agriculture in 2007, there were 12,549 farms in the United States operating through a community-supported agriculture arrangement.

The end of the decade roughly coincided with the end of Regan's presidency in 1988 and the stock market collapse of 1987, in which the Dow Jones Industrial Average fell 22.61 percent in one day. High-salary, status-seeking, image-conscious Americans suddenly were feeling the effects of the stock market collapse and the junk bond savings and loan scandals. Some people lost their jobs, others lost their investments, and others received pay cuts. Excessive flaunting of wealth was out, and this affected food trends. People stopped spending at extravagant restaurants. Many of the high-end restaurants closed, and others chose to simplify their menus and lower their prices. Americans turned to comfort food—familiar, simple food, such as meatloaf, noodle burgers, casseroles, two-bean salad, spaghetti and meatballs, lasagna, Jell-O, and grilled cheese sandwiches. Midwest cooking became popular as people welcomed the return of dishes from the past.

People were staying at home rather than going out to restaurants. The only problem was that after a decade of going out or buying take-out, most people did not know how to cook. This problem was compounded by the fact that more and more mothers were working outside of the home and did not have as much time to cook. Relying on the advent of the microwave, the United States turned to microwavable TV dinners and out-of-the-box meals, and corporate America marketed convenience. At the beginning of the decade in 1981, Stouffer's introduced Lean Cuisine frozen dinners and entrées. The brand is marketed as a fast, nutritional, and low-calorie line of meals. In 1984, Lean Cuisine outsold Weight Watchers frozen entrees. In 1985, General Mills introduced Hamburger Helper, Taco Bake Dinner, and Tuna Helper Tetrazzini. All are boxed pasta bundled with a packet or packets of powdered sauce and seasonings intended to be mixed with either hamburger meat or canned tuna for the family on the go. The mascot for Hamburger Helper commercials was a talking "helping hand." In 1988, Boboli Pizza provided prefabricated crusts so that people could make their own pizza at home. In 1989, Healthy Choice introduced the Fresh Express "salad in a bag" for those who would rather not take the time to chop vegetables and toss lettuce.

More than 500 microwaveable food products were introduced to the market in 1987 alone. By the mid-1980s, microwaves were found in 25 percent of American households. This trend was facilitated by the falling cost of microwave technology, which coalesced with the improved methods for transporting frozen foods. According to a report from Highbeam Business, almost 90 percent of consumers owned a microwave oven by 1990.

Entries

Alcohol: Beer and Wine

In the 1980s, the dichotomy between localized and globalized production was easy to see in the beer industry. On the one hand, national marketing of standardized beers called for market consolidation as major players emerged. Yet on the other hand, the United States was experiencing the beginnings of the microbrew and craft brew revolution. The culture of small breweries in the United States was nearly completely destroyed by Prohibition. Prohibition drove the majority of breweries into bankruptcy. Some of the only breweries to survive were the larger ones, including Anheuser-Busch and Pabst, which survived by making malts for other purposes. The larger breweries survived by producing "near-beer," a term used during prohibition to refer to malt beverages that contained less than 0.5 percent alchohol. After Prohibition was repealed, these large producers, lead by Anheuser-Busch and Pabst, were able to quickly regain market control. During the booming 1980s, global brands gained prominence, and Budweiser became the dominant beer in the United States. Budweiser was the flagship brand of the Anheuser-Busch Companies, Inc., and gained more popularity through strategic advertising on television and at sporting events. Budweiser is a light lager with mild flavor, which uses rice and corn, unlike most European beers. The company brought Bud Light to market in 1982. Bud Light was a lower-calorie version of Budweiser and quickly gained a significant market share. Simultaneously, the 1980s were the decade of microbrewing in the United States. In 1975, there were no microbreweries in the United States, but by the end of the 1980s, every major U.S. city had a microbrewery, while Oregon had more than half a dozen, and they were even sprouting up in less populous areas such as Maine and Wyoming. Americans, more and more of whom had traveled abroad and sampled beers that tasted nothing like beer at home, began to demand a higher-quality and more varied product. Microbrews took Old World tradition and combined it with American hops and grains to produce the world's best beers. The American wine industry, too, had been almost

---

Spirits and Liquor

As a result of Prohibition, bourbon sales remained low up until the 1980s. In the 1980s, the bourbon industry responded to interest in small-quantity yet high-quality liquor. Blanton's Bourbon, a single-barrel bourbon, was introduced in 1984, and four years later, Booker's small-batch bourbon was released. Meanwhile, in California, several small distilleries began producing high-quality local spirits. St. George Spirits in Alameda began producing eau de vie in 1982. A year later, Charbay began production of vodka and other spirits. Their neighbors in Oregon, Clear Creek Distillery, began making eau de vie from pears in 1985.

---

destroyed by Prohibition. After repeal, the vast majority of wine consumed in the United States was imported. However, by the 1980s, California wines were competing successfully with the best French wines. This was mainly due to the unprecedented and monumental win for California wine at the Judgment of Paris in 1976, at which California wine beat French wine for the first time ever in a blind taste test by European wine critics. Suddenly, American wine connoisseurs no longer looked to France for quality wine, and California wine became an in-vogue commodity. In fact, California wines were being shipped to wine lovers in France. As a result of the increased number of microbreweries, the number of small wineries also grew. Public desire to support the local economy also facilitated these developments and, in response to this social and environmental consciousness, the first organic winery in the United States was bonded in 1980 in Mendocino County—California's Frey Vineyards.

American Southwest Cuisine

Southwestern cuisine exploded in American during the 1980s. The American Southwest offers New American cuisine combinations such as cooking inspired by Cal-Mex, Tex-Mex, and Santa Fe. This cuisine including grilling, corn, blue corn, beans, chilies, cilantro, limes, salsa, and squash, certainly made its way into defining New American cuisine. At the start of the 1980s, chili was the best-selling canned food in the United States. California chefs promoted this region's cooking style incorporating beans, corn, fresh and dried chilies, cilantro, grilled food over mesquite, and pico de gallo. Pecan pie was the most popular Southern-style Texas dish, especially if made with chocolate. Chefs took this simple old food, as they did with the food of various regions around the United States, and reinvented it. Mark Miller opened Coyote Café in Santa Fe in 1986 and put his own twist on Mexican food with dishes such as smoked chili pasta with duck and green chili stew. Dean

Fearing became the executive chef of The Mansion on Turtle Creek in Dallas toward the end of the 1980s and became known as the Father of Southwestern Cuisine, according to *Restaurant Hospitality* magazine. Fearing made his contribution to New American cuisine using Texas ingredients and techniques, for example, lobster taco with yellow tomato salsa, quail demi-glace, cold smoked pheasant, and smoked corn. Fearing cooking incorporates concepts and techniques from Italian, Thai, Southern, Cajun, and Mexican cuisines. Her Majesty the Queen of England and Presidents George Bush and Bill Clinton have dined at The Mansion on Turtle Creek in Dallas. Stephen Pyles, native Texan, opened ultra-trendy Routh St. Café in Dallas in1983 with John Dayton. The Café had a cooking style similar to Fearing's, for example, lobster enchilada with red pepper crème fraiche and caviar, catfish mousse with crayfish sauce, and Colorado lamb with Texas pecans and garlic. The walls were adorned with art by Jasper Johns and David Hockney. Pyles later opened two similar restaurants in the Midwest. *Bon Appétit* credited Pyles with almost single-handedly changing the cooking scene in Texas. Pyles was enamored by the produce and seafood he had been exposed to in California, so when he opened Routh St. Café, he was importing specialty produce from Southern California, such as baby carrots and yellow bell peppers. Today, the Southwest style is firmly a part of American Cuisine.

California Cuisine

The trend of fusion cooking in California was the rage around the country in the 1980s. California cuisine focused on blending ideas and ingredients from different regions (Mexico, Italy, the Mediterranean, China, and Japan) with classic ingredients and using freshly prepared local ingredients where possible. Alice Waters, co-owner and co-founder of Berkeley, California's Chez Panisse and Jeremiah Tower, head chef of Chez Panisse from 1972 to 1978, have been credited with creating and developing California cuisine. Chez Panisse presentation was always, casual, chic, and upscale. Celebrity chef Michael McCarty set the style for California restaurants with Michael's in Santa Monica in 1979. Waiters dressed in chinos and pink oxford shirts. Michael's was, like Chez Panisse, casual but chic in décor, and expensive. The dishes were flavored with vinaigrettes and cream sauces, and the plates were decorated with colorful vegetables or berries, artfully displayed. Roasted vegetables were a big part of California cuisine. Red peppers could be grilled on the BBQ, broiled, charred over a gas flame, or baked at high temperature until blackened. While grilling was trendy in the 1970s, roasting vegetables was the craze in the 1980s. Jeremiah Towers and Alice Waters introduced roasting whole garlic at Chez Panisse. Jeremiah Tower continued to set trends during the 1980s with his three restaurants: Balboa Café, Santa Fe Bar and Grill, and Stars—all in San Francisco. In 1982, *Chez Panisse Menu Cookbook* was published, further popularizing California Cuisine. Chez Panisse restaurant's popularity has endured, and as recently as 2006 to 2008, it was voted among the top 50 restaurants in the world by *Restaurant* magazine. The Chez Panisse menu, geared toward fresh ingredients that are in season, grown locally, symbolizes the growing interest in taking individual responsibility for the environment by making food choices that have a minimal impact, such as eating locally and organically. The 1980s brought a growing awareness of the consequences of international shipment of mass-produced food, in that it uses a tremendous amount of resources, including fuel, and also does not taste as good as freshly harvested produce, and locally harvested meat and fish. Celebrity chefs leaped to the rescue by offering and encouraging the consumption of local, sustainably produced ingredients. To exemplify this shift in consciousness in food choices, Niman-Schell Beef became a mark of distinction on northern California menus, such as Stars, Zuni Café, and Chez Panisse. Niman Ranch is a San Francisco Bay area-based ranch, meat processor, and distributor of high-quality "natural" beef, lamb, and pork, founded by rancher Bill Niman. The beef, for example, came from cattle raised without using antibiotics to stave off gastrointestinal-tract ailments and without growth hormones, which dramatically shorten the time it takes the cattle to reach slaughtering size. Niman-Schell kept the calves with their mothers for as long as they needed to nurse and, afterward, placed them in proximity to the mother cows. All of his cows were fed all-natural feed. Niman Schell beef's popularity was based on the taste and the environmental benefit of it being prepared in a humane, eco-friendly, small-farmer fashion. The popularity of the beef spread from these northern California restaurants to restaurants around the country.

Spa Cuisine

Beginning as early as 1981, trend-setting restaurants began to offer spa cuisine, which catered to upscale health-conscious clients who desired small, portioned, healthy yet complicated food dishes. According to Sylvia Lovgren, Four Seasons Hotel's diet menu included spa cuisine items such as sautéed cod fillet with steamed spaghetti squash and red pepper coulis and brown and wild rice pilaf with wheat. The idea behind spa cuisine was that one would take a break from a sauna or massage at the spa to eat one of the nourishing concoctions.

Cajun Food

Louisiana had a lot to offer to New American cuisine in the way of Cajun and Creole cooking—both of which combine French and African cooking techniques. The foodies went wild for it. By the mid-1980s, just about every major American city had a Cajun restaurant, and each added its own region's accent. Cajun cooking was popularized by celebrity chef Paul Prudhomme in the 1980s with dishes such as duck gumbo or spot prawn jambalaya. Prudhomme is the owner and chef of K-Paul's Louisiana Kitchen, and his most famous dish was blackened red fish. After the 1984 publishing of his cookbook, *Louisiana Kitchen,* blackened redfish was replicated around the country so often that redfish was put on the endangered species list. Other Cajun dishes such and bread pudding became staples on trendy menus around the country. The word "Cajun" references a person of French-Acadian descent whose ancestors on one or both sides of the family come from the land of Acadie, particularly modern-day New Brunswick or Nova Scotia. French Acadians, kicked out of Nova Scotia in the 1700s, found homes in the bayous of south Louisiana and brought with them unique foods such as blackened fish, gumbo, and jambalaya—

often served alongside or made with a combination of bell pepper, onion, celery, parsley, bay leaf, green onions, and cayenne pepper. Cajun cuisine is heavy on game meats supplemented with rice or corn. While Creole cuisine blends French, Portuguese, Spanish, Caribbean, Mediterranean, deep Southern American, Indian, and African influences, Cajun cuisine is simpler and spicier. By the end of the decade, Cajun cooking went out of style but has continued to be a style of cooking that is undoubtedly American.

Celebrity chef Paul Prudhomme made Cajun cooking popular across the United States in the 1980s. (AP/Wide World Photos)

Cheese

Similar to the return to localized, small-scale production of alcohol seen in the microbrewery revolution, artisan cheese making experienced a renaissance during the 1980s. According to *Harvard Magazine*, anthropologist Heather Paxson describes artisan cheese making as "the process of using sensory evaluation in cheese making, such as running a finger through freshly set curd to decide if it's ready to cut." With advances in farming technology during the twentieth century, small farmers could not compete, and many went out of business. As a result, mass production ruled all aspects of the food industry, processed cheese took over the market, and marketplace diversity in cheese diminished. Due to a renewed interest in taste and growing concern over the social and environmental consequences of the origins of food, people grew disillusioned with the industrially produced foods that had low-grade, tasteless ingredients. Furthermore, the rise of foreign travel exposed many Americans to the European artisan tradition. More and more small producers and dairies were making unpasteurized cow, goat, and sheep cheeses. They paid greater attention to what the animals were eating and how they were raised. Today, there are hundreds of small, artisan producers in the country, especially in Vermont, Wisconsin, and northern California.

Desserts

Fruit sorbet was a popular desert during the 1980s, and it went perfectly with America's obsession with exotic fruits. Sorbets were flavored with passion fruit, raspberry, blood orange, black currant, and, of course, kiwi. Trendy restaurants offered sorbet between courses as palate refreshers and for color and display. Frozen food in general was popular, especially premium high-fat ice creams. Ronald Reagan declared July National Ice Cream Month in 1984. In addition to Häagen-Dazs, there was Ben & Jerry's—a company that applied a concept akin to the popular trend in fusion cooking and the trend in wild pizza toppings. Ben & Jerry's was the pacesetter in the land of mix-in ice cream. They mixed in anything—candy, cookies, nuts—and produced novel flavors such as Heath Bar Crunch and Cherry Garcia. Other twists on ice cream that were popular in the 1980s include Jell-O Pudding Pops—frozen creamy pudding on a stick, made popular by comedian Bill Cosby serving as the star in their commercials. Also introduced in the 1980s was the ice cream cookie sandwich. For an ice cream substitute, the health-minded hurried to eat a soybean curd frozen dessert called Tofutti. Tofutti was popular among the lactose-intolerant, kosher, vegetarian, and vegan consumers who wanted to join in on the ice cream craze.

Chocolate

Among sorbet and mix-in ice cream, another desert craze during this decade, trendier than exotic fruit deserts, was chocolate. Dessserts included cakes, chocolate tortes filled and frosted with chocolate, Chocolate-covered fruit, chocolate truffles flavored with nuts and liquors, chocolate pecan pie, chocolate brownies, and chocolate chip cookies. To satisfy consumers' desire to be distinctive, white chocolate caught on. Chef Michel Fitoussi concocted white chocolate mousse in New York and, in fact, mousse was the most popular of white chocolate desserts. White chocolate was being used in truffles, brownies, desert sauces, cakes, tortes, tartes, cheesecake, ice cream, and even white chocolate chip cookies. It offered the unique advantage of being supple and easily molded into decorations. White chocolate caught on beyond the elitist crowd, and in 1987, Nestlé introduced Alpine White, America's first white chocolate bar.

Exotic Fruits and Vegetables

To go along with the pattern of interest in everything new, New American cooking enthusiasts became fascinated by exotic produce. Consumption of kiwi, the most fashionable of the exotic fruits, increased sevenfold from 1980 to 1985. Beyond kiwi, people were interested in cooking with fruit in general, including strawberries, raspberries, passion fruit, mango, jicama, star fruit, radicchio, and blood oranges. To fill their need for exotic vegetables, chefs would strive to include such rare items as enokidake mushrooms, blue potatoes, blue corn, mesclun, arugula, and green peppercorns. New methods for shipping and handling made this possible. The kiwi, with its bright green center dotted with black seeds, was attractive as a garnish. In general, these unusual and striking fruits and vegetables not only added unique flavor to a plate but also brightened up the presentation and elevated the dish to a work of art. Examples of dishes that incorporated exotic produce include mango chutney, pineapple-corn kernel salsa, blood-orange buerre blanc, carambola (star fruit) sorbet, and raspberry chicken.

Fast Food

Fast food, especially the hamburger, is the most-consumed type of food in the United States. According to Jean Anderson, in *The American Century Cookbook*, fast-food chains sold 200 hamburgers per second during the 1980s. This was true despite the news in 1982 that new infectious agents, prions, were first discovered in the brains of cattle in the European Union, and prions caused a disease in cattle known as mad cow disease. It soon became common knowledge in the United States that cattle were routinely being fed the flesh of other cattle on factory farms and that this feeding practice was causing the disease of the brain in cattle. Still, Americans' love for the hamburger barely diminished, and around the world, the United States is famous if not infamous for the hamburger. McDonald's was the recipient of much criticism in the 1980s for selling junk food. In response, McDonald's began selling salads, reducing the fat content of its hamburgers, and changing the way it made fries. Burger King also addressed these concerns by offering a salad bar beginning in 1983. In 1983, McDonald's introduced Chicken McNuggets to add variety to the menu and soon became the second-largest purchaser of chicken in the United States. The intention behind the introduction of Chicken McNuggets was to create a product that could easily be eaten while driving. This single product changed the way chickens were raised and processed, so that the majority of chickens were no longer sold whole. Burger King also began changing its menu to keep up with the competition. In 1982, it introduced the bacon double cheeseburger. Three years after the introduction of the McNugget at McDonald's, Burger King introduced Chicken Tenders. Wendy's hamburger chain gained a tremendous amount of attention in 1984 when its "Where's the beef?" ad campaign debuted, which featured three elderly ladies inspecting a hamburger from a hypothetical competitor that had a huge bun and a tiny hamburger inside. One of the women exclaims, "Where's the beef?" The commercial was parodied on TV comedy shows for years.

Italian Cooking

Novelty, innovation, and a break from tradition characterized Italian cooking in the 1980s. Colored pastas tinted with tomato, spinach, beets, saffron, or squid ink were all the rage. In-vogue pasta was not served with meatballs, but with three cheeses. Simultaneously, pasta offered a good answer to the health craze objective to have high carbohydrates, lower protein, and low-fat-intake diets. Chef Craig Claiborne started the rage for pasta salads. Pasta was great because it could be served with olive oil sauces not too heavy in cream, cheese, or eggs, such as Genoese pesto. Italian grain dishes were also trendy in the 1980s, including polenta and risotto. Chez Panisse was the first non-Italian restaurant to serve polenta, and it soon became a common starch at trendy restaurants.

Popular pasta dishes are served with lighter olive oil-based sauces, such as pesto. (Akross/ Dreamstime.com)

New American Cuisine

When dining out, yuppies did not choose restaurants based on the quality of the food or ambiance but on the hipness of the chef and the extent to which the restaurant was considered in vogue. Status dictated restaurant choice. This was the dawning of the age of the celebrity chef. The celebrity chefs were rock stars, restaurant activists, cooking TV show stars, and authors who were popularized through food magazines and cookbooks read by housewives trying to create an impressive dinner party. The James Beard Foundation, founded during the 1980s and headquartered in Beard's Greenwich Village townhouse, publicly honors chefs with what are often called "the Oscars of the food world." Each celebrity chef was trying to reinvent "New American cuisine" during the 1980s. "New American cuisine" is a term for expensive, elitist, modern cooking that was a natural result of both the influence of increased migration to the United States and an increase in European travel among Americans. It was essentially la nouvelle cuisine of France prepared with American ingredients. It combines flavors from America's melting pot with traditional techniques—a blending a local food with migrant food. Each major city of the country had its unique contribution to the definition of New American cuisine, as presented to the world through its local celebrity chef and promoted in publications such as *Vogue* and *Harper's Bazaar*. New American chefs used regional dishes for inspiration instead of *cuisine classique* dishes. New techniques were embraced and modern equipment was often used; chefs even used microwave ovens. The chefs paid close attention to the dietary needs of their guests and were extremely inventive in creating new combinations and pairings. According to Sylvia Lovgren, dishes were marked by exotic, trendy ingredients, such as raspberry vinegar, green peppercorns, pink peppercorns, foie gras, onion marmalade, walnut oil, and sun-dried tomatoes. The plates were carefully composed platters of edible art. The chefs used squeeze bottles filled with colored sauces to create photoworthy, edible, aesthetically decorative food.

Pizza: California Style

California celebrity chefs set trends in pizza—crazy pizza with the wildest toppings each chef could dream up. Jeremiah Towers was the first to make the nontraditional pizzas at Chez Panisse in 1974, where he made stylish individual pizzas. However, it was Wolfgang Puck who really popularized unusual pizzas; Puck is best known for his California-style brick oven pizza. He made nontraditional pizza at his restaurant, Spago, on Sunset Boulevard in Los Angeles, with ingredients such as smoked salmon, duck sausage, goat cheese, caviar, Black Forest ham, artichokes, wild mushrooms, and even American chocolate chip cookies. At some of Puck's restaurants, the chef would cook the pizza right in front of the customer. Spago was a hit overnight and required reservations be made months in advance, and eventually small pizzas were found on the appetizer menus at many trendy restaurants around the country. In 1985, chefs Rick Rosenfield and Larry Flax continued the pizza trend by opening the first California Pizza Kitchen in Beverly Hills, California. CPK served pizzas with unusual toppings such as BBQ chicken and broccoli and slanted toward being healthy. Currently there are 240 full-service CPK restaurants as per their website, and CPK pizzas are currently available frozen in supermarkets. Other toppings that appeared during the crazy pizza fad included roasted red peppers, tuna fish, capers, smoked salmon, crème fraiche, and caviar.

Wolfgang Puck

Wolfgang Puck was the most famous of star chefs, mostly because he refused to take haute cuisine seriously. He was born in Austria and trained in France. He took over Ma Maison in Los Angeles in the 1970s, which quickly became the hottest restaurant in town. His *Modern French Cooking for the American Kitchen* (1981) was one of America's best-selling "French" cookbooks. By 1981, Puck's career and fame were clear, and the stage was set for expression of his creative culinary visions. Puck made his contribution to fusion California cuisine in 1983 when he opened a popular Chinese-French restaurant called Chinois on Main in Santa Monica, California. Chinois on Main's menu included dishes such as lobster with rice-wine and ginger cream sauce and rack of lamb with cilantro and miso. Chinois on Main gradually became as big a success as Puck's Spago, which was wildly popular just a year before this restaurant opened. Similar to Chinois on Main, La Petite Chaya in southern California was a popular Japanese-French restaurant. The Asian influence on American cuisine

Celebrity chef Wolfgang Puck, pictured here in 2006, made a name for himself with his extremely popular fusion cooking. (AP/Wide World Photos)

stemmed from the 1981 easement of immigration restrictions, which facilitated immigrants entering the United States from all over China, Taiwan, and Hong Kong and from Southeast Asia. The majority of these immigrants settled in the western part of the United States.

Soft Drinks

Although Coke was invented in 1886 and had enjoyed a majority of the market share, by 1981, Pepsi was making inroads into the market and eventually outsold Coca-Cola in certain markets. In response, Coca-Cola began introducing new varieties of its classic beverage. In 1982, Coke and Pepsi introduced Diet Coke and Diet Pepsi, respectively. Diet Coke was different from Coke in that it contained aspartame, an artificial sweetener that has only 4 calories per gram. Aspartame had just been approved by the Food and Drug Administration in 1981 for use in food, and it is used in a wide range of diet foods. By the late 1980s, the market was flooded with diet drinks, including Diet Mountain Dew. In 1985, Cherry Coke was introduced, and, in that same year, New Coke, which encompassed a change in the classic formula. New Coke turned out to be wildly unpopular but worked to the company's advantage in the long run when it reintroduced Coca-Cola Classic. Snapple bottled drinks, an all-natural juice derived from a carbonated apple juice, became a craze during the 1980s. The product, advertised as "Made from the best stuff on Earth," was popular among those interested in a healthier alternative to sodas. Interestingly, until 2009, Snapple was made with high fructose corn syrup. When Snapple introduced its real brewed iced tea in 1987, sales began to skyrocket. Consumers increasingly chose it over its carbonated competitors. Bottled water became trendy among the yuppies in the mid- to late 1980s. Sought after for its snob value or for its supposed cleanliness, bottled water seemed to be an excellent alternative for health and fitness fanatics.

Further Reading

Anderson, Jean and Hanna, Elaine. *The New Doubleday Cookbook*. Garden City, NY: Doubleday, 1985.

Brody, Jane E. *Jane Brody's Good Food Book: Living the High-Carbohydrate Way.* New York: Norton, 1985.

Civitello, Linda. *Cuisine and Culture: A History of Food and People*. Hoboken, NJ: John Wiley & Sons, Inc., 2004.

Kamp, David. *The United States of Arugula*. New York: Broadway Books, 2007.

"Melting Pot Cuisine: The State of American Cuisine." http://www.james beard.org/files/jbf_state_of_american_cuisine.pdf

Prudhomme, Chef Paul. *Chef Paul Prudhomme's Louisiana Kitchen*. New York: William Morrow, 1984.

Puck, Wolfgang. *Wolfgang Puck's Pizza, Pasta, and More!* New York: Random House, 2000.

Tsuda, Nobuko. *Sushi Made Easy*. New York: Weatherhill, 1981.

10

1990s

Margaret Haerens

The 1990s were a decade informed by a number of interesting trends in American cuisine. On the one hand, food companies continued to have great success with packaged and frozen foods, coming out with variations on established products and experimenting with different flavors and packaging. Fast food was a staple in American diets, especially with low-income families or with families too busy to have a home-cooked meal every night. It seemed that the 1990s were continuing trends toward fast food and packaged foods that originated in earlier decades. However, beneath the surface, there was a growing concern about where food was coming from and what was in certain products. Consumers demanded nutritional labeling and consistent standards for food adjectives such as "organic," hormone free, "low fat," or "lean." Information on how crops and animals meat were raised, especially what chemicals and hormones were used, was more available to consumers and became an important factor in many consumers' food choices. Food professionals and consumers were more interested in food science—how certain processes worked and why some worked better than others. The influence of food television, particularly the up-and-coming Food Network, facilitated renewed interest in cooking, food, and entertaining and had a profound impact on the rise of the celebrity chef in American popular culture.

The resurgence of interest in food, cooking, and food culture was reflected in the popularity of cookbooks and cooking magazines. Established periodicals such as *Gourmet* and *Bon Appétit* saw a dramatic increase in subscriptions during the decade. *Cook's Illustrated,* a new food and

Barefoot Contessa Ina Garten prepares fruitcake cookies in her East Hampton, New York, kitchen, which doubles as the set for her television show. (AP/Wide World Photos)

cooking magazine that often compared different recipes, cooking processes, and packaged brands, proved successful in attracting and keeping readers. Cooking shows on PBS and cooking segments on morning television and talk shows remained a draw for many viewers interested in cooking. Martha Stewart and the Barefoot Contessa (a brand created by Ina Garten) established their reputations as two of the most successful food and entertainment brands in the United States on the basis of their popular cookbooks, food and cooking products, and media appearances. With more and more Americans taking an interest in cooking and food, television executives determined the time was right for an American cable network devoted completely to cooking and food programming.

The Food Network debuted on November 23, 1993. From the beginning, the network featured well-known chefs and culinary personalities, explored issues related to food and food preparation, and offered exciting food competitions and cook-offs. It was an immediate success, as viewers tuned in to instructional cooking programs during the day and food entertainment shows at night. It also featured a number of American chefs who quickly became celebrities and television personalities because of their success on the Food Network. The first celebrity chef to emerge was Emeril

Lagasse, whose energetic and engaging Cajun cooking style on his show *The Essence of Emeril* led to skyrocketing ratings for the fledgling network. Bobby Flay was another Food Network personality to achieve celebrity chef status. Flay hosted and competed in several popular shows, including *Boy Meets Grill, BBQ with Bobby Flay, Throwdown! with Bobby Flay*, and *Hot Off the Grill with Bobby Flay*. Viewers loved his spicy Southwestern culinary style and his engaging approach to cooking and food. Mario Batali also became a celebrity chef and well-known television personality because of his success on the Food Network. For years he was the host of *Molto Mario* and *Mario Eats Italy*, which established him as one of the top American chefs specializing in Italian cuisine. Another recognizable television personality who emerged from Food Network during the 1990s was Alton Brown. The creator and host of *Good Eats*, a program that examines the science behind cooking, Brown often analyzes cooking equipment and discusses the chemistry of cooking and food. His clever and knowledgeable approach to food science leads commentators to describe Brown as a combination of Mr. Wizard and Bill Nye the Science Guy.

Brown's interest in food and cooking science was a reflection of a larger 1990s trend. Scientists, chefs, and consumers were focusing greater attention on the physical and chemical reactions in cooking processes. There was a renewed curiosity as to why certain food preparation processes worked the way they did and how scientists and chefs could manipulate and deconstruct food to create culinary innovation. Molecular gastronomy was a result of that renewed and unbridled curiosity. Both a scientific discipline and a culinary movement, molecular gastronomy considers the chemistry and physics behind the preparation of food. Scientists focus on the science, while chefs then apply these scientific principles to their own cooking to create experimental and avant-garde dishes. An example of a dish created with molecular gastronomy is the foam sauces that began appearing on a number of menus in restaurants around the country during that time. Food enthusiasts flocked to restaurants featuring such innovations to taste these dishes and to have a truly unique dining experience. American chefs associated with the culinary movement of molecular gastronomy are Grant Achatz, Wylie Dufresne, and Michael Carlson.

A different kind of science was applied to crops and animal breeding during the decade. Scientists made breakthroughs in crop development and protection with the invention of genetically modified (GM) foods. Realizing that modifying the DNA structure of plants and animals could produce advantageous traits, scientists began to experiment in the 1990s with genetically modified crops and livestock. The most common modification

A plant physiologist compares Florida-grown Endless Summer tomatoes to his greenhouse-grown fruit. The tomato is the first commercially grown genetically engineered product to enter supermarkets. (Agricultural Research Service/ USDA)

was to make crops less reliant on herbicides and pesticides for protection against disease. The first commercially grown genetically modified crop was a tomato, the Flavr Savr, that was genetically altered to stay fresh longer. At first, GM foods were hailed as a way to alleviate world hunger and as a boon to developing countries. As controversy erupted over GM products, more and more countries considered limiting or banning the use or import of GM foods. In America, GM crops are a staple in food production. Most food that Americans buy in supermarkets contains at least one genetically modified ingredient—if not several. While the rest of the world seems to be highly concerned about the impact of GM foods, the United States does not show the same level of worry.

If the development of GM foods is a prime example of the progress food science made in the 1990s, the backlash against GM foods is an example of the increasing concern with food ethics. Critics of GM foods worry about the long-term safety of scientifically modified foods as well as the effect they might have on biodiversity. As in earlier decades, there is always a certain segment of the American consumer interested in the ethics of livestock and agricultural practices. During the 1990s, families were concerned more than ever with eating healthy food. These consumers questioned where their food came from and how it was grown or raised. This led to a growing movement against the use of factory farms, which are industrialized farms that raise one kind of animal in close quarters to maximize production. Hormones and other chemicals are often injected into animals to keep them healthy or to make them larger or meatier. Animals are kept in cages so small they are unable to move around—or even turn around. For the growing number of consumers ethically opposed to such practices, meat and dairy from organic and free-range farms became more accessible and affordable. Organic farms follow farming methods modeled on natural ecosystems, using crop rotations, compost, animal grazing, and careful cultivation to raise food with little or no fertilizer. Animals are treated more humanely and are not injected with needless hormones or other chemicals. A free-range environment means that animals have some room to move around, can graze off the land, and often interact with other animals. For many consumers, it was worth paying a little more to ensure that the products they purchased were raised or grown organically and humanely.

The U.S. government came to the aid of concerned consumers by passing the Organic Foods Production Act of 1990. This law created the National Organic Program (NOP), which set the uniform minimum standards for food classified as organic in the United States. Before the passage of the bill, private and state agencies had been certifying organic practices, but there was no uniformity in standards between states and, therefore, no guarantee that "organic" meant the same thing from state to state. As a result, many food companies were calling their products "organic" when they were not. The law remedied that situation by allowing food producers that met NOP standards to affix a "Meets the USDA Organic Requirements" label on their products.

Nutritional labeling became an issue early in the decade. In 1990, Congress passed the Nutrition Labeling and Education Act, which allowed the Food and Drug Administration (FDA) the authority to require nutritional labeling of most packaged food sold in the United States. The law required that all nutrient claims made by food manufacturers met the FDA's strict standards. This law was put in place to discourage food manufacturers from making false or misleading claims about their products' nutritional value, such as calling their ice cream "low fat" if that wasn't true. These provisions were meant to provide consumers with information to make informed decisions about the products they ate and fed their families.

The growing concern over food ethics and the promotion of organic food led to a strong movement to support local foods and traditions. The slow food movement exemplified this trend; the Slow Food International organization was established to preserve local cuisines, traditions, and cultures that the members perceived as being at risk from globalization, industrialized farming, and the rapid growth of fast-food culture. During the decade, there was a growing awareness of eco-gastronomy, or the connections between food and the plants it came from. The controversy over

The Movement against Factory Farms

In the 1990s, Americans grew increasingly concerned with healthy eating. Part of that concern involved investigating where their food came from and how it was grown and raised. As a result, a movement against factory farms developed. Factory farms raise one kind of animal —fish, chicken, pigs, turkeys, or cows—at high densities and often indoors in poor conditions. For example, in some factory farms animals cannot walk around or are kept in cages so tightly that they cannot turn around or move freely. Animals are injected with growth hormones, antimicrobial agents, or vitamin supplements to produce unusually large animals, or to enlarge a specific part—such as to produce a chicken with more breast meat than a normal chicken. Animals are bred to feature a specific characteristic or to produce animals more suited to the confined spaces. These poor conditions and treatments are meant to produce the most meat, eggs, or dairy products at the lowest cost. However, when Americans became aware of these conditions, some rejected food from factory farms and began to search out food coming from organic farms or free-range farms, where animals are allowed some semblance of free movement and are given humane treatment. As the decade wore on, more and more organic and free-range products became available for American consumers concerned with food ethics and the chemicals that were injected into our food products.

GM foods is another aspect of this movement. As individuals considered the connection between the way food is grown or raised, their own food choices, and the impact on local and global ecosystems, the 1990s became a time during which more information was made available for concerned activists and consumers to make informed choices about food. More and more Americans became aware of the food industry and how they could make a difference in their own lives as well as on a larger scale through educating themselves and then implementing ethical and conscientious food practices and choices. This focus on making well-informed decisions on food is a trend that has become more prevalent in the twenty-first century as today's consumers draw from progress made in the 1990s.

Entries

Artisan Bread Movement

Artisan breads are baked in small batches rather than mass produced. Although artisan breads have always been available at bakeries and some stores, during the 1990s, there was a surge in popularity for crafted, preservative-free bread. Many observers trace the rise of artisan breads in the United States to the San Francisco Bay Area's bread revolution of the 1970s and 1980s. Examples of artisan breads are focaccia, ciabatta,

Artisan bread sits in baskets on display at a farmers' market. The popularity of artisan bread increased with consumers' requests for fewer preservatives. (Alisonh29/Dreamstime.com)

stoneground wheat bread, and farm-style bread. Artisan breads are characterized by the use of centuries-old baking techniques and their lack of chemicals, especially the preservatives that are found in most supermarket breads. They are made up of four core ingredients: flour, water, yeast, and salt. Sourdough is added for some breads. Others require eggs and sugar. A variety of ingredients can be added to make flavored artisan bread: onions, olive oil, cheese, fruit, sun-dried tomatoes, or nuts. Rustic breads use whole grain flours. The ingredients and processes are fundamentally the same as they were throughout history. Ingredients are mixed, slowly fermented, hand crafted, and then baked in masonry ovens. While baking, loaves are exposed to steam, which creates a shiny surface. While the outside may be crusty or chewy, the interior is always moist. Breads are "scored" with decorative cross-cuts, along which the bread cracks while rising and baking to allow steam to escape. The emphasis is on high-quality ingredients and careful baking. Artisan breads have a much shorter shelf life than brand-name breads sold as supermarkets because they are made without preservatives.

Barefoot Contessa

A brand of cookbooks, cooking mixes and products, and television program, the Barefoot Contessa is the brainchild of Ina Garten, who has created a simple and elegant style of cooking and entertainment for American audiences and readers. Garten was born on February 2, 1948, in Brooklyn, New York, and was raised in Stamford, Connecticut. Early on, she was drawn to science as well as to cooking. She attended Syracuse University but postponed her education to get married in 1968. Her husband, Jeffrey Garten, was in the military, and the newlyweds moved to Fort Bragg, North Carolina. It was there that she began to pursue her interest in cooking and entertaining while her husband served in the Vietnam War. After his military stint was over, the couple traveled to Paris, where Ina fell in love with French cuisine and the use of fresh herbs, fruits, vegetables, and other ingredients she found in farmers' markets around the city. She incorporated these interests into her cooking once she returned to the United States, featuring her distinctive cooking style at weekly dinner parties she hosted at her home in Washington, DC, in 1972. She also went back to school, earning her MBA at George Washington University. Hired as a government aide at the U.S. State Department, she eventually worked her way up to the position of budget analyst on nuclear energy issues. In 1978, she bought a specialty food store in the Hamptons, New York, which became the Barefoot Contessa. Over the years, Garten's store was acclaimed for its elegant style and delicious food. Although she had no formal culinary training, she honed her style with the aid of cookbooks and feedback from friends and customers. In 1996, she sold the store and began to write her renowned cookbook, *The Barefoot Contessa Cookbook*. She followed that with a series of popular Barefoot Contessa cookbooks: *Barefoot Contessa Parties!* in 2001; *Barefoot Contessa Family Style* in 2002; *Barefoot in Paris* in 2004; *Barefoot Contessa at Home* in 2006; and *Barefoot Contessa: Back to Basics* in 2008. Her Food Network show, *Barefoot Contessa*, first aired in 2002. Taped mostly in her own home kitchen, it features Garten preparing simple yet elegant dishes efficiently, with an emphasis on entertaining friends in a warm, welcoming atmosphere.

Mario Batali

One of America's most recognizable chefs, Mario Batali was born on September 9, 1960, in Yakima, Washington. He began cooking at an early age with his family, often helping his grandmother make pies and jams.

In 1975, he moved with his family to Spain but returned to the United States to study at Rutgers University in New Jersey. He graduated from Rutgers in 1982 and later attended Le Cordon Bleu in London. He found culinary school boring, however, and decided to leave in favor of further training in a high-pressure professional kitchen. He apprenticed in the kitchen of the legendary chef Marco Pierre White. After a few other stints, he drastically changed his career by moving to the northern Italian village of Borgo Capanne in 1989 to apprentice in the kitchen at La Volta. He aimed to master the style of Italian cooking renowned in the region; it took him three years. He returned to the United States to open his first restaurant, Po, in 1993. He has opened several restaurants, including Babbo Ristorante e Enoteca in 1998 (with business partner Joseph Bastianich), Lupa in 1999; and Del Posto in 2005. Batali has written three cookbooks and has also become a popular TV personality. For years he was the host of *Molto Mario* and *Mario Eats Italy* on the Food Network. He is also one of the Iron Chefs on *Iron Chef America*. His PBS travel series called *Spain...On the Road Again* aired in 2011. In 2002, he received the James Beard Foundation's Best Chef: New York City award. He is also one of the recipients of the 2001 D'Artagnan Cervena Who's Who of Food & Beverage in America.

Alton Brown

Known as the erudite and witty creator and host of the Food Network show *Good Eats,* Alton Brown is one of the most recognizable food personalities on American television. Born on July 30, 1962, Brown attended the University of Georgia and studied drama. He worked for several years in cinematography and film production. He then graduated from the New England Culinary Institute in 1995. Interested in creating a smart, interesting cooking show for television, he developed the pilot for *Good Eats* for PBS. The show launched in July, 1998, airing on the Chicago PBS affiliate WTTW. It focused on the science behind cooking, often analyzing cooking equipment and devices as well as the cooking process. A year later, the show was picked up by the Food Network. *Good Eats* is celebrated for its scientific approach to food and cooking, and Brown is often described as a combination of Mr. Wizard and Bill Nye the Science Guy. In 2003, his first book, *I'm Just Here for the Food*, received a James Beard Foundation/KitchenAid Book Award. He has written several other instructional cooking books and has contributed to a number of food and lifestyle magazines.

In 2004, he began a continuing stint as the announcer and expert analyst for another Food Network series, *Iron Chef America*. That same year, *Bon Appétit* magazine named him Cooking Teacher of the Year. In 2006, Brown developed a mini-series called *Feasting on Asphalt* for the Food Network. In its limited run, Brown traced the history of food found while traveling the United States. He developed a variation on *Feasting on Asphalt* called *Feasting on Waves*, which explores local Caribbean cuisine he encountered while on a Caribbean boat trip. He also designed a series of Shun Cutlery, which bears his image.

Chocolate Molten Lava Cake

Also called chocolate fondant pudding or chocolate lava cake, chocolate molten lava cake is a chocolate dessert that became popular during the 1990s in American restaurants. It can be described as a rich chocolate cake with a soft, creamy chocolate center. Although there are several variations of the basic recipe, the cake comprises four main ingredients: butter, eggs, sugar, and chocolate. The origins of the cake are in dispute. Jean-Georges Vongerichten, the renowned chef, maintains that he invented it when he pulled a chocolate sponge cake from the oven before it had finished baking in 1987. However, the legendary French chocolatier Jacques Torres counters that a version of the chocolate molten lava cake was already on menus in French restaurants years before that. The rise of the chocolate molten lava cake in American restaurants is attributed to Vongerichten, who championed the dessert and put it on the menu of his prominent restaurants. Soon, other chefs took notice and created versions for their restaurants. During the 1990s, chocolate molten lave cake was a staple in American dessert cuisine.

Cook's Illustrated

Created by editor and food writer Christopher Kimball, *Cook's Illustrated* is a popular and influential American cooking magazine published by Boston Common Press bimonthly. Each issue is 32 pages in length, features no advertising, and offers about 10 recipes. The article accompanying each recipe traces its development, then focuses on solving problems associated with the recipe or offering time-saving techniques. The author often cooks the recipe several times, testing variations on ingredients or techniques to achieve consistent or superior results. A panel of tasters then tests each finished product. Readers love the staff's emphasis on simplifying recipes, careful testing, practical tips, detailed instructions, and helpful explanations of why certain processes work better than others. They also enjoy the taste tests of different products in order to find the brands that work and taste the best. In 1980, Kimball first launched *Cook's Magazine*, and it was published until 1989. Kimball hired several of *Cook's* editors, writers, and business staff to launch a new version of the magazine. He titled it *Cook's Illustrated*, and the first edition was published in 1993. The magazine proved to be a big hit; initially, the circulation was about 25,000 but jumped to 600,000 by 2004. Three years later, more than one million subscribers got the magazine every other month. In 2011, the magazine reports more than 1.3 million subscribers. By these numbers, *Cook's Illustrated* is regarded to be an industry star. The magazine's website has also had success—it has 300,000 paid subscribers. The staff of *Cook's Illustrated* has developed a television cooking show, *America's Test Kitchen*, which airs on PBS. They also publish a series of cookbooks, and have created a sister magazine called *Cook's Country,* which features home-style cooking.

The Cosmopolitan

This cocktail catapulted into American popular culture because of its frequent mention on the popular TV show *Sex and the City.* The cosmopolitan is a combination of lemon vodka, triple sec, cranberry juice, and lime juice, with a lime wedge as a garnish. Cointreau is often substituted for cheaper triple sec to provide a cleaner taste. The cosmopolitan is sometimes classified as a type of martini and is served in a martini glass. The origins of the drink are in dispute. The legend is that the cosmopolitan emerged from the gay community in Provincetown, Massachusetts, in the 1970s. Other sources claim that a bartender in Minneapolis created the drink in 1975. Some people think the cocktail was based upon the Harpoon, a drink designed to promote Ocean Spray cranberry juice during the 1960s. When a recipe for a gin-based version of the cosmopolitan was discovered in the 1934 book *Pioneers of Mixing at Elite Bars,* drink historians maintained that bartenders identified it as the source for the modern, vodka-based recipe. Another account attributed the cosmopolitan to a South Beach bartender named Cheryl Cook. Whatever the origins, it is known that the drink can be traced back to 1987, when Toby Cecchini made what we now recognize as the cosmopolitan in Manhattan, working from a second-hand description of Cheryl Cook's version of the cocktail. Cecchini's recipe is considered to be the standard. The drink was always popular, but became a household name with its appearance on *Sex and the City.* As the regular drink of Carrie Bradshaw and her three friends, the Cosmopolitan became the drink of choice for many viewers of the show and was publicized in the media as an elegant and hip cocktail. Observers note that the popularity of the Cosmopolitan introduced a new generation of drinkers to the cocktail and recognize it as one of the most famed cocktails of the past 20 years.

Bobby Flay

A critically acclaimed chef and restaurateur, Bobby Flay caught the attention of Americans with his award-winning cookbooks and popular shows on the Food Network in the 1990s. Born on December 10, 1964, in New York City, Flay started his cooking career by working at Joe Allen's, a famed restaurant in Manhattan's Theater District. He went on to study at the French Culinary Institute, receiving the school's Outstanding Graduate award in 1993. He began to develop his culinary style, which features flavors and dishes from the American Southwest. In 1991, he opened his first restaurant in New York City, Mesa Grill. A few years later, he opened another restaurant, Bolo Restaurant & Grill. Flay received the James Beard Foundation's Rising Star Chef of the Year award in 1993. He opened another Mesa Grill in Las Vegas in 2004, Bar Americain in Manhattan in 2005, Bobby Flay Steak in Atlantic City, and a third Mesa Grill in the Bahamas in 2007. He also opened a chain of burger shops in various locations in New York, New Jersey, Pennsylvania, and Connecticut. Flay is also a staple on the Food Network, where he has hosted and competed in several popular shows, including *Boy Meets Grill, BBQ with Bobby Flay, Throwdown! with Bobby Flay,* and *Hot Off the Grill with Bobby Flay.* In *Throwdown!* Flay challenges cooks known for certain dishes or a specific style to a cooking competition featuring their signature dish. He is also recognized as one of the Iron Chefs in *Iron Chef America* and is a contributor to *The Early Show* on CBS, starring in a cooking segment every week. For the past couple of decades, Flay has been one of the more prolific restaurateurs and television personalities in American cuisine.

Frappuccino

A registered trademark of Starbucks Coffee, frappuccinos are iced coffee drinks—a mix of coffee, water, milk, ice, and various syrups. As to the exact recipe, Starbucks keeps it a secret, although customers with allergies can ask if a certain ingredient is included. Frappuccino-style drinks can be

---

The Rise of the Food Network

The Food Network is a cable TV network devoted to food and cooking. The shows that appear on the network feature well-known chefs and culinary personalities, explore issues related to food and food preparation, and offer exciting food competitions and cook-offs. Originally called the TV Food Network, the concept for the network was developed by Joe Langhan in 1991. The Food Network went live on November 23, 1993, and debuted during the week of Thanksgiving. It attracted a following from the beginning—before the Food Network, cooking shows had been limited to public television, and viewers were happy to get a variety of food programming all through the day and night. The first Food Network celebrity chef to emerge was Emeril Lagasse, whose energetic and engaging Cajun cooking style on his show *The Essence of Emeril* led to good ratings for the young network. Shows featuring Mario Batali and Bobby Flay also proved popular and established both chefs as celebrities in their own rights. In 1996, the Food Network was sold to the A.H. Belo Corporation, then later sold to E.W. Scripps. Today, the Food Network is available in an estimated 100 million U.S. homes and is broadcast in England and Asia. During the day, the network airs mainly instructional cooking programs; in the evening, it offers a range of food entertainment fare.

---

traced back to a Boston-area coffee chain called Coffee Connection. The name is rooted in New England as well: *frappe* is a type of milkshake unique to New England, and a cappuccino is an Italian coffee topped with frothed milk. In 1994, Starbucks purchased the Coffee Connection chain, took over the recipe for the frappuccino, and made it a global sensation. Starbucks customers particularly enjoyed the frappuccino as a warm-weather drink. The company soon introduced a range of different flavors, such as mint and chocolate, caramel, espresso, mocha, and peppermint. Some flavors are available only in certain countries for limited times. Vegan, light, decaffeinated, and cream versions of the frappuccino are also available. Some frappuccinos use tea instead of coffee. In 2006, Starbucks introduced the Frappuccino Juice Blend, a combination of real fruit juices with tea and ice. Flavors include lemonade, pomegranate, tangerine, and strawberry lemonade. Starbucks also bottled the frappuccino to sell it in stores; it is believed that the store version is a different recipe than the one sold at Starbucks. There are several flavors of the bottled frappuccinos available, including mocha, vanilla, coffee, caramel, and dark chocolate raspberry. Because Starbucks has more than 16,000 stories in more than 50 countries, frappuccinos are widely available in a variety of flavors at any given time, cementing its position as one of the most popular iced coffee drinks in the world.

Genetically Modified (GM) Foods

In the 1990s, scientists began inserting specific genes into plants or animals in order to modify their genetic structure and produce traits that hold a perceived advantage for the producer or consumer. With genetic engineering, for example, you can create a plant that produces human insulin. Another common modification was to make crops less reliant on herbicides and pesticides for protection against disease. In fact, most of the GM foods are plant products like soybean, corn, canola, and cotton seed oil that have been modified to resist viruses and chemicals. Animals have also been genetically modified. The first commercially grown genetically modified crop was a tomato, the Flavr Savr, that was genetically altered to stay fresh longer. During the 1990s, the popularity of GM products spread across the world, especially in developing countries. In the United States, GM products are a staple in food production. In fact, the Grocery Manufacturers of America estimate that 75 percent of all processed foods in the United States contain a GM ingredient. With the rapid growth of GM products worldwide, controversy erupted over its growing use. Critics of GM foods argue that there has not been enough testing of the ill effects of the affected food products, and therefore there is a doubt as to the ultimate safety of GM foods. Critics also want more analysis of the effects of GM products on ecosystems, particularly their impact on biodiversity. Supporters of GM foods have cited tests that show no adverse health effects from the consumption of such products and maintain that they bring higher yields and profitability to many farmers, including those in developing nations. They also note that GM products allow for reduced use of pesticides, which means fewer chemicals in the air and ground. The controversy over GM food has led to many countries considering bans on it. In Europe, food and animal feed containing more than 0.5 percent GM ingredients must be clearly labeled for consumers.

Grape Tomatoes

Grape tomatoes are sweet, flavorful tomatos that are grown in bunches and shaped like grapes. Grape tomatoes have a higher sugar content than many cherry tomatoes and, therefore, have become a popular snack food for kids and adults. They are also a popular ingredient in salads, sauces, and other dishes. First developed by farmers in Asia, grape tomatoes first appeared in the United States when Andrew Chu, a vegetable farmer in Florida, grew a batch in 1996 after a recommendation from a Taiwanese friend. At first, the product was limited and marketed only to Asian consumers; but Chu quickly realized grape tomatoes held a mainstream appeal. Before long, commercial vegetable growers agreed, and the new tomatoes were being grown all over the United States. The rush to capitalize on the burgeoning popularity of the new tomato devolved into a controversial battle over copyright issues and the supply of seed to grow grape tomatoes. Legal proceedings over these issues proved contentious. Despite the behind-the-scenes battle amongst tomato growers, the American public embraced the new product. In fact, grape tomatoes are one of the most popular types of tomatoes sold in the country today, loved for their sweet taste and convenient shape. Tomatoes are widely recognized as a healthy food, containing certain compounds that have been proven to help prevent cancer, heart disease, cataracts, and other illnesses. Tomatoes also contain lycopene, an antioxidant, and lutein, which is important for eye health.

Emeril Lagasse

One of the most successful and recognizable chefs of his era, Emeril Lagasse is a celebrated chef, restaurateur, author, and television personality. Growing up in Fall River, Massachusetts, Lagasse often cooked with his mother, Hilda, at home. When he was a teenager, he began his culinary career as a baker while working at a Portuguese bakery. Determined to become a professional chef, he attended Johnson and Wales University's College of Culinary Arts, graduating in 1978. He traveled to Paris and Lyon to learn the basic techniques of classic French cuisine. Returning to the United States, he worked at restaurants in New York, Boston, and Philadelphia before he took over an executive chef position at the New Orleans restaurant, Commander's Palace, in 1982. There Lagasse became a culinary star. In 1990, he opened his first restaurant, Emeril's, in New Orleans. His style drew from the Creole and Cajun cooking of the region. The success of Emeril's spawned several other restaurants; Lagasse is the executive chef and proprietor of 13 restaurants around the country. In 1991, Lagasse was named Best Southeast Regional Chef by the James Beard Foundation. In 1998, he was chosen Chef of the Year by *GQ* magazine. In 2006, he was inducted into the MenuMasters Hall of Fame by *Nation's Restaurant News*. Lagasse is also a celebrated television personality. He has hosted more than 1,500 shows on the Food Network and was one of the network's first breakout stars. He is perhaps best known for his first show, *Essence of Emeril,* which launched in 1994. Lagasse is also the author of 14 bestselling books and has established the Emeril Lagasse Foundation in

2002 to support children's education and nonprofit organizations with culinary, nutrition, garden, arts, and life skills programs. In 2008, Lagasse joined the Martha Stewart family of brands.

Iron Chef

Produced by Fuji Television, *Iron Chef* is a Japanese cooking competition that ran from 1993 to 1999. The show featured a group of resident iron chefs—top Japanese chefs specializing in various cuisines (Japanese, Italian, French, and Chinese) who were challenged by experienced chefs from around the world. Each cooking battle was built around a certain ingredient, which had to be featured in each dish. Presided over by the fictional character of flamboyant Chairman Kaga in his Kitchen Stadium, the competition was narrated by two regular commentators as well as one or two guest commentators, who analyzed the competition in real time (1 hour), providing background information and context and speculating on the dishes while the chefs and their assistants competed. In the United States and other English-speaking countries, the show was dubbed in English. During each show, several dishes were produced, a panel of judges assessed the results, and a winner was chosen. The show did well in Japan. When the original series aired in the United States on the Food Network, it quickly became a surprise cult favorite, and executives decided to adapt it for American television. The show's success spawned a couple of spin-offs: an unsuccessful American version, *Iron Chef USA*, in 2001; an Israeli version, *Krav Sakinim*, in 2007; and the Food Network version, *Iron Chef America*, which featured renowned American cooking personalities as iron chefs, including Bobby Flay and Mario Batali, as well as one of the original iron chefs, Masaharu Morimoto. Alton Brown was cast as the commentator and analyst, and American food critics, media figures, and celebrities were chosen as judges. First airing in 2004, *Iron Chef America* eventually added other iron chefs: Cat Cora, Michael Symon, and Jose Garces.

Molecular Gastronomy

Molecular gastronomy is a scientific discipline and a culinary movement that studies the chemistry and physics behind the preparation of food. Molecular gastronomists analyze the physical and chemical processes that occur while cooking, and chefs then apply these scientific principles to their own culinary styles to create experimental and avant-garde dishes. The movement can be traced back to 1988, when Hungarian physicist Nicholas Kurti and French physical chemist Hervé coined the term "molecular gastronomy" to describe their work. This established a scientific discipline to encompass their own investigations into the science behind traditional cooking practice. The two scientists held a series of workshops in Italy in 1992 to provide a forum for scientists and chefs to exchange research, ideas, and practices related to the science of cooking and cooking practices. They deemed the five goals of the new scientific discipline to be: "(1) to collect and investigate old wives' tales about cooking; (2) to model and scrutinize existing recipes; (3) to introduce new tools, products, and methods to cooking; (4) to invent new dishes using knowledge from the previous three aims; and (5) to use the appeal of food to promote science." This surging interest in the scientific aspects of food preparation intrigued bright, adventurous chefs all over the world. These chefs began to apply ideas learned through the investigations of molecular gastronomists to their own cooking to improve cooking processes and to create culinary innovations. Inventions of molecular gastronomy were avant-garde and included fruit caviar, hot ice cream, and foam sauces. This style of cooking has also become known as molecular gastronomy, but it is also called culinary alchemy, scientific cooking, scientific cuisine, experimental cuisine, or molecular cooking. A number of American chefs became renowned for their experiments with molecular gastronomy, such as Grant Achatz, Wylie Dufresne, and Michael Carlson.

Nutritional Labeling and Education Act of 1990

This law gives the Food and Drug Administration (FDA) the authority to require nutritional labeling of most packaged food sold in the United States. These labels inform the consumer about what is actually in the product they are about to buy or eat. The law also allows the FDA to require that all nutrient claims made by food manufacturers meet FDA standards. In practical terms, this means that if a food product is advertised as being low fat, it actually must be low fat by FDA standards. The Nutritional Labeling and Education Act was signed into law on November 8, 1990. Specific provisions of the law cover the following: require food manufacturers to reveal the fat, cholesterol, sodium, sugar, fiber, protein, and carbohydrate content in their products; require labeling for the top-selling fruits, vegetables, fish, and shellfish; exclude meat, poultry, and egg products; and

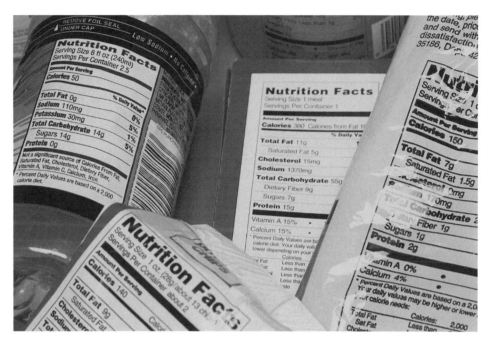

Nutrition labels on packaged foods are required by the FDA and provide consumers with information on calorie, fat, and nutritional content. (PhotoDisc, Inc.)

set standards for food descriptors such as "reduced," "low," "lite," and so on. These provisions were put into place to enable consumers to make informed decisions about the products they eat and feed their families. In 1993, the FDA and the U.S. Department of Agriculture (USDA) implemented regulations that designate the format and content of nutrition labels on most foods, including processed meat and poultry products. In 2006, a new criterion was added: the nutrition fact labels on packaged food products are now required to list how many grams of trans fat are contained within one serving of the product.

Olestra

Olestra is a fat substitute that gained prominence in the 1990s before flaming out in the early 2000s. Discovered by Procter & Gamble researchers F. Mattson and R. Volpenhein in 1968, olestra molecules are used as a fat substitute because they are so large and fatty that they cannot be metabolized by enzymes and bacteria in the stomach and are therefore neither absorbed nor digested. Olestra also binds cholesterol, vitamins, and other fat-soluble drugs; in fact, Procter & Gamble initially considered olestra to be a prime cholesterol drug. In 1987, P&G petitioned the FDA to approve olestra as a fat substitute to be used in fast foods, chips, shortenings, and other food products. Before it was even approved, however, some product analysts and media figures identified olestra as the next big thing in the food industry—a fat substitute that added no fat, cholesterol, or calories to products was a breakthrough in food production. Other industry experts were wary of olestra, noting that P&G warned that the product caused "anal leakage" in some people during testing and also interfered with the absorption of vitamin E. Responding to these critics, P&G modified the structure. After years of controversy, debate, further research, and patent extensions, the FDA approved the use of olestra in savory snacks such as chips, crackers, and tortilla chips. However, every package of snacks containing olestra must have a label that states: "Olestra may cause abdominal cramping and loose stools. Olestra inhibits the absorption of some vitamins and other nutrients. Vitamins A, D, E, and K have been added." Not long after products containing olestra hit the market, reports of adverse reactions came to light, including diarrhea, fecal incontinence, and abdominal cramps. After investigation, the FDA concluded that olestra could not be considered the culprit and that it should be classified as a safe product. As a result of the complaints and the controversy, sales of olestra products plummeted and no new products containing the fat substitute are planned.

The Organic Foods Production Act (OFPA) of 1990

In an attempt to clearly define organic farming practices, the U.S. government passed the Organic Foods Production Act of 1990, which was part of that year's farm bill. OFPA created the National Organic Program (NOP), which set the uniform minimum standards for food classified as organic in the United States. The act states that "the principal guidelines for organic production are to use materials and practices that enhance the ecological balance of natural systems and that integrate the parts of the farming system into an ecological whole." Until that time, private and state agencies had been certifying organic practices, but there was no uniformity in standards among states and, therefore, no guarantee that "organic" meant the same thing from state to state. Moreover, many food producers were calling their products "organic" when they were not. The organic food industry as well as the National Association of State Departments of Agriculture, the American Farm Bureau Federation, and the Center for

Science in the Public Interest pushed U.S. politicians to pass OFPA. These groups felt that federal regulation would end consumer confusion and provide a strong advantage for American products in the international organic market. Under OFPA, food must meet the law's standard to be certified. Companies that do not meet the standards but still use the classification will be prosecuted for breaking the law. To enforce the standards, private and state certifiers visit producers, processors, and handlers to check that their companies meet the standards set by OFPA. If they do, they are allowed to affix a "Meets USDA Organic Requirements" label on their products. OFPA allows states to pass standards that are more restrictive than the federal standards, but they must be approved by the USDA. The act also maintains that states cannot discriminate against out-of-state products that meet the federal standards.

Red Bull

A very popular energy drink worldwide, Red Bull contains taurine, glucuronolactone, caffeine, B vitamins, sucrose, phenylalanine, and glucose. Red Bull, the company that owns the drink, boasts that it improves performance and endurance while increasing concentration and stimulating your metabolism. Red Bull was created by an Austrian entrepreneur, Dietrich Mateschitz. In 1982, Mateschitz discovered a Thai energy drink called Krating Daeng (which translates to "red bull" in Thai) that cured his severe jet lag and gave him energy. He decided to adapt Krating Daeng for the European market and worked for years with TC Pharmaceutical to come up with a suitable version. The result was carbonated and less sweet than Krating Daeng. Meanwhile, Mateschitz formed a company called Red Bull with his business partner, Chaleo Yoovidhya. Each man invested $500,000 and received 49 percent of the new company. In 1987, they launched Red Bull in a limited area and then began to offer it in different markets in the 1990s. It wasn't introduced into the United States until 1997. It quickly became the most popular energy drink on the market and a renowned brand in American popular culture. Red Bull was a worldwide hit. In 2009, controversy erupted in Hong Kong when Red Bull Cola drinks imported from Austria were found to contain trace amounts of cocaine. Testing showed that an individual with a low tolerance for cocaine would have to drink two million cans of Red Bull in a single sitting before becoming seriously ill from the drug. However, concerns remained high, and some countries attempted to ban Red Bull in their markets. The company is an active sponsor of various sports and activities ranging from extreme sports to art shows and video games. In the United States, the company sponsors the Red Bull New York, a team in Major League Soccer.

Slow Food Movement

This is an international movement that aims to counteract the disappearance of local food traditions and cuisine by promoting local farming and regional foods and culture. According to the philosophy of Slow Food International, "We believe that everyone has a fundamental right to pleasure and consequently the responsibility to protect the heritage of food, tradition and culture that make this pleasure possible. Our movement is founded upon this concept of eco-gastronomy—a recognition of the strong connections between plate and planet." The movement can be traced back to 1986, when Carlo Petrini formed an organization, Arcigola, to protest the opening of a McDonald's near the Spanish Steps in Rome. This action spawned an entire movement to fight the proliferation and globalization of fast-food franchises and a greater appreciation for local cuisines and ingredients. In 1989, the movement took a step forward, with the founding manifesto signed by slow food delegates from 15 countries. A year later, the first International Food Congress was convened. Slow Food International became a legal entity in 1996, which was the same year the international office was opened. In 2000, Slow Food USA was established. The movement has since expanded globally to more than 100,000 members in 132 countries. It continues to draw followers interested in preserving local food traditions and regional cuisines against the encroachment of fast food and packaged products. According to the movement's official philosophy, "Slow Food works to defend biodiversity in our food

A gardener sows a seedling plant in prepared soil. Gardening and farming are becoming more popular with the slow food movement. (Elifranssens/Dreamstime.com)

supply, spread taste education and connect producers of excellent foods with co-producers through events and initiatives."

Further Reading

"An Unpretentious Chef Has Many Fans." *The New York Times* (25 November 1998).

Balzer, Harry. "The Ultimate Cooking Appliance." *American Demographics* 15, no. 7 (1993): 40–41.

"Chefs on the Hot Plate." *People Weekly* 27 (1998): 52.

Frederick, Heather Vogel. "From Soup to Nuts: Celebrity Chefs and Downhome Fare Are Just Two of the Ingredients Heating Up Publishers' Seasonal Stews." *Publishers Weekly* 244, no. 28 (1997): 31–34.

Gvion, Liora and Naomi Trostler. "From Spaghetti and Meatballs through Hawaiian Pizza to Sushi. The Changing Nature of Ethnicity in American Restaurants." *Journal of Popular Culture* 41, no. 6 (December 2008): 950–74.

Howard, Theresa. "Quick-Comfort Segment Marks New Generation of Fast Food." *Nation's Restaurant News* 28, no. 42 (1994): 41–42.

Jay, Sarah. "Surfing the Food Network: Notes of an Armchair Cook." *The New York Times* (17 April 1998).

Narayan, Shoba. "Where the Kitchen Is Mostly a Men's Club." *New York Times* (27 May 2001).

Pollan, Michael. "Cruising on the Ark of Taste." *Mother Jones* (May–June 2003): 74–77.

Pollan, Michael. *In Defense of Food: An Eater's Manifesto.* New York: Penguin Press, 2008.

Spiegler, Marc. "The Cocktail Nation." *American Demographics* 20, no. 7 (21 November 2010): 40–41.

Bibliography

Anderson, Jean. *American Century Cookbook: The Most Popular Recipes of the 20th Century*. New York: Clarkson Potter, 1997.

Beard, James. *James Beard's American Cookery*. New York: Galahad Books, 1972.

Bundy, Beverly. *The Century in Food: America's Fads and Favorites*. Portland, OR: Collector's Press, 2002.

Child, Julia. *The French Chef Cookbook*. New York: Alfred A. Knopf, 2009.

Cohen, Rich. *Sweet and Low: A Family Story*. New York: Farrar, Strauss, Giroux, 2006.

D'Amico, Joan and Karen Eich. *The United States Cookbook: Fabulous Foods and Fascinating Facts from All 50 States*. New York: John Wiley and Sons, 2000.

Deutch, Tracey. *Building a Housewife's Paradise: Gender, Politics, and American Grocery Stores in the 20th Century*. Chapel Hill: University of North Carolina Press, 2010.

Diner, Hasia R. *Hungering for America: Italian, Irish, and Jewish Foodways in the Age of Migration*. Cambridge: Harvard University Press, 2001.

Fischer, M. F. K. *The Art of Eating*. Hoboken, NJ: John Wiley and Sons, 2004.

Fussell, Betty Harper. *Masters of American Cookery: M.F.K Fischer, James Andrews Beard, Raymond Craig Claiborne, Julia McWilliams Child*. New York: Times Books, 1983.

Gabaccia, Donna R. *We Are What We Eat: Ethnic Food and the Making of Americans*. Cambridge, MA: Harvard, 1988.

Gardner, Bruce L. *American Agriculture in the 20th Century: How It Flourished and What It Cost*. Cambridge: Harvard University Press, 2000.

Jackle, John A. and Keith A. Sculle. *Fast Food: Roadside Restaurants in the Automobile Age*. Baltimore: Johns Hopkins University Press, 1999.

Johnson, Ronald. *The American Table: More Than 400 Recipes That Make Accessible for the First Time the Full Richness of American Regional Cooking*. New York: William Morrow, 1984.

Jones, Evan. *American Food: The Gastronomic Story.* New York: Vintage Books, 1981.

Katzen, Molly. *The Moosewood Cookbook.* Berkeley, CA: Ten Speed Press, 1992.

Lappe, Francis Moore. *Diet for a Small Planet.* New York: Ballantine Books, 1991.

Lee, Jennifer 8. *The Fortune Cookie Chronicles.* New York: Twelve Books, 2008.

Levenstein, Harvey A. *Paradox of Plenty: A Social History of Eating in Modern America.* New York: Oxford University Press, 1993.

Levenstein, Harvey A. *Revolution at the Table: The Transformation of the American Diet.* New York: Oxford University Press, 1988.

Lovegren, Sylvia. *Fashionable Food: Seven Decades of Food Fads.* Chicago: University of Chicago Press, 1995.

Mariani, John F. *The Encyclopedia of American Food and Drink.* New York: Lebhar-Friedman Books, 1999.

Mariani, John and Galina. *The Italian-American Cookbook.* Boston, MA: The Harvard Commons Press, 2000.

McFeely, Mary Drake. *Can She Bake a Cherry Pie? American Women and the Kitchen of the 20th Century.* Amherst: University of Massachusetts Press, 2000.

McNamee, Thomas. *Alice Waters and Chez Panisse: The Romantic, Impractical, Often Eccentric, Ultimately Brilliant Making of a Food Revolution.* New York: Penguin Press, 2007.

Nathan, Joan. *The New American Cooking.* New York: Knopf, 2005.

O'Neill, Molly. *American Food Writing: An Anthology with Classic Recipes.* New York: Library of America, 2009.

Ozersky, Josh. *The Hamburger: A History.* New Haven, CT: Yale University Press, 2008.

Reichl, Ruth, ed. *The Gourmet Cookbook: More Than 1000 Recipes.* Boston: Houghton Mifflin, 2006.

Rombauer, Irma S. *Joy of Cooking: 75th Anniversary Edition.* New York: Scribner, 2006.

Smith, Andrew F., ed. *The Oxford Companion to American Food and Drink.* New York: Oxford University Press, 2007.

Villas, Steve. *Pig: King of the Southern Table.* Hoboken, NJ: John Wiley and Sons, 2010.

Articles

Dyson, Lowell K. "American Cuisine in the 20th Century." *Food Review* 23: (January–April 2000) 2–7.

Hess, John L. "Good American Cookery—An Endangered Species." *The New York Times*, January 7, 1974, p. 37.

McKenzie, Catherine. "A Challenge to American Cookery: An Enforced Shift in Diet Suggests That We Make Plentiful Foods More Palatable." *The New York Times*, January 13, 1935, p. SM14.

Miller, Tim. "The Birth of the Patio Daddy-O: Outdoor Grilling in Post-War America." *Journal of American Culture* 33: 1 (March 2010), pp. 5–11.

Perenyi, Eleanor. "What Ever Happened to American Cooking?" *The Saturday Evening Post* 236: 23. (June 15, 1963), pp. 68–70.

Schnetzer, Amanda Watson. "The Golden Age of American Cooking." *Policy Review* 97 (October–November 1999), pp. 53–65.

Websites

Food History News—http://www.foodhistorynews.com/.

Food in America: Culture and History—http://library.jwu.edu/research/websites/food_america.htm

The Food Timeline—www.foodtimeline.org

National Hot Dog and Sausage Council—http://www.hot-dog.org/

Serious Eats: A Food Blog and Community—http://www.seriouseats.com/

U.S. Agriculture in the 20th Century—http://eh.net/encyclopedia/article/gardner.agriculture.us

What's Cooking America—http://whatscookingamerica.net/

Index

About the Editor and Contributors

Editor

Sherri Liberman is a senior librarian for the New York Public Library. A freelance writer, she is also the author of three young adult titles for Rosen Publishing, *Historical Atlas of Azerbaijan*, *Historical Atlas of the Industrial Age and the Growth of American Cities*, and the biography *Lynne Reid Banks*. Her great affection for all things culinary was the primary motivation for writing this book, as was a desire to sort out her dysfunctional relationship with frozen and canned foods. Sherri lives in Brooklyn, NY, with her cat, Mimi.

Contributors

Margaret Haerens is a freelance writer and editor living in Brooklyn, NY. She has worked in reference publishing for 18 years on a variety of reference works. Cooking is one of her favorite hobbies, along with reading, embroidery, kung fu, and flamenco dancing.

Hilary Schenker is a writer and illustrator living in Brooklyn, NY. She works at the New York Public Library on Manhattan's Lower East Side as an adult literacy educator and holds a BA in English from Barnard College. She loves food and is a member of the Park Slope Food Coop.

Margaret Rose Siggillino is a librarian at the New York Public Library with an interest in culinary fiction, culinary history, and all things food-related. A writer, she submitted "The Development of Culinary Fiction in Relation to the Obsession with Food in Western Culture: A Content Analysis" as the final thesis project for her Masters of Library and Information Science at Queens College. She is a former pastry chef, baker, and cookie decorator. She continues to cook, bake, explore various musical genres, write, and exercise in her spare time.

Judith Yablonski is both a freelance writer and attorney based in the Northwest. She has authored a children's reference book titled *Plant and Animal Cells: Understanding the Differences Between Plant and Animal Cells* and several newspaper articles on environmental issues. She enjoys supporting healthy living through diet by frequenting her weekly local organic farmers' markets.